GG.

Saber Marionette J

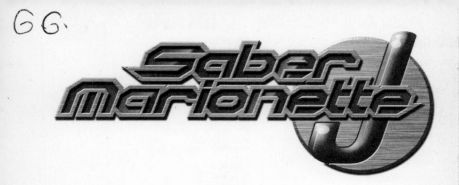

ALSO AVAILABLE FROM ⊙TOKYOPOP®

Volume 1

Written by
Satoru Akahori
Art by
Yumisuke Kotoyoshi

TOKYOPOP®

LOS ANGELES • TOKYO • LONDON

Translation - Jeremiah Bourque
English Adaptation - Paul Morrissey with Tim Beedle
Associate Editor - Tim Beedle
Retouch and Lettering - John Lange
Cover Layout & Graphic Design - Raymond Makowski

Senior Editor - Mark Paniccia
Managing Editor - Jill Freshney
Production Coordinator - Antonio DePietro
Production Manager - Jennifer Miller
Art Director - Matthew Alford
Director of Editorial - Jeremy Ross
VP of Production & Manufacturing - Ron Klamert
President & C.O.O. - John Parker
Publisher & C.E.O. - Stuart Levy

Email: editor@TOKYOPOP.com
Come visit us online at www.TOKYOPOP.com

A 🔷 **TOKYOPOP**® Manga

TOKYOPOP® is an imprint of Mixx Entertainment, Inc.
5900 Wilshire Blvd. Suite 2000, Los Angeles, CA 90036

SABER MARIONETTE 'J' Volume 1 ©SATORU AKAHORI•JUKKI HANADA•YUMISUKE KOTOYOSHI 2003.
First published in Japan in 1997 by KADOKAWA SHOTEN PUBLISHING CO., LTD., Tokyo. English
translation rights arranged with KADOKAWA SHOTEN PUBLISHING CO., LTD., Tokyo through
TUTTLE-MORI AGENCY, INC., Tokyo. English text © 2003 by Mixx Entertainment, Inc.
TOKYOPOP is a registered trademark of Mixx Entertainment, Inc.

ISBN: 1-59182-386-2

First TOKYOPOP® printing: July 2003

10 9 8 7 6 5 4 3 2
Printed in the USA

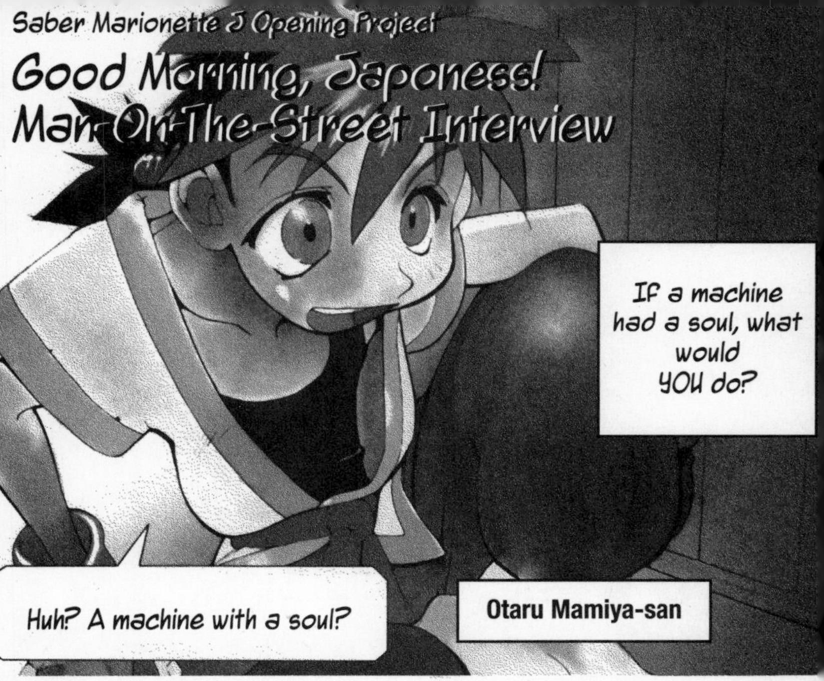
Saber Marionette J Opening Project
Good Morning, Japoness! Man-On-The-Street Interview
If a machine had a soul, what would YOU do?
Otaru Mamiya-san
Huh? A machine with a soul?

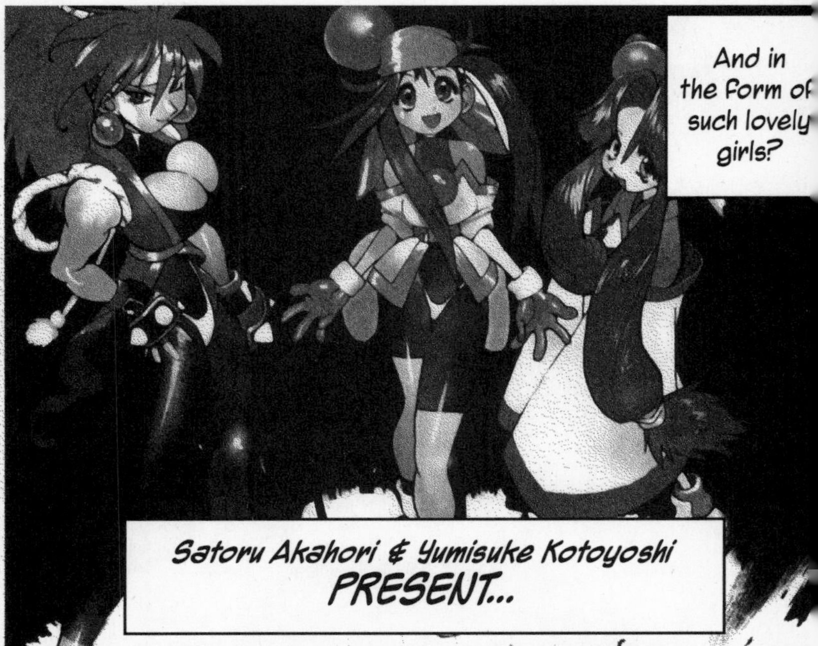
And in the form of such lovely girls?
Satoru Akahori & Yumisuke Kotoyoshi PRESENT...

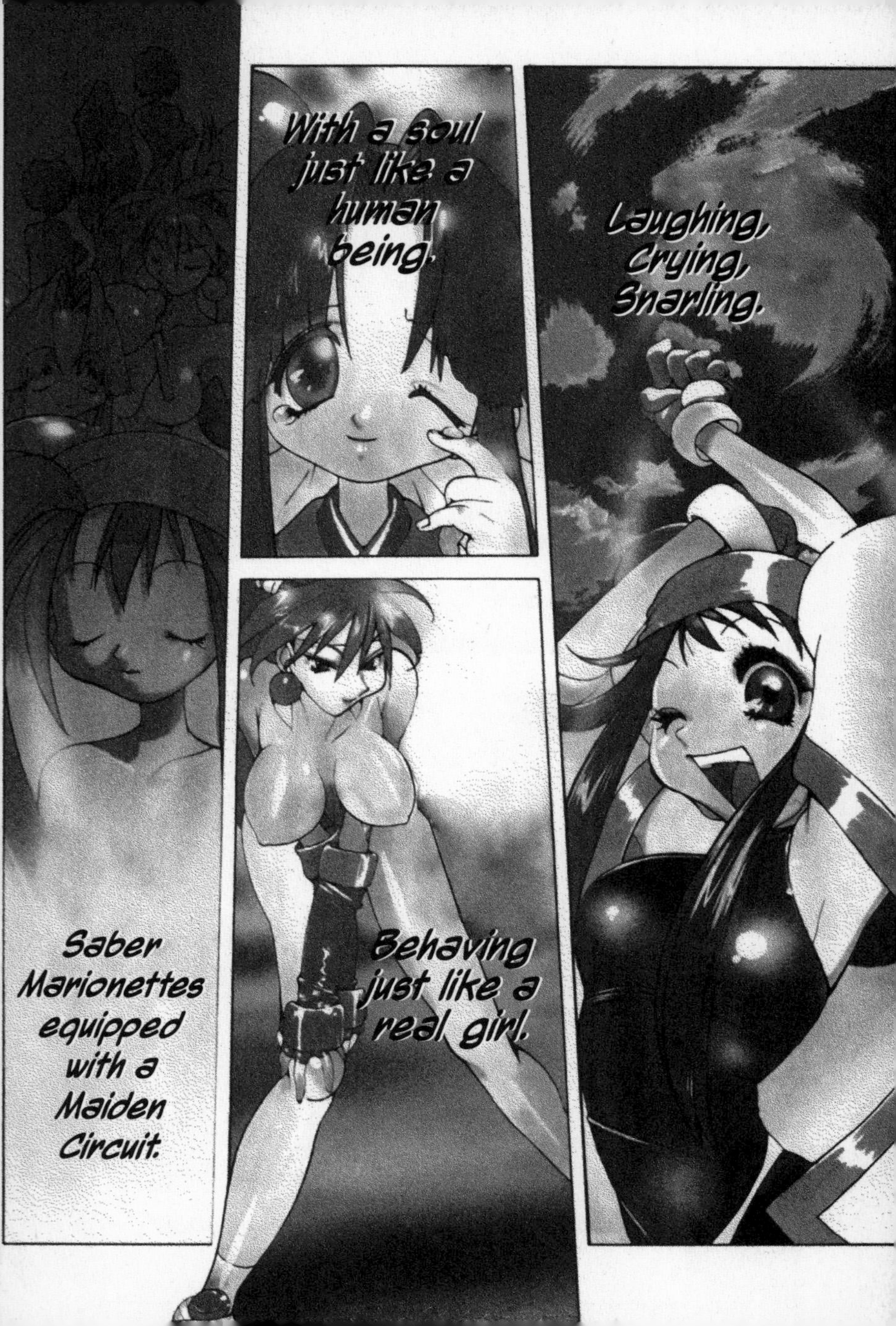
Laughing, Crying, Snarling.
With a soul just like a human being.
Behaving just like a real girl.
Saber Marionettes equipped with a Maiden Circuit.

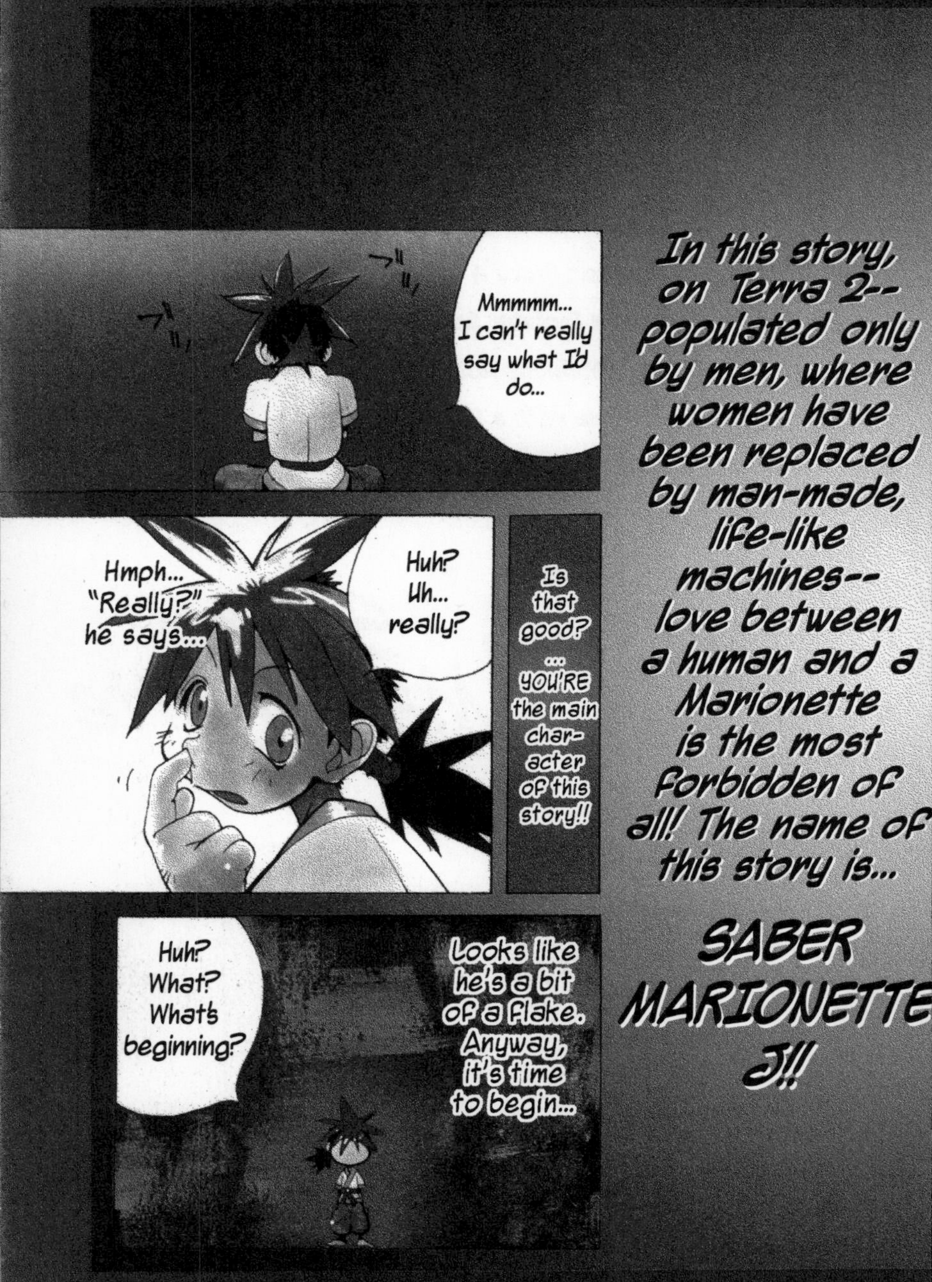
In this story, on Terra 2--populated only by men, where women have been replaced by man-made, life-like machines--love between a human and a Marionette is the most forbidden of all! The name of this story is...
SABER MARIONETTE J!!
Mmmmm... I can't really say what I'd do...
Is that good? ... YOU'RE the main character of this story!!
Huh? Uh... really?
Hmph... "Really?" he says...
Looks like he's a bit of a flake. Anyway, it's time to begin...
Huh? What? What's beginning?

CONTENTS

Saber Marionette J

Writing/ Satoru Akahori
Scenarios/ Juuki Hanata
Character Design/ Tsukasa Kotobuki
Art/ Yumisuke Kotoyoshi

Chapter 1: Planet Terra 2

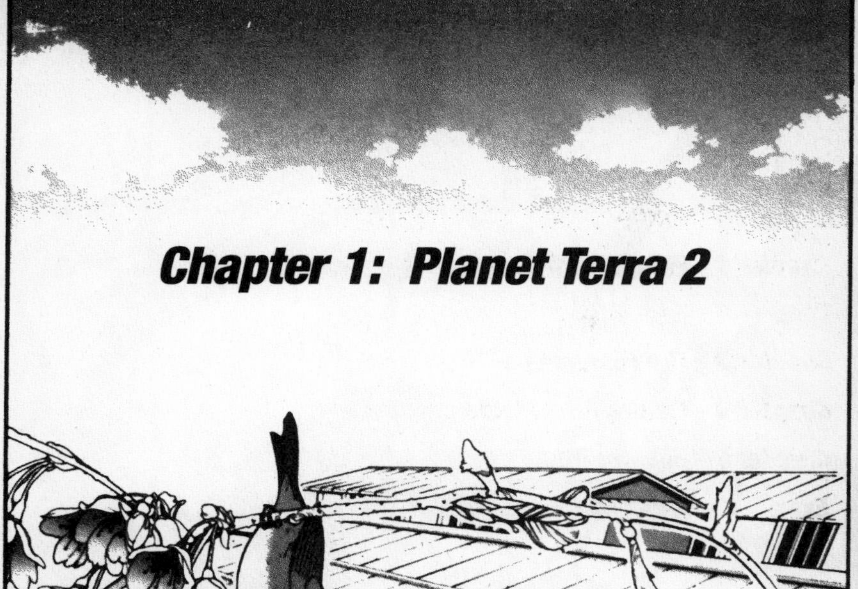

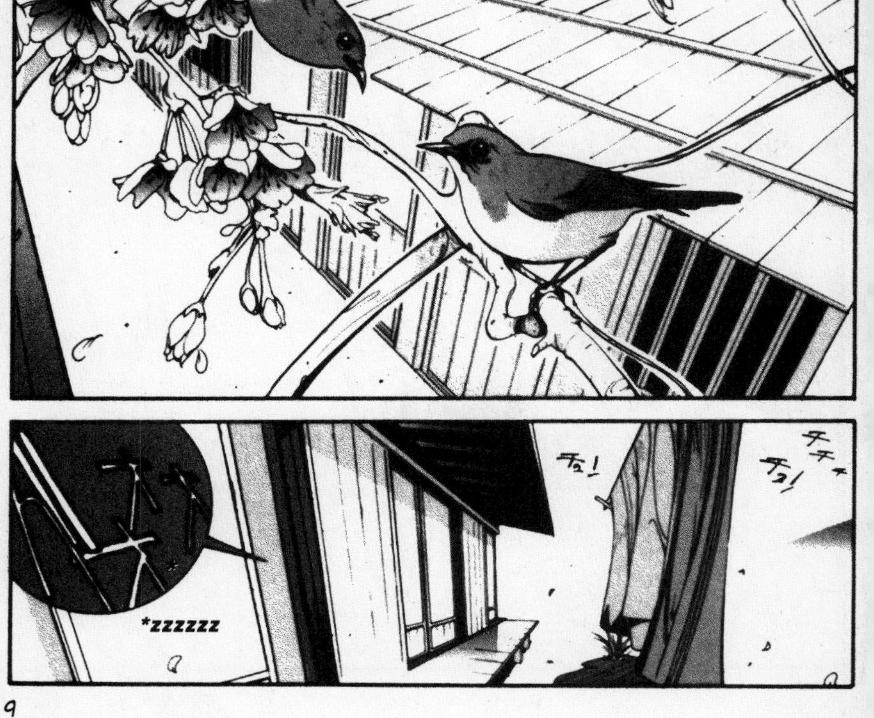
*zzzzzz

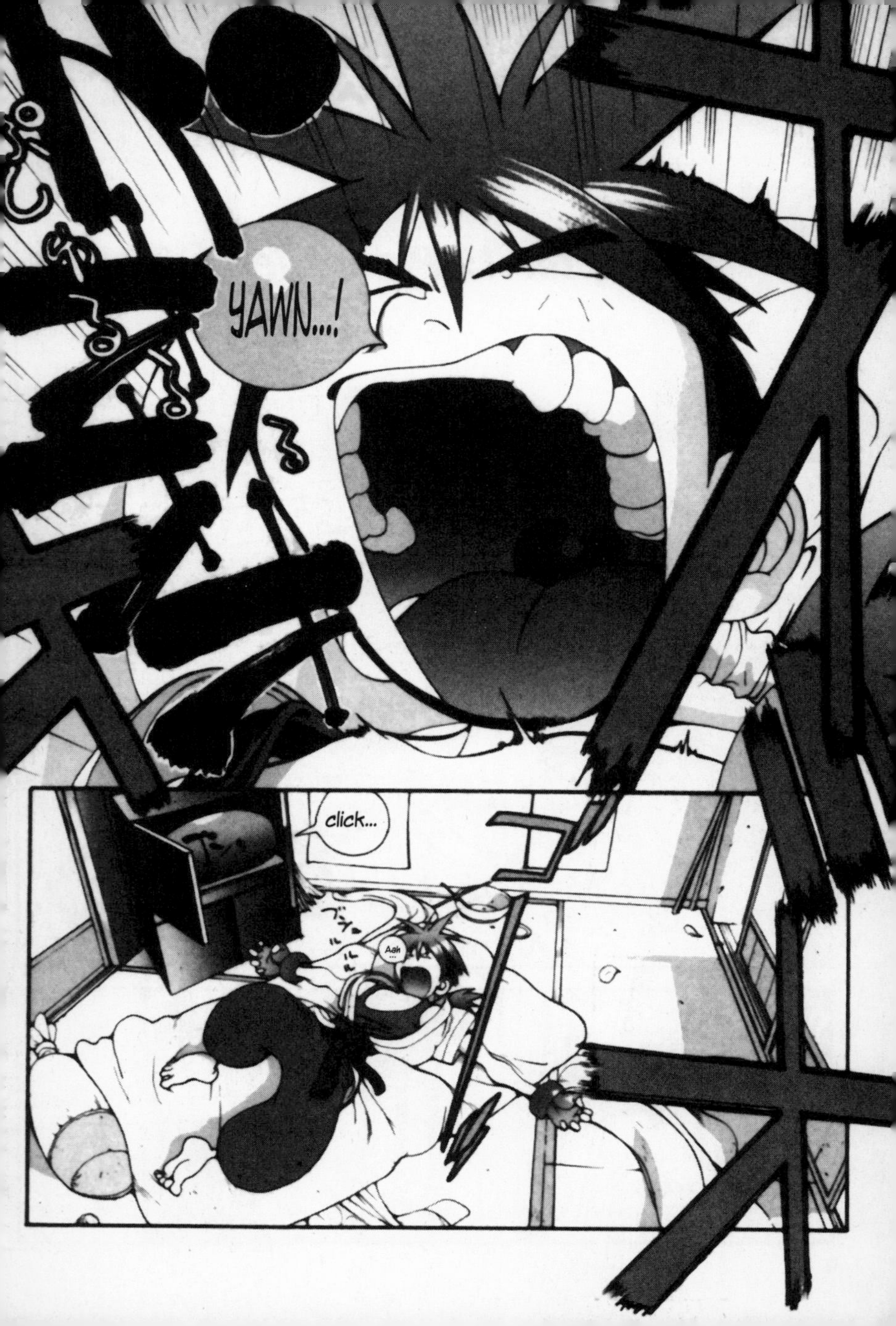
YAWN...!
click...
Aah...

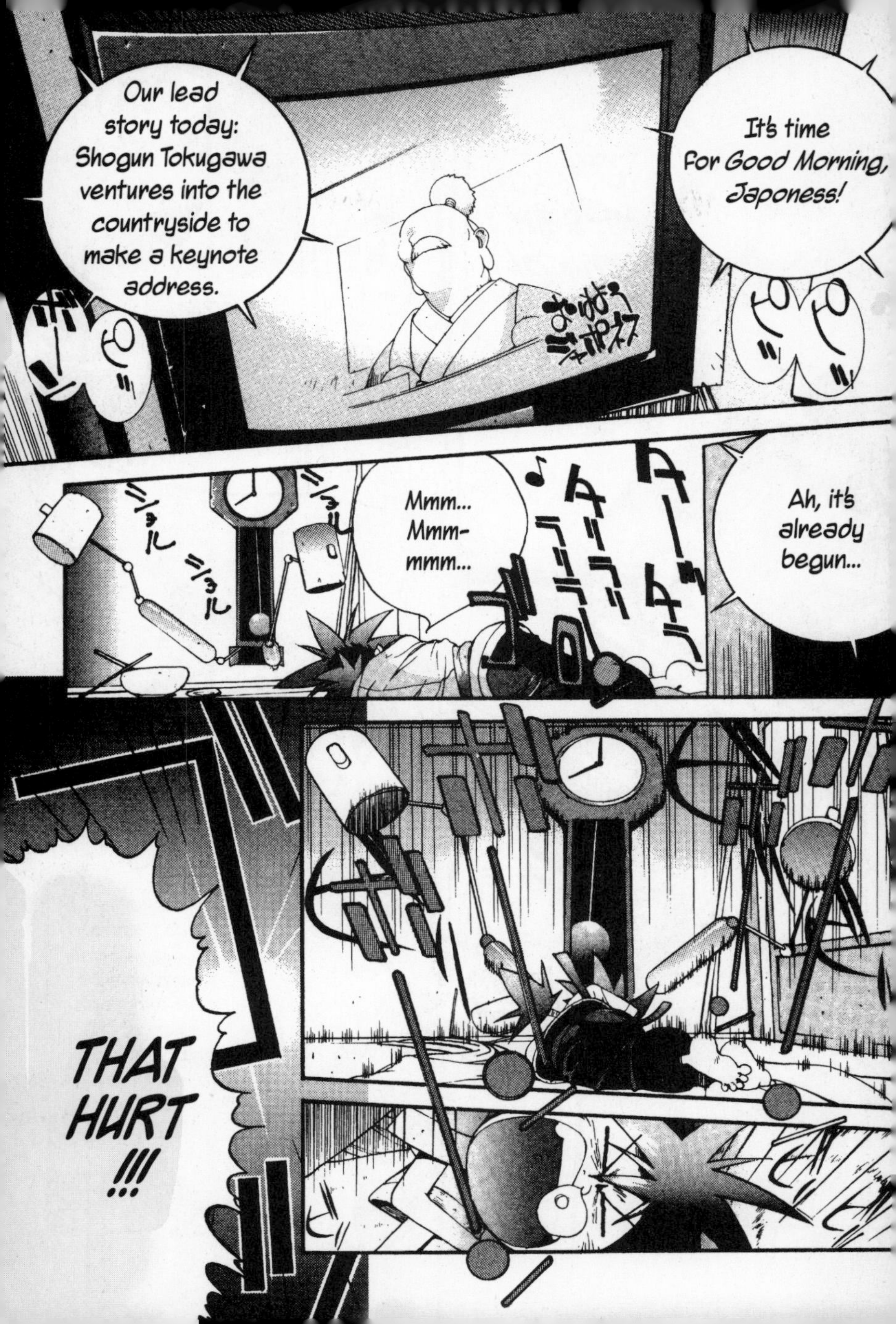
It's time for Good Morning, Japoness!
Our lead story today: Shogun Tokugawa ventures into the countryside to make a keynote address.
Ah, it's already begun...
Mmm... Mmm-mmm...
THAT HURT!!!

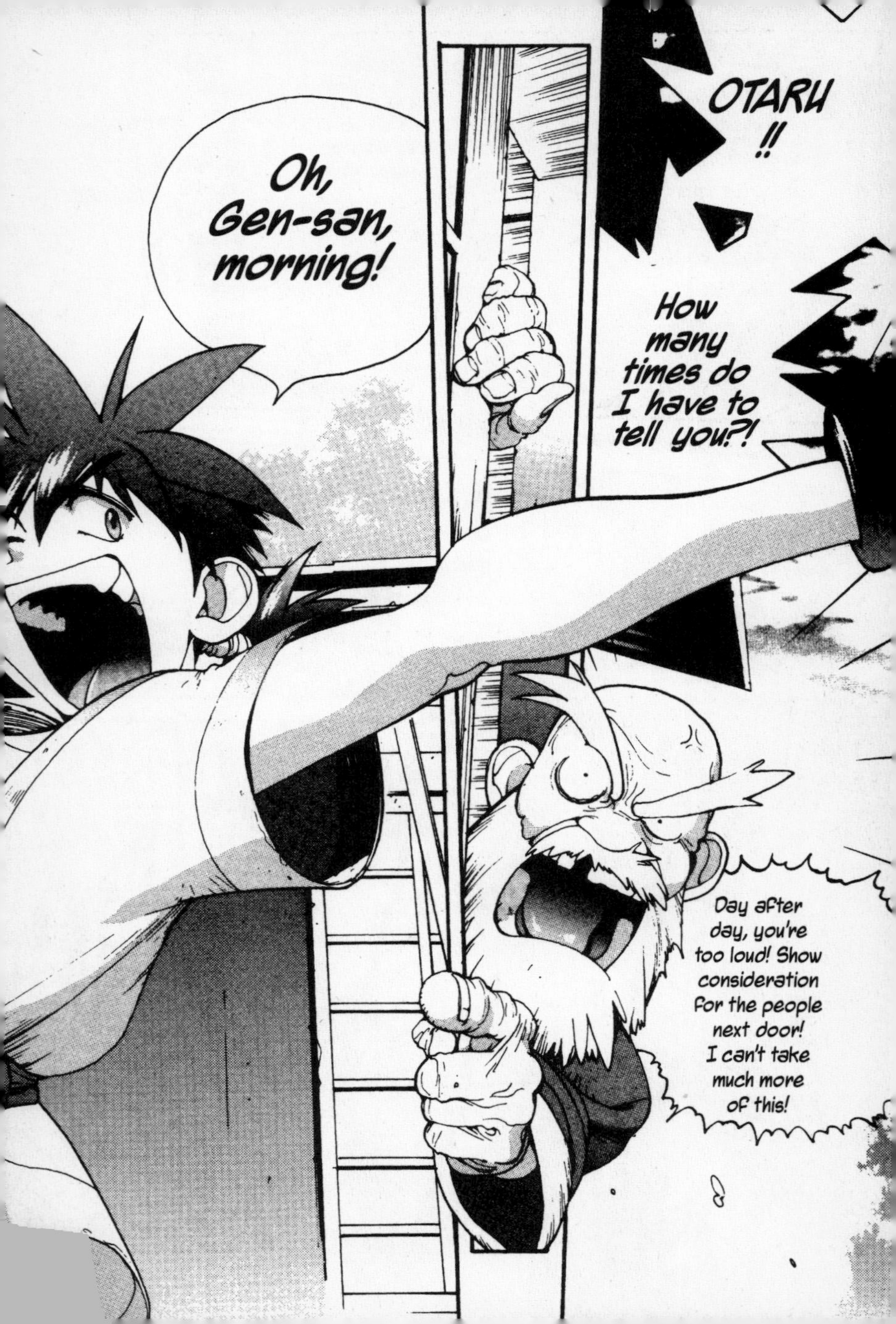
OTARU !!
How many times do I have to tell you?!
Oh, Gen-san, morning!
Day after day, you're too loud! Show consideration for the people next door! I can't take much more of this!

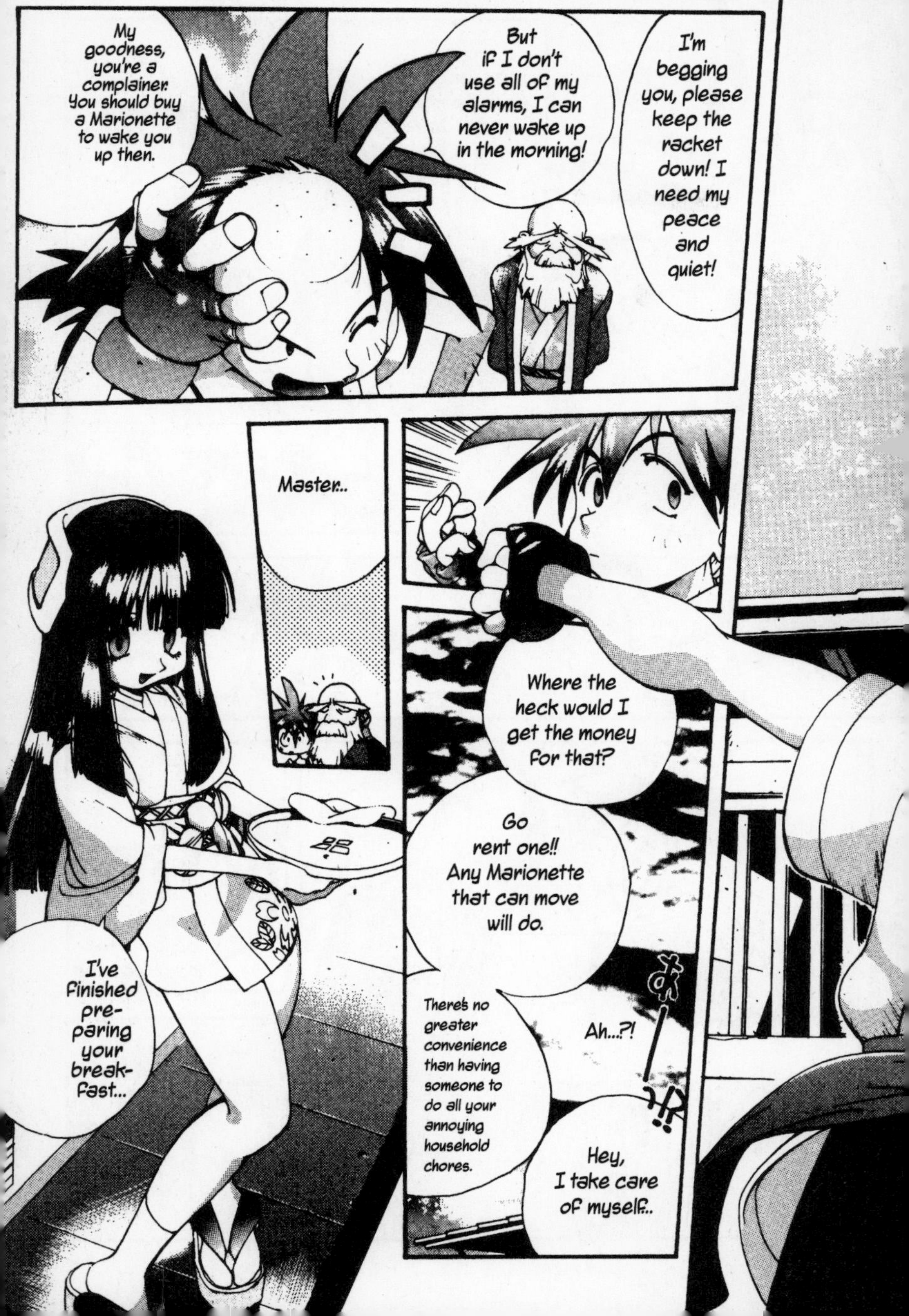
I'm begging you, please keep the racket down! I need my peace and quiet!
But if I don't use all of my alarms, I can never wake up in the morning!
My goodness, you're a complainer. You should buy a Marionette to wake you up then.
Where the heck would I get the money for that?
Go rent one!! Any Marionette that can move will do.
There's no greater convenience than having someone to do all your annoying household chores.
Hey, I take care of myself..
Ah...?!
Master..
I've finished pre-paring your break-fast...

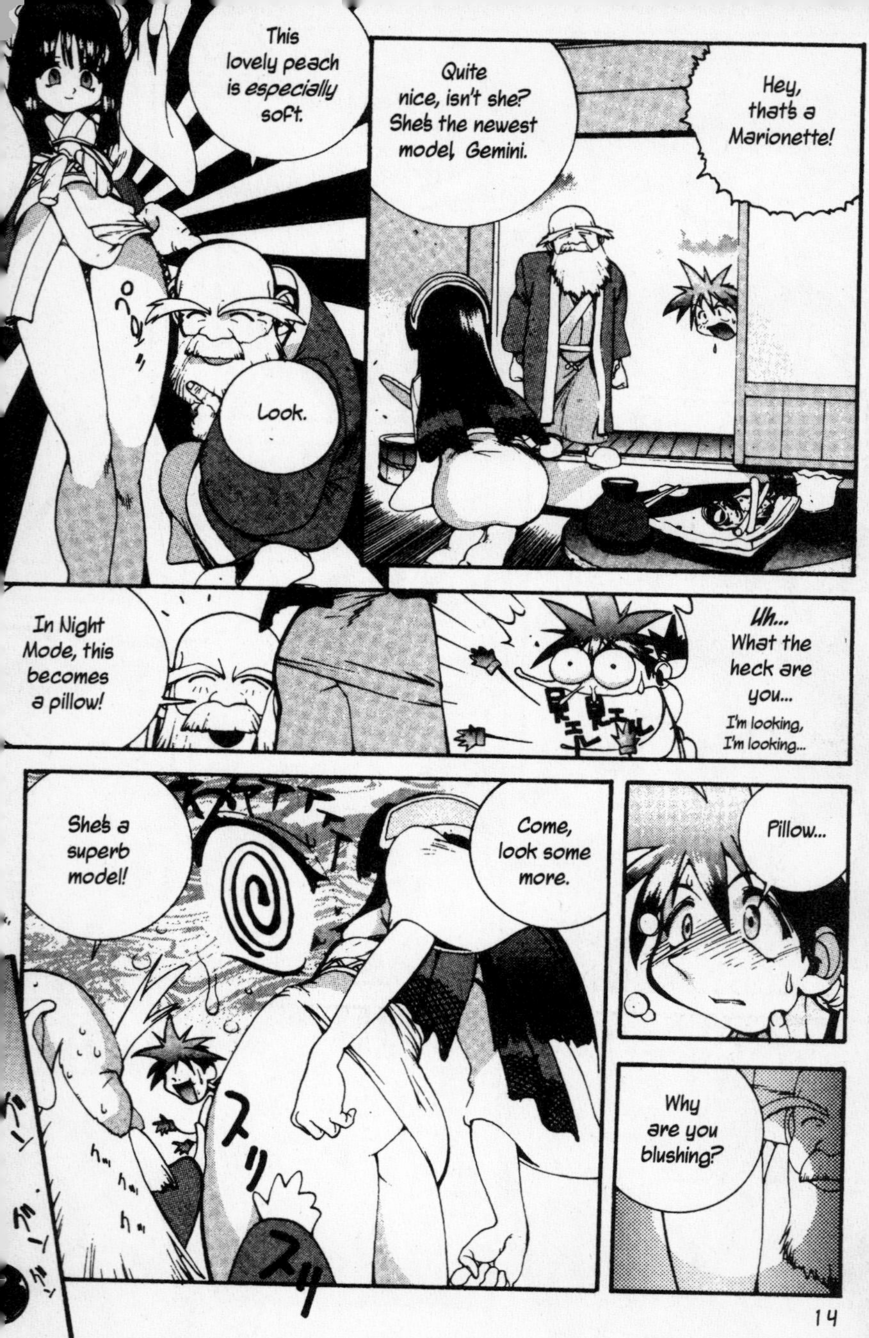
Hey, that's a Marionette!
Quite nice, isn't she? She's the newest model, Gemini.
This lovely peach is *especially* soft.
Look.
Uh... What the heck are you...
I'm looking, I'm looking...
In Night Mode, this becomes a pillow!
Pillow...
Why are you blushing?
Come, look some more.
She's a superb model!

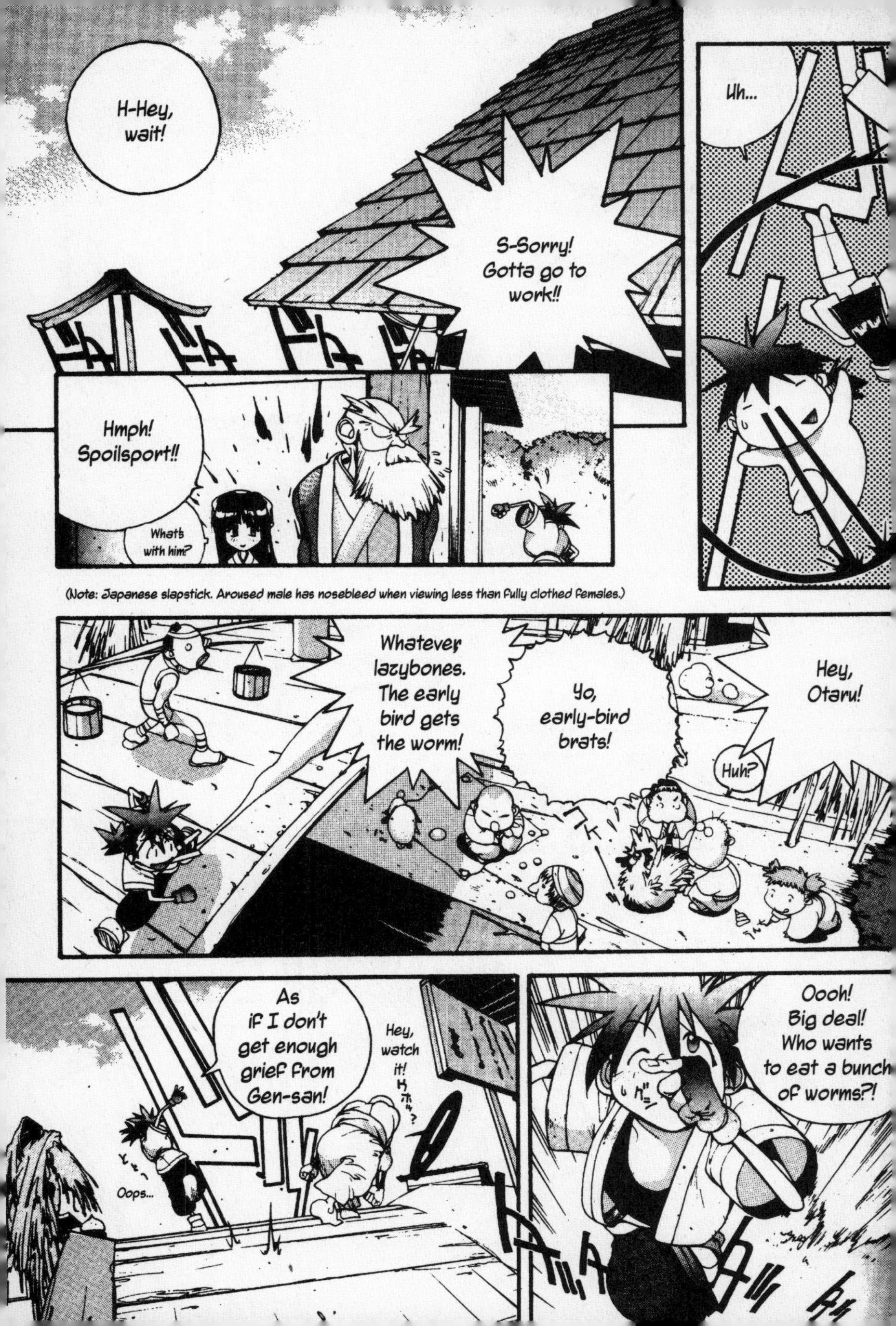
Uh...
H-Hey, wait!
S-Sorry! Gotta go to work!!
Hmph! Spoilsport!!
What's with him?
Hey, Otaru!
Huh?
Yo, early-bird brats!
Whatever, lazybones. The early bird gets the worm!
Oooh! Big deal! Who wants to eat a bunch of worms?!
Hey, watch it!
As if I don't get enough grief from Gen-san!
Oops...
(Note: Japanese slapstick. Aroused male has nosebleed when viewing less than fully clothed females.)

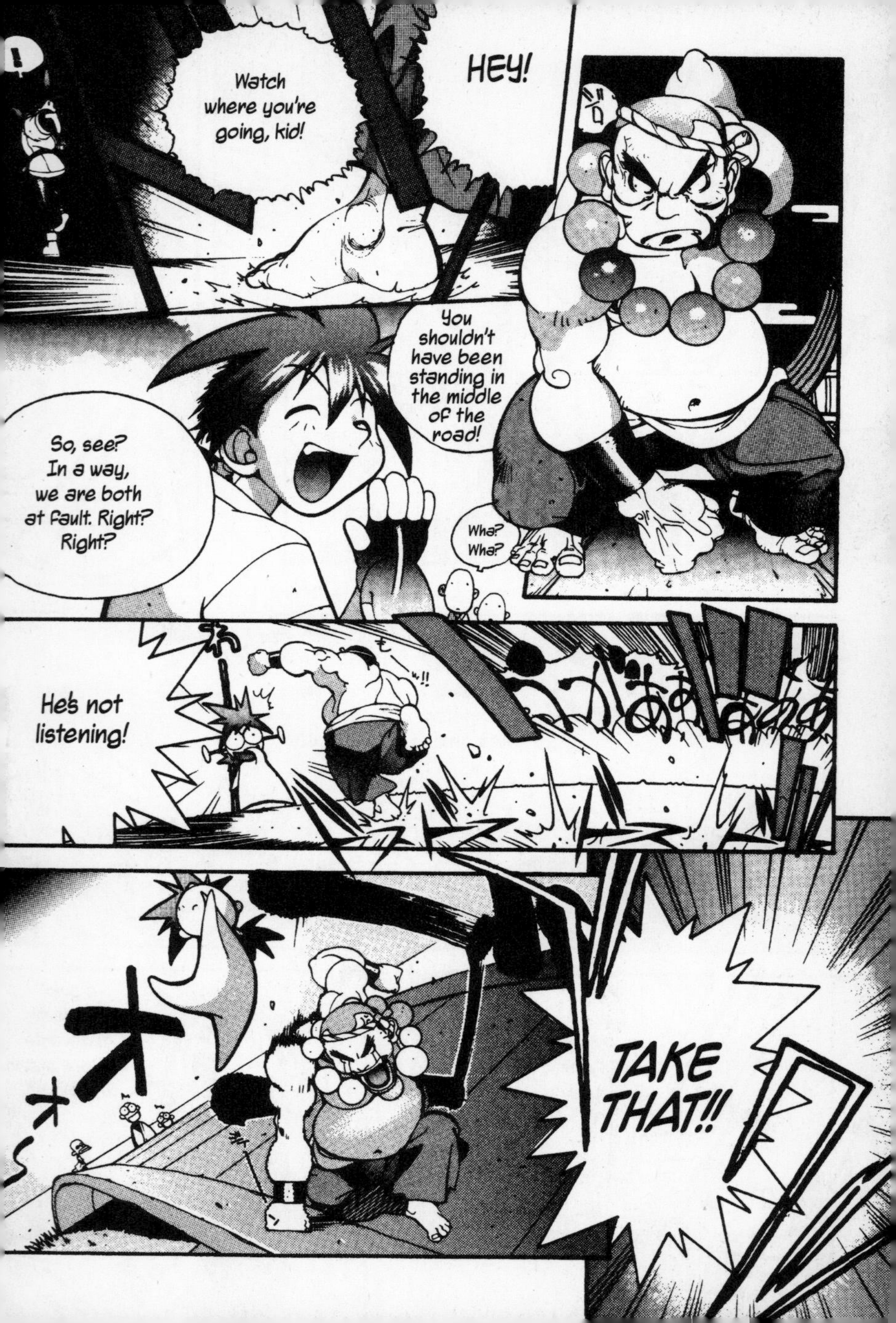
HEY!
Watch where you're going, kid!
You shouldn't have been standing in the middle of the road!
So, see? In a way, we are both at fault. Right? Right?
Wha? Wha?
He's not listening!
TAKE THAT!!

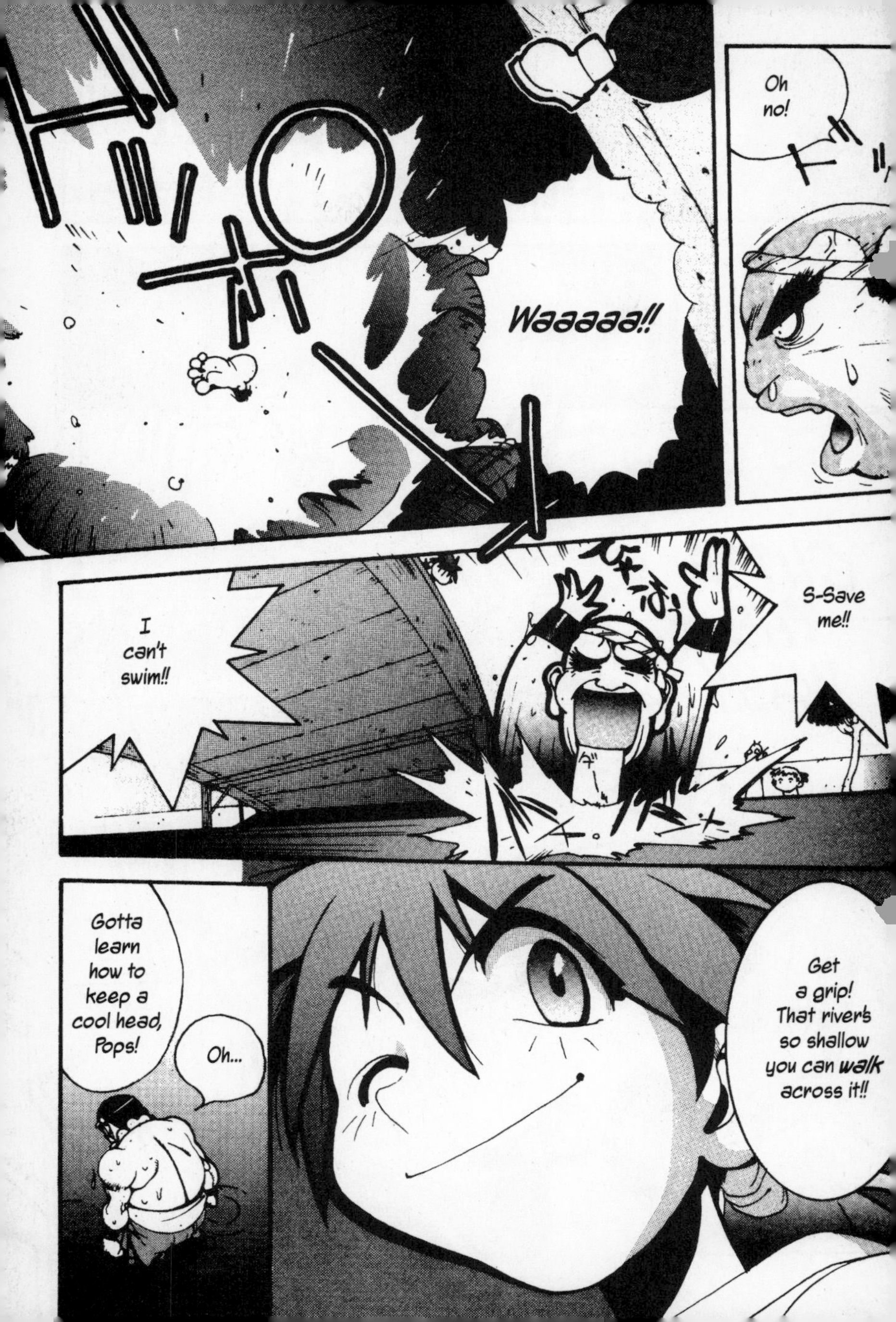
Oh no!
Waaaaa!!
S-Save me!!
I can't swim!!
Get a grip! That river's so shallow you can *walk* across it!!
Gotta learn how to keep a cool head, Pops!
Oh...

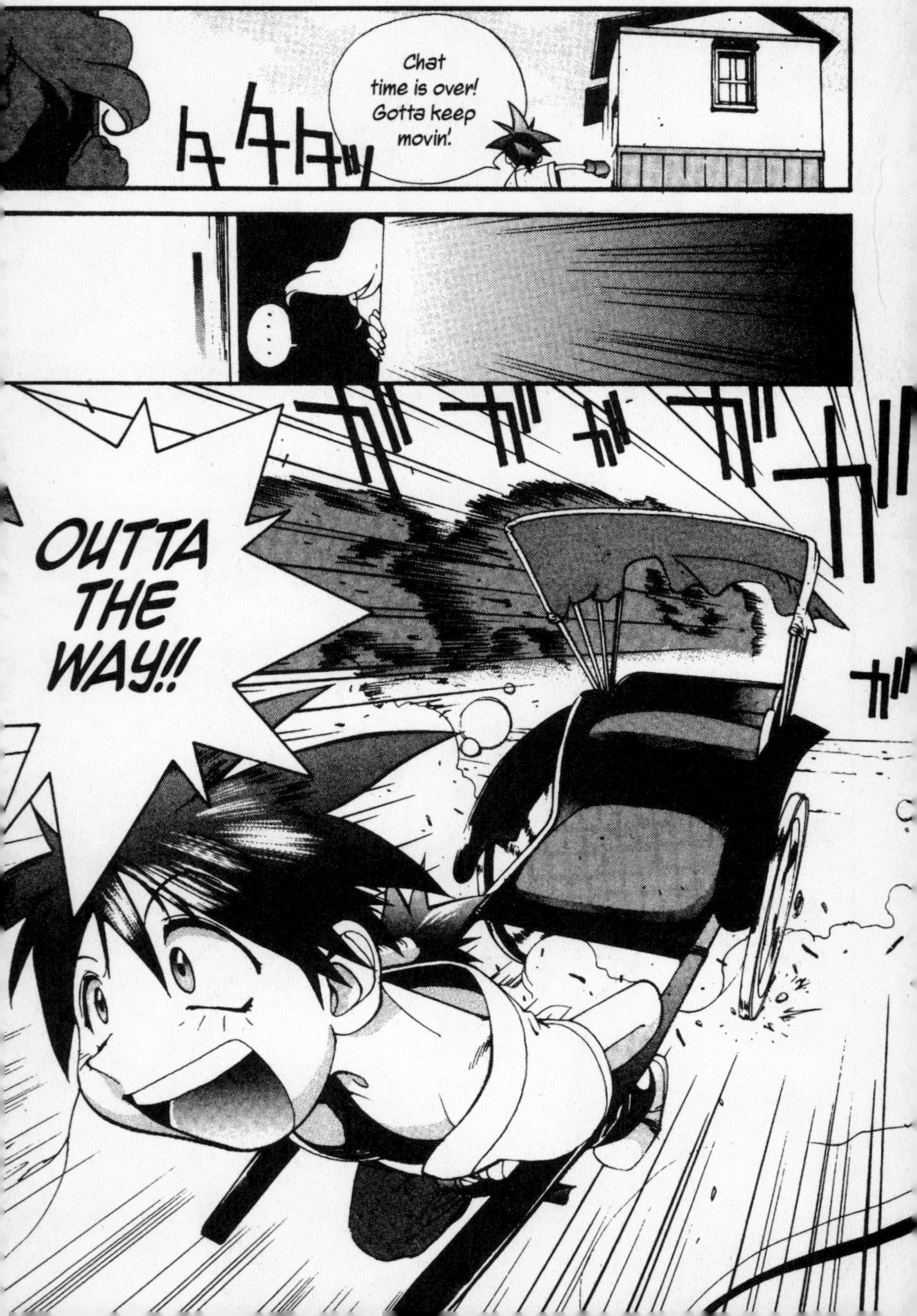
Chat time is over! Gotta keep movin'!
...
OUTTA THE WAY!!

My name's Otaru Mamiya. This big city's called Japoness. I'm a born and bred Japoness kid!
You're not a true blue Japoness kid unless you hate small-minded jerks and love a big party!
OUTTA MY WAY!! OUTTA MY WAY!!!

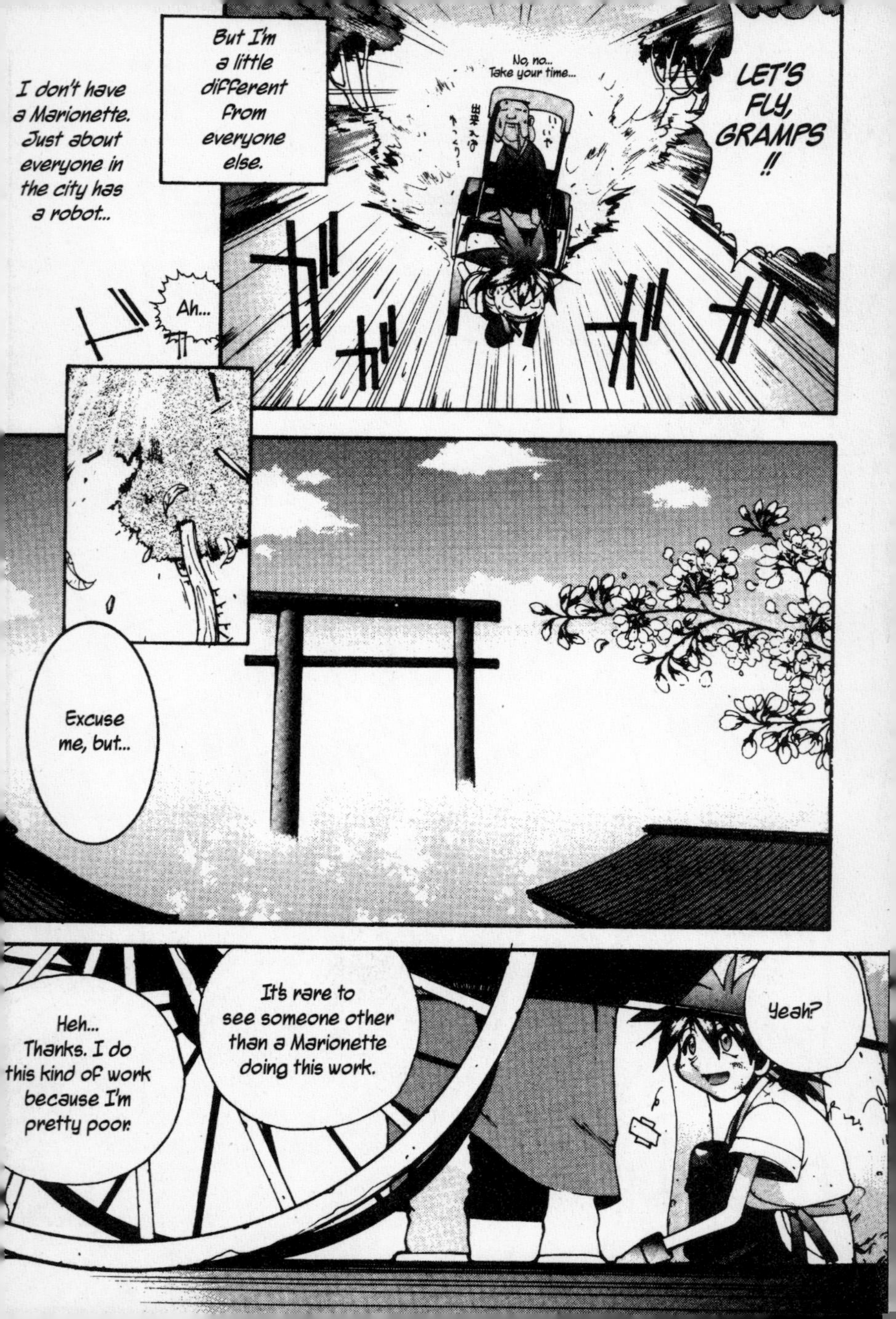
LET'S FLY, GRAMPS!!
No, no... Take your time...
But I'm a little different from everyone else.
I don't have a Marionette. Just about everyone in the city has a robot...
Ah...
Excuse me, but...
Yeah?
It's rare to see someone other than a Marionette doing this work.
Heh... Thanks. I do this kind of work because I'm pretty poor.

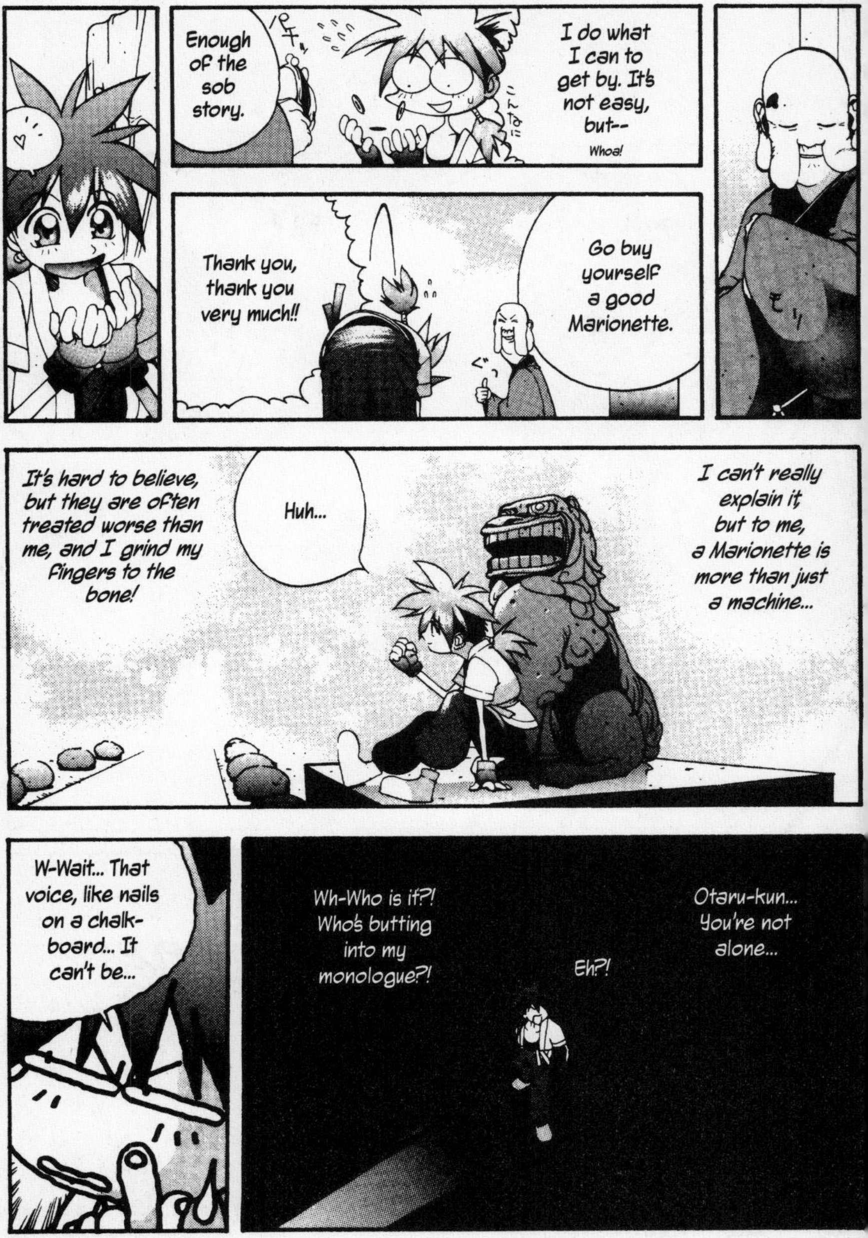
I do what I can to get by. It's not easy, but--
Whoa!
Enough of the sob story.
Go buy yourself a good Marionette.
Thank you, thank you very much!!
I can't really explain it, but to me, a Marionette is more than just a machine...
Huh...
It's hard to believe, but they are often treated worse than me, and I grind my fingers to the bone!
Otaru-kun... You're not alone...
Eh?!
Wh-Who is it?! Who's butting into my monologue?!
W-Wait... That voice, like nails on a chalk-board... It can't be...

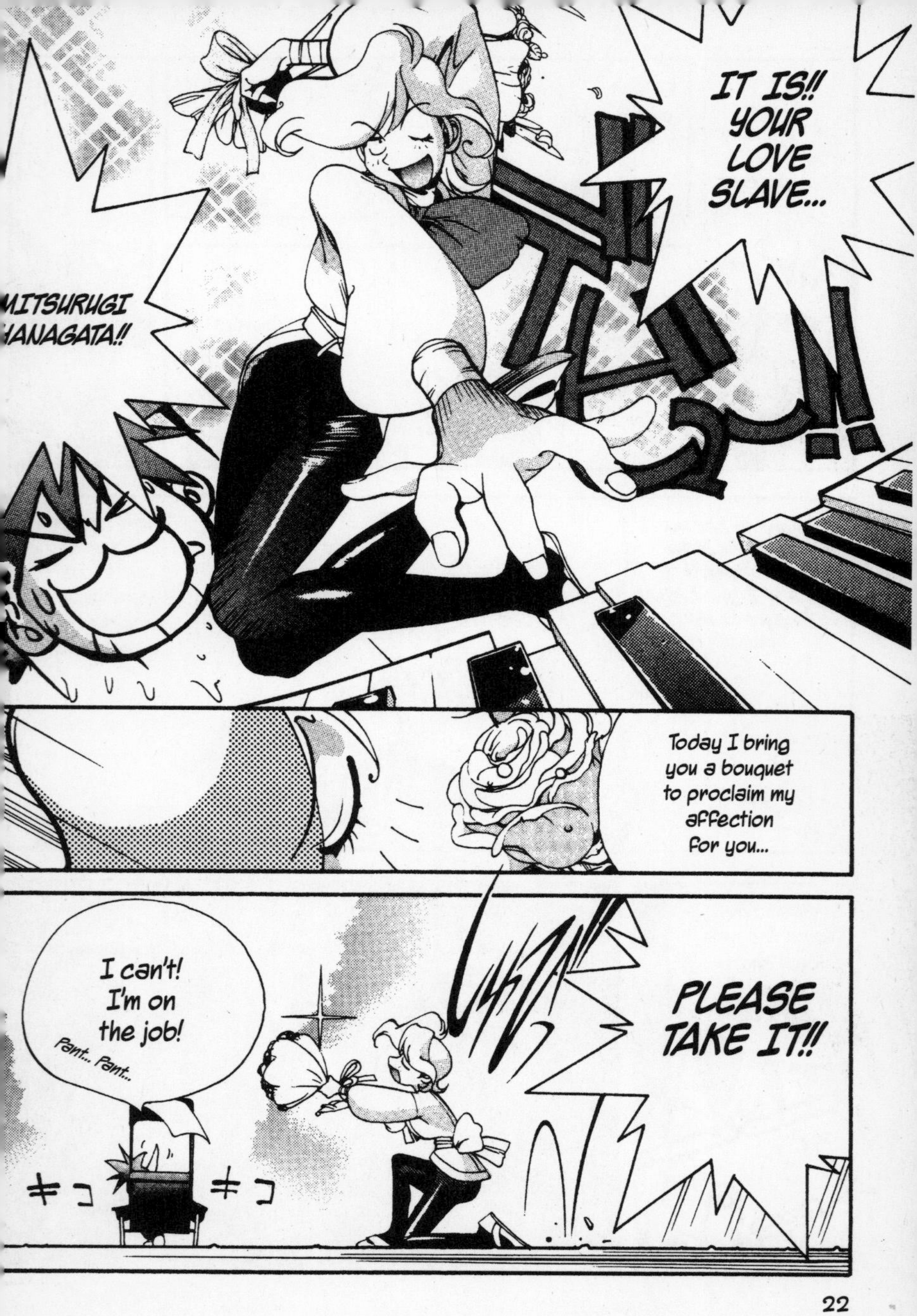
IT IS!! YOUR LOVE SLAVE...
MITSURUGI HANAGATA!!
Today I bring you a bouquet to proclaim my affection for you...
PLEASE TAKE IT!!
I can't! I'm on the job!
Pant... Pant...
キコ キコ

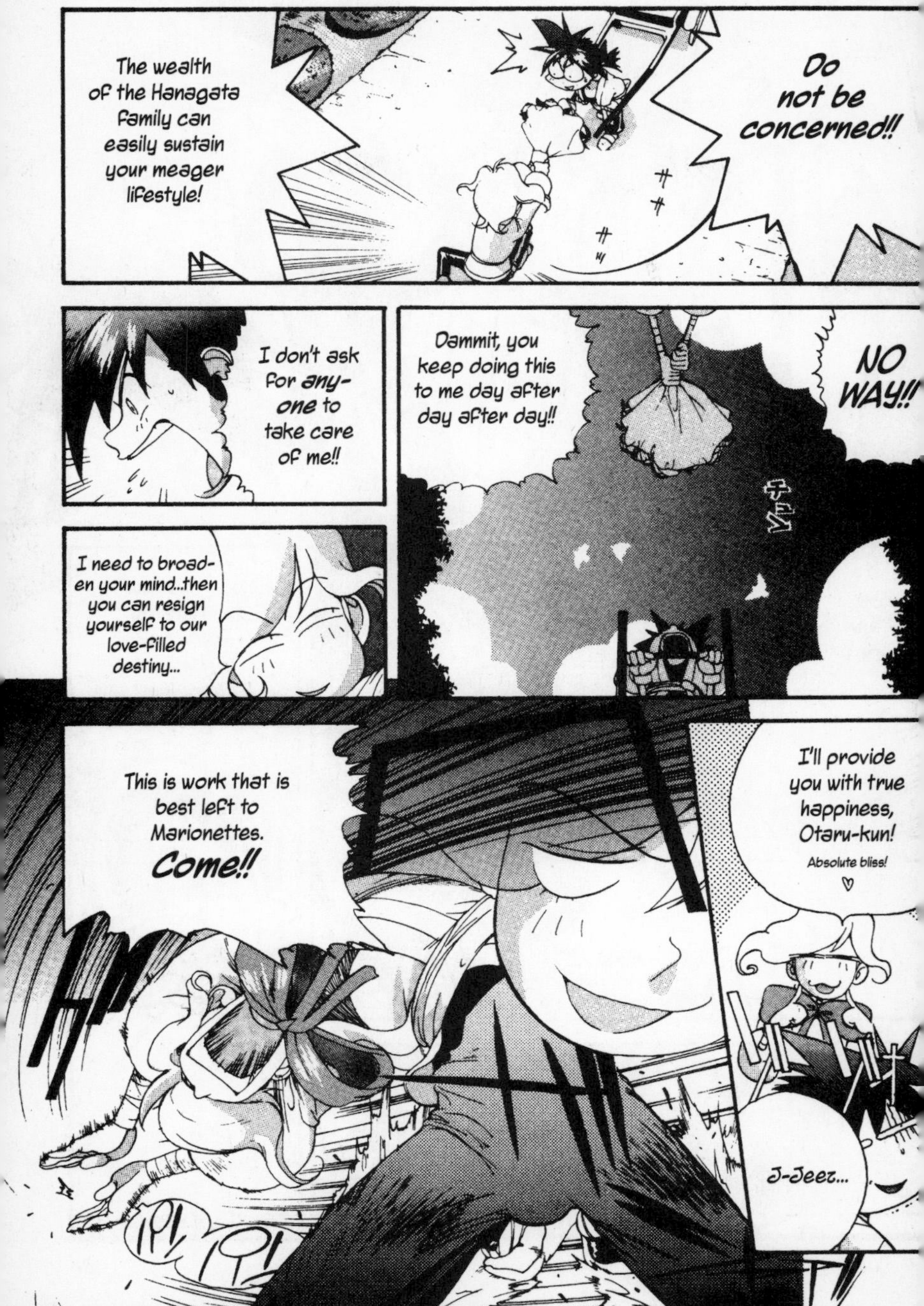
Do not be concerned!!
The wealth of the Hanagata family can easily sustain your meager lifestyle!
NO WAY!!
Dammit, you keep doing this to me day after day after day!!
I don't ask for anyone to take care of me!!
I need to broaden your mind...then you can resign yourself to our love-filled destiny...
I'll provide you with true happiness, Otaru-kun!
Absolute bliss!
J-Jeez...
This is work that is best left to Marionettes.
Come!!

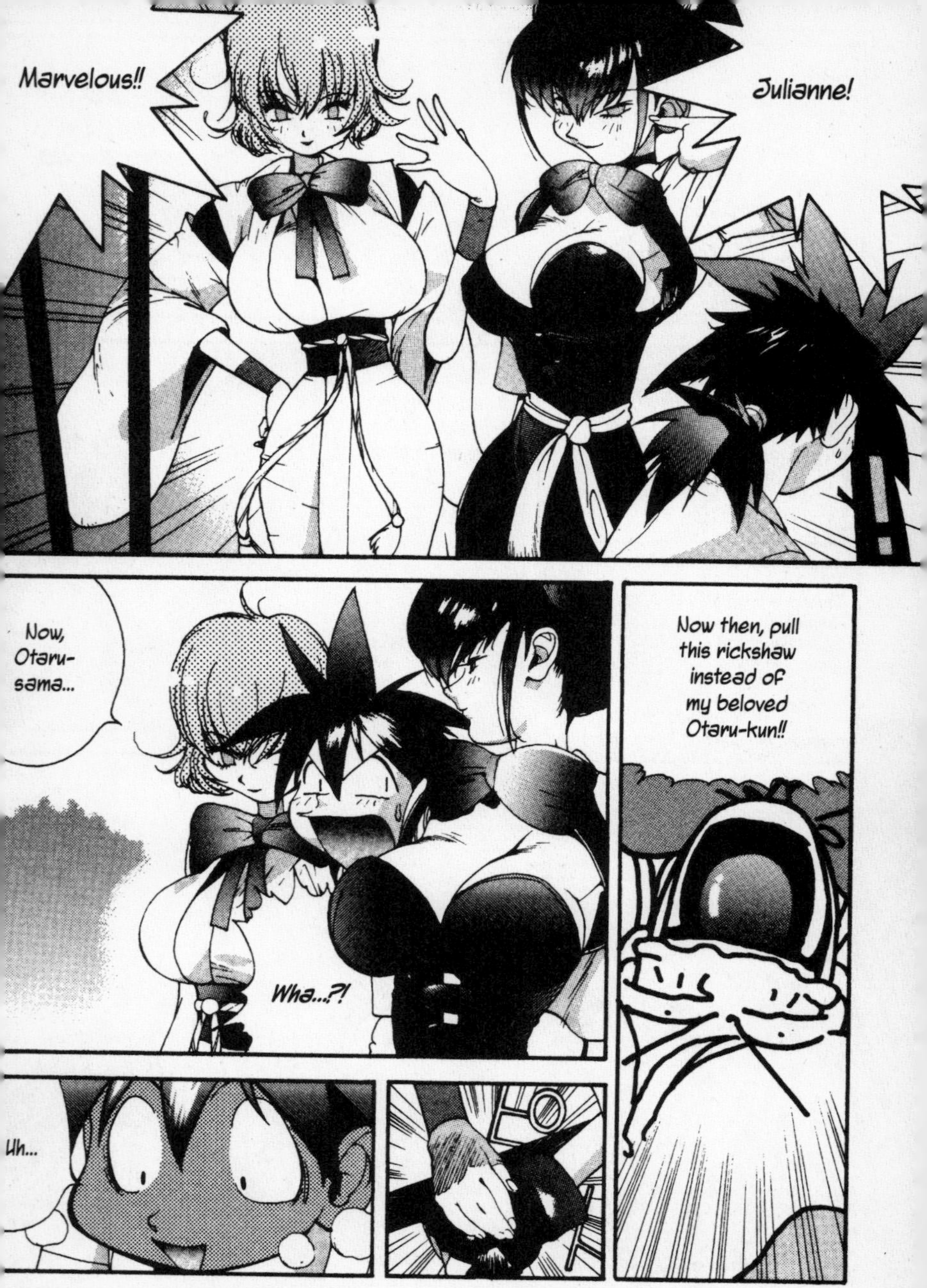
Julianne!
Marvelous!!
Now then, pull this rickshaw instead of my beloved Otaru-kun!!
Now, Otaru-sama...
Wha...?!
Uh...

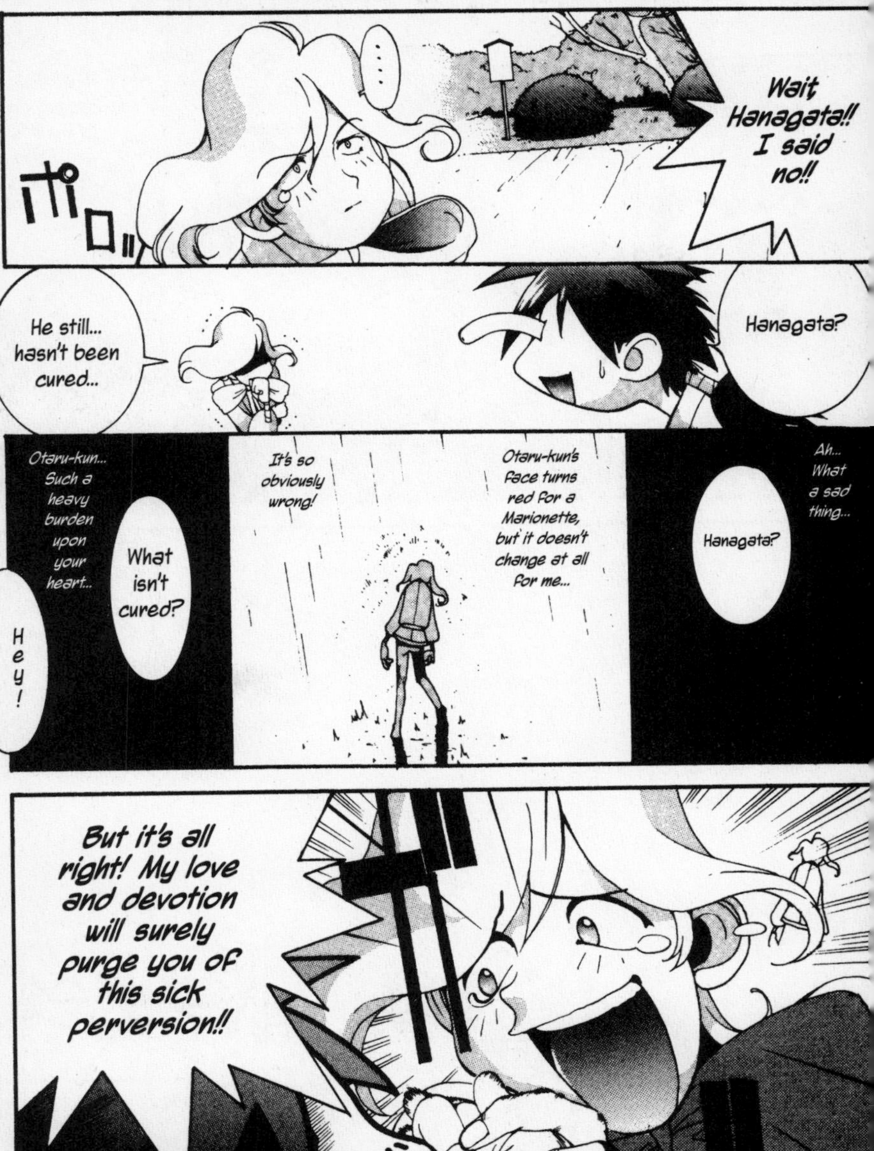
Wait, Hanagata!! I said no!!
...
Hanagata?
He still... hasn't been cured...
Ah... What a sad thing...
Hanagata?
Otaru-kun's face turns red for a Marionette, but it doesn't change at all for me...
It's so obviously wrong!
Otaru-kun... Such a heavy burden upon your heart...
What isn't cured?
Hey!
But it's all right! My love and devotion will surely purge you of this sick perversion!!

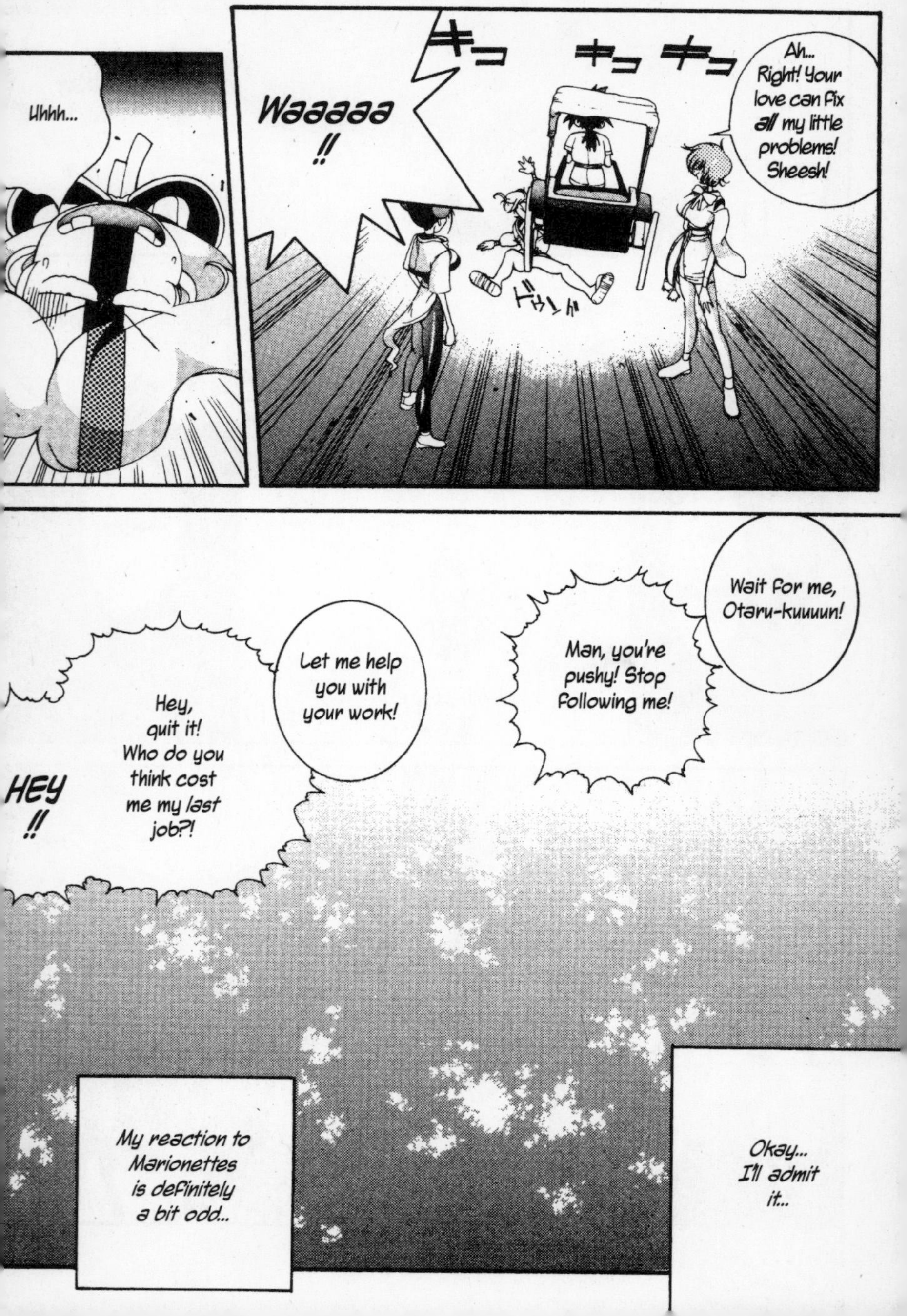
Ah... Right! Your love can fix all my little problems! Sheesh!
キッ キッ キッ
Waaaaa !!
Uhhh...
Wait for me, Otaru-kuuuun!
Man, you're pushy! Stop following me!
Let me help you with your work!
Hey, quit it! Who do you think cost me my last job?!
HEY !!
Okay... I'll admit it...
My reaction to Marionettes is definitely a bit odd...

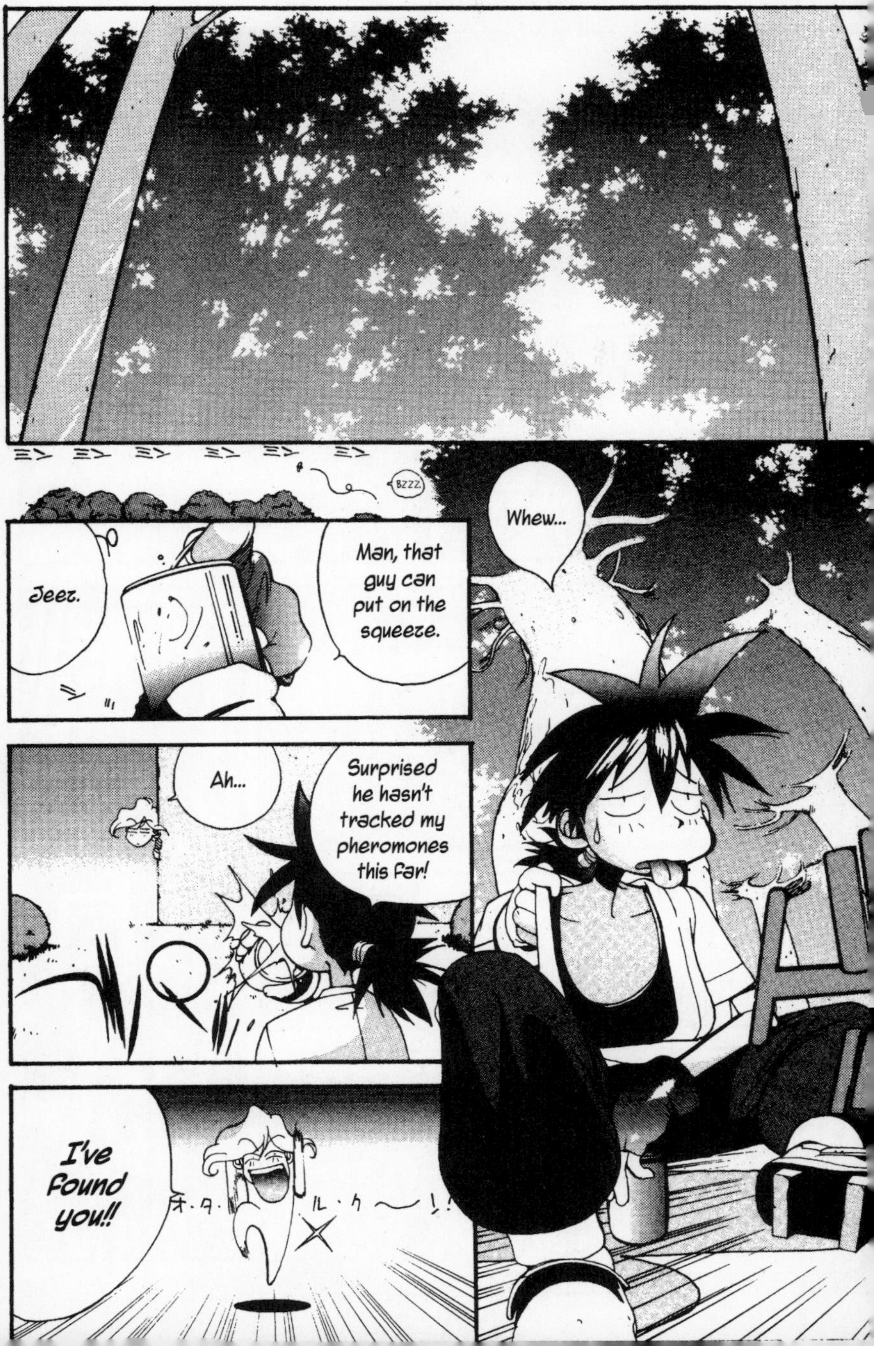
Whew...
BZZZ
Man, that guy can put on the squeeze.
Jeez.
Surprised he hasn't tracked my pheromones this far!
Ah...
I've found you!!
オ・タ・ル・ク～！！

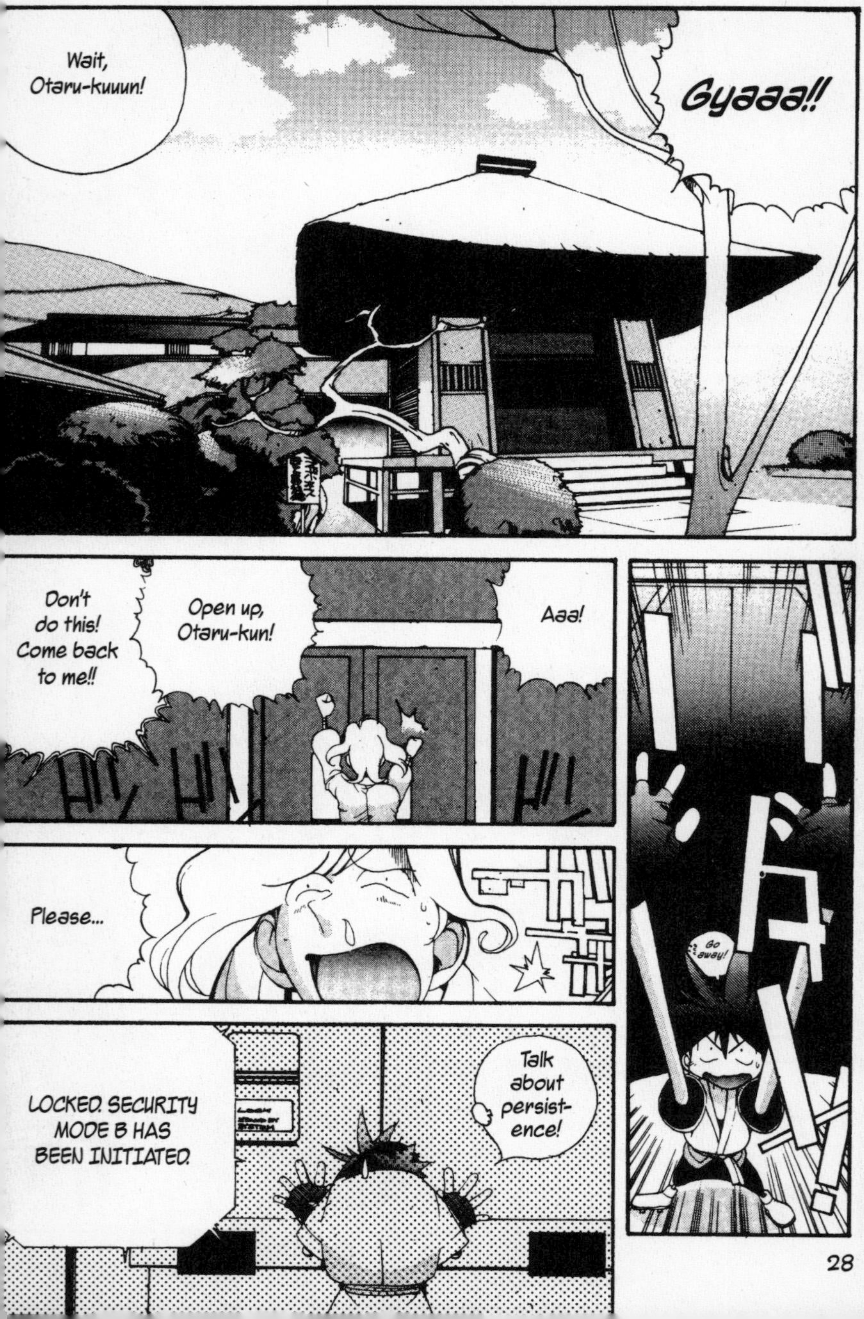
Gyaaa!!
Wait, Otaru-kuuun!
Go away!
Aaa!
Open up, Otaru-kun!
Don't do this! Come back to me!!
Please...
Talk about persist-ence!
LOCKED. SECURITY MODE B HAS BEEN INITIATED.

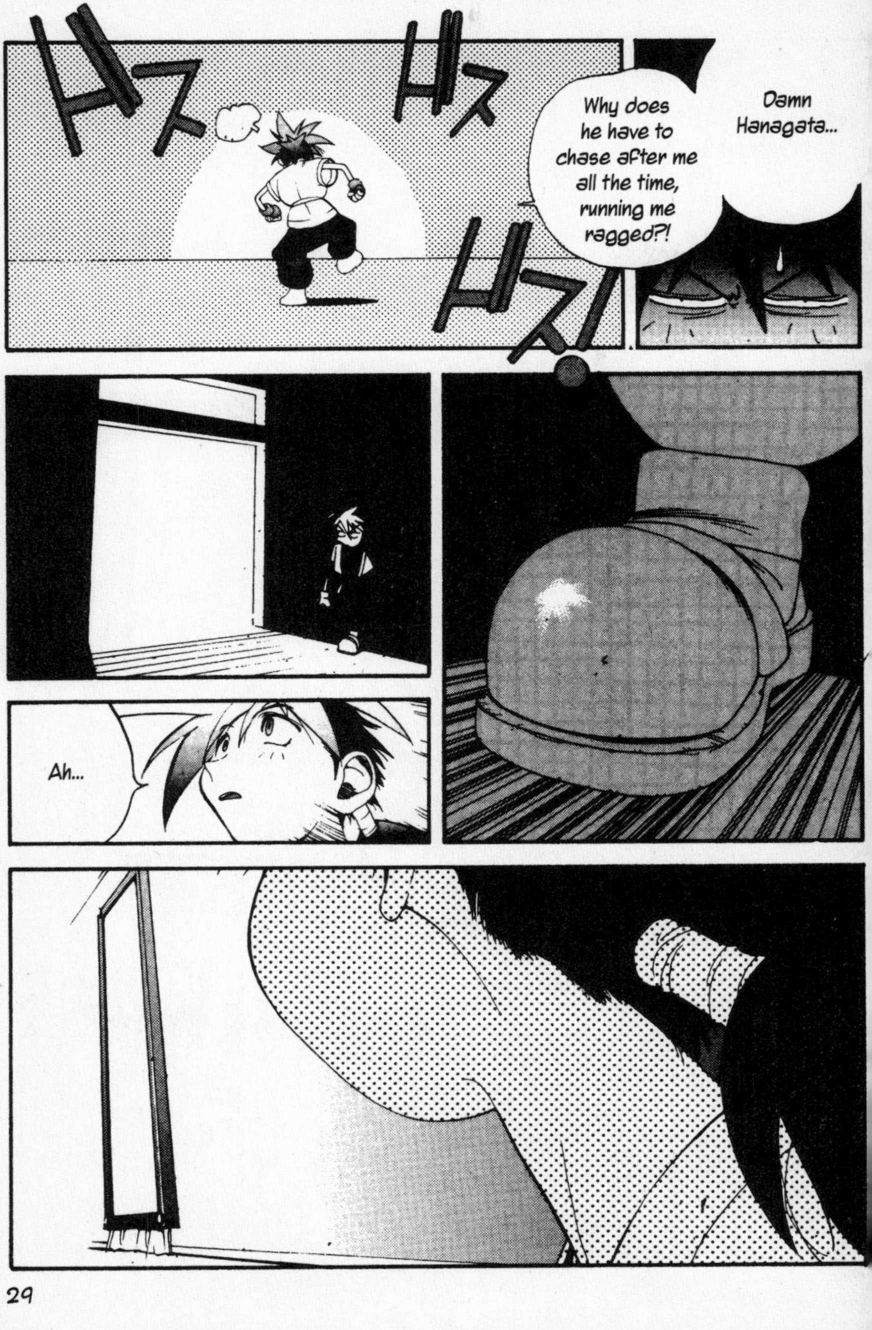
Damn Hanagata...
Why does he have to chase after me all the time, running me ragged?!
Ah...

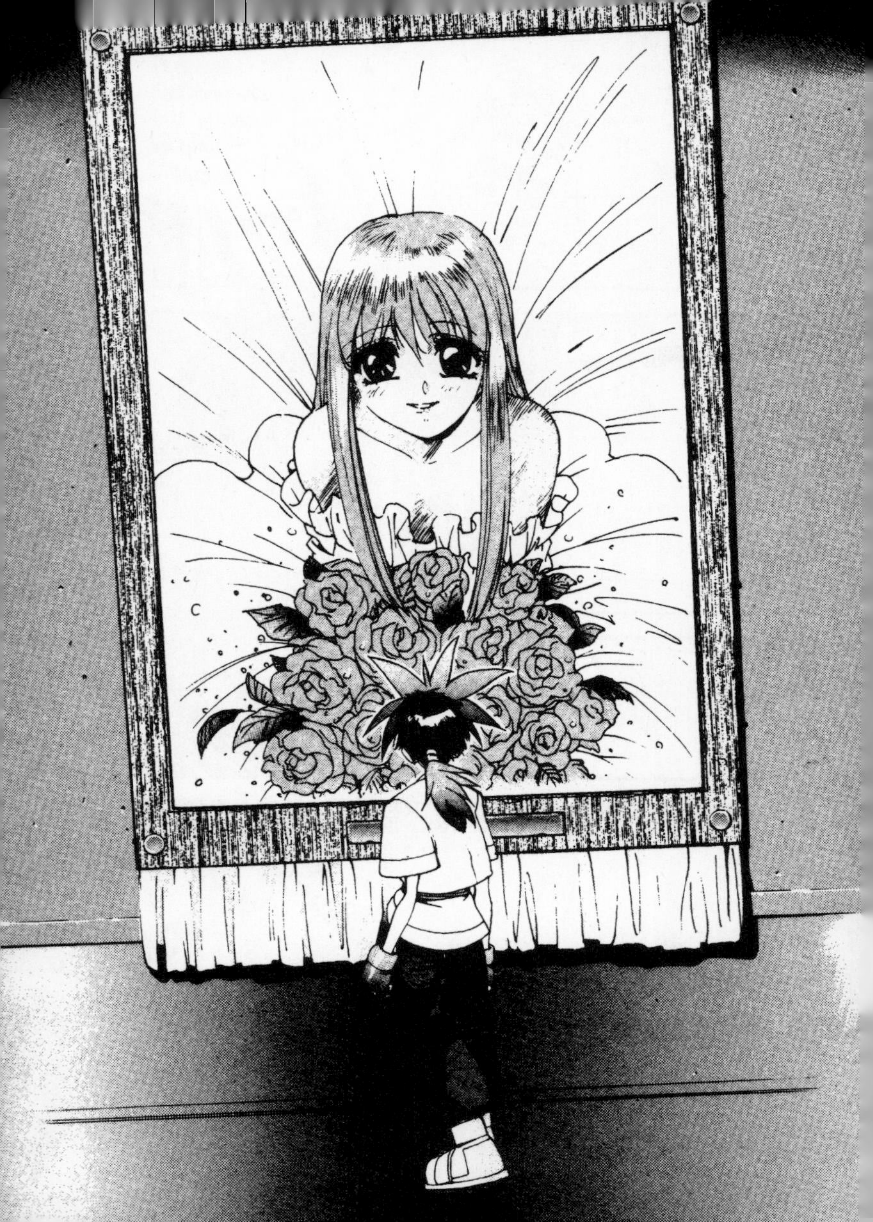

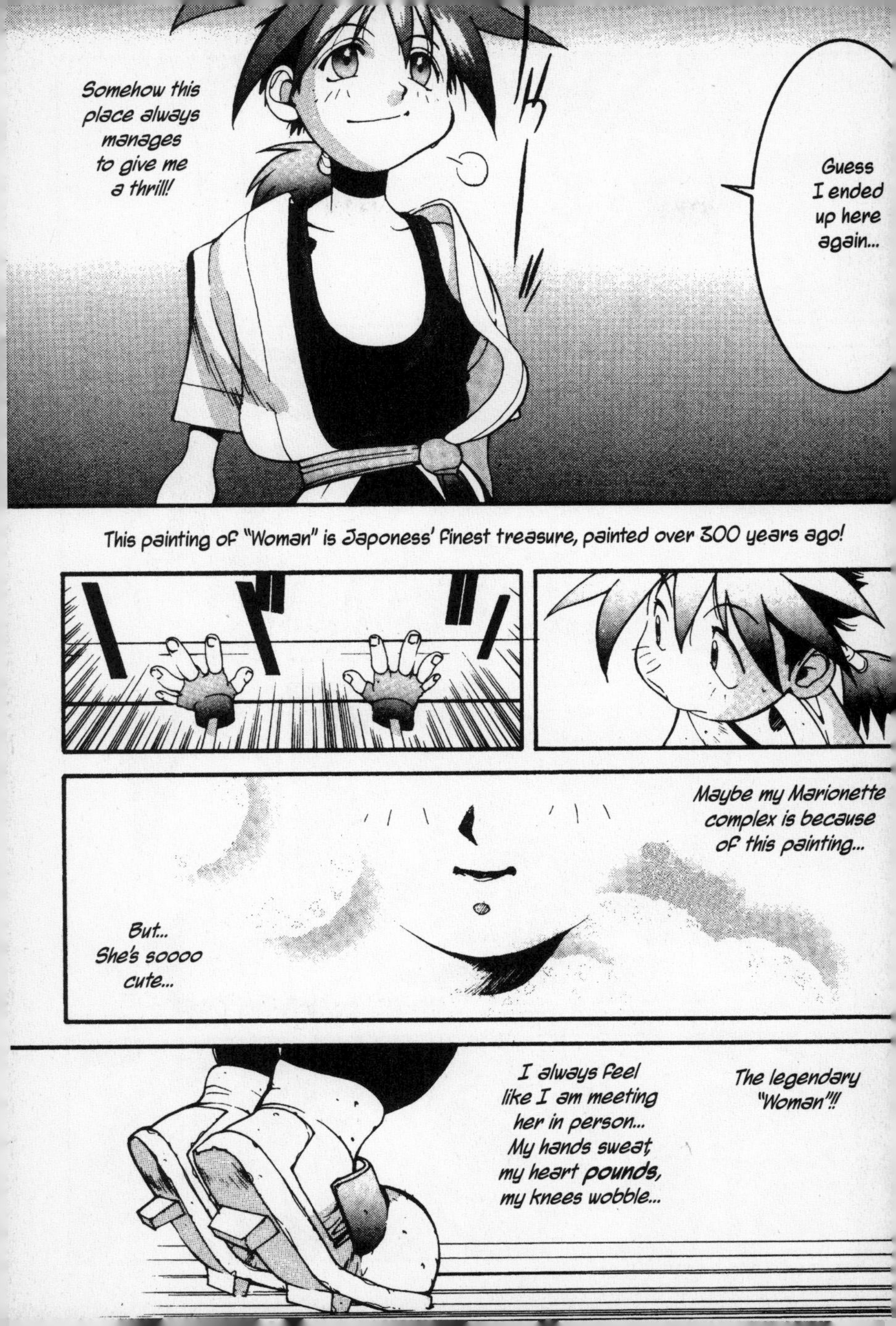
Guess I ended up here again...
Somehow this place always manages to give me a thrill!
This painting of "Woman" is Japoness' finest treasure, painted over 300 years ago!
Maybe my Marionette complex is because of this painting...
But... She's soooo cute...
The legendary "Woman"!!
I always feel like I am meeting her in person... My hands sweat, my heart pounds, my knees wobble...

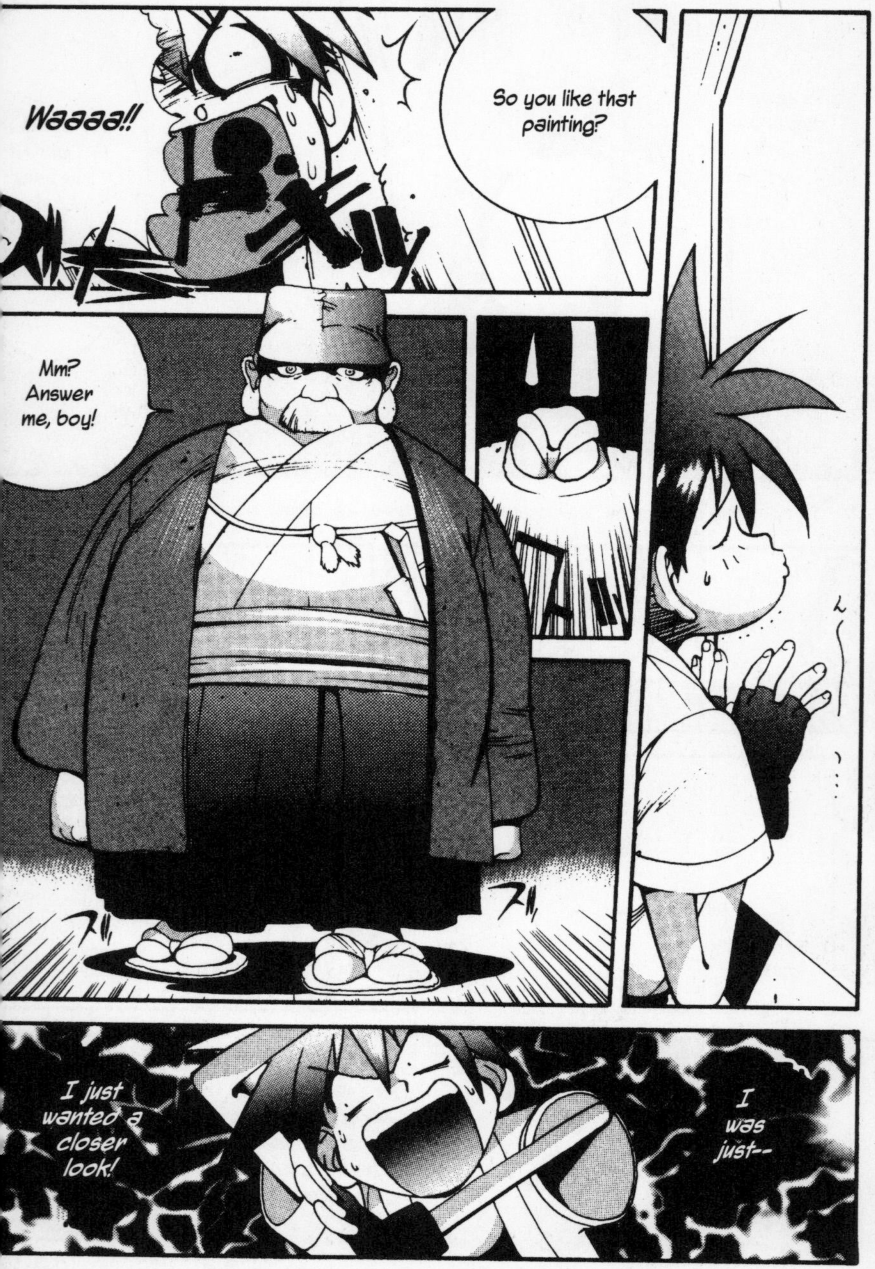
So you like that painting?
Waaaa!!
Mm? Answer me, boy!
I was just--
I just wanted a closer look!

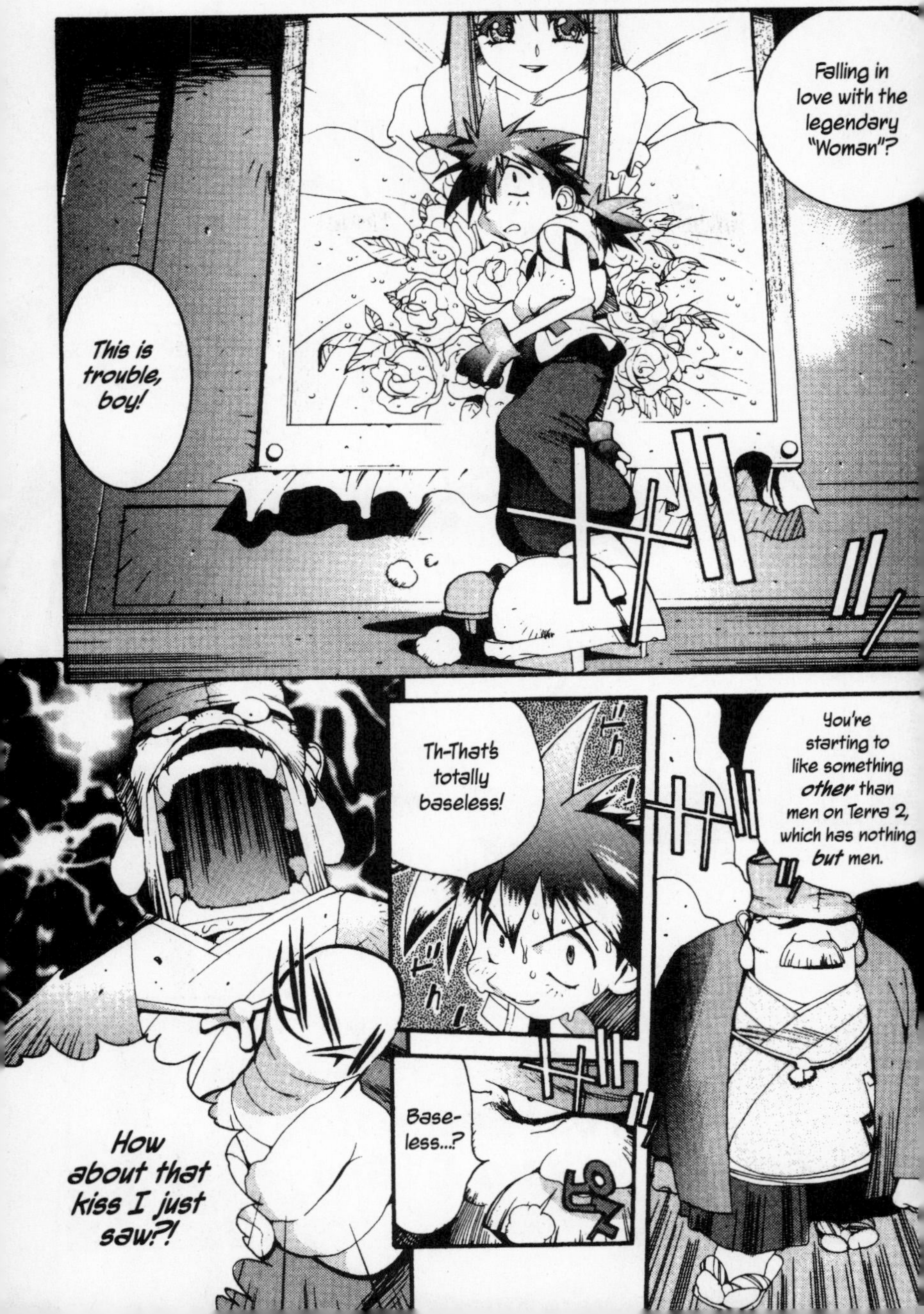
Falling in love with the legendary "Woman"?
This is trouble, boy!
You're starting to like something *other* than men on Terra 2, which has nothing *but* men.
Th-That's totally baseless!
Base-less...?
How about that kiss I just saw?!

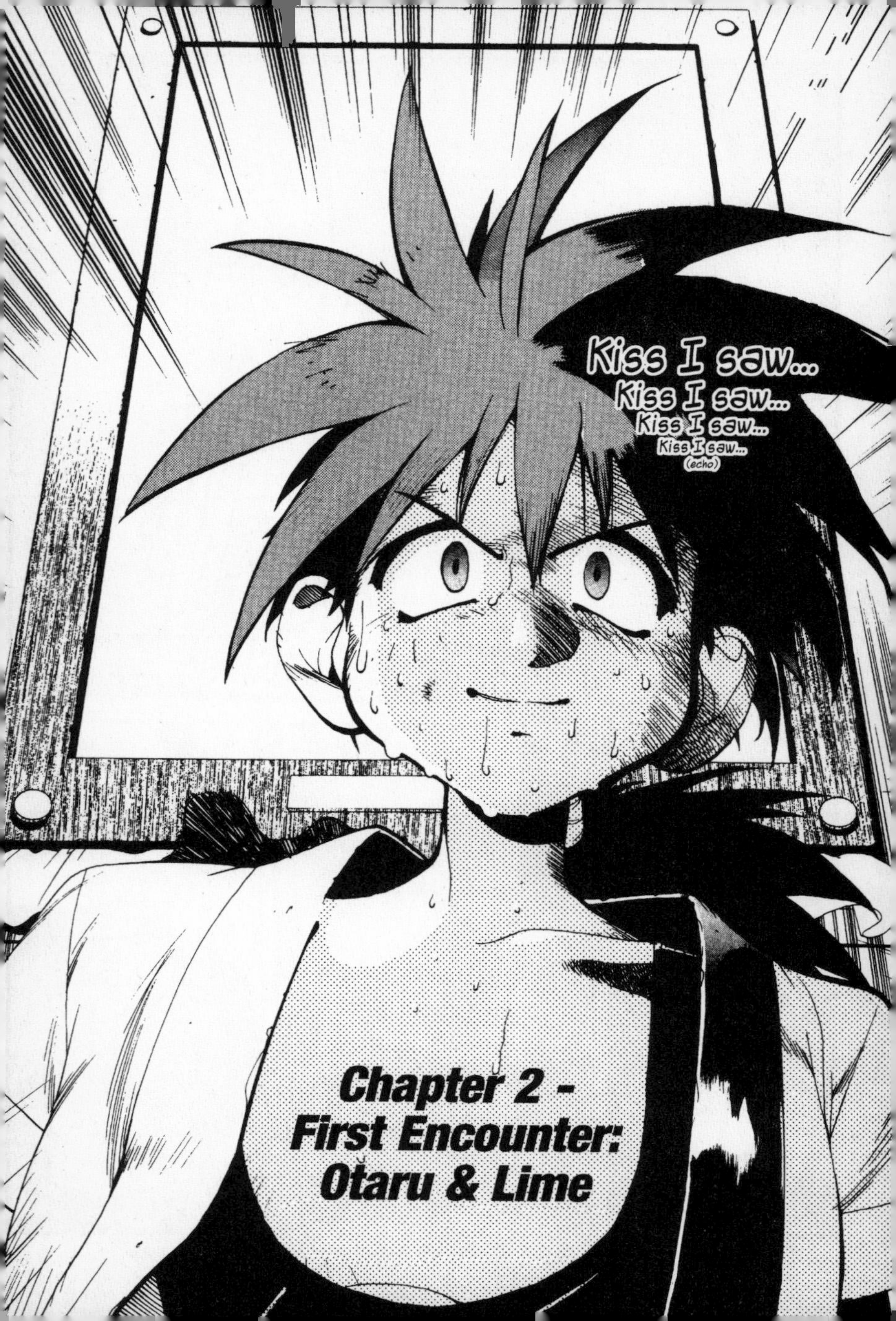
Kiss I saw...
Kiss I saw...
Kiss I saw...
Kiss I saw...
(echo)
Chapter 2 - First Encounter: Otaru & Lime

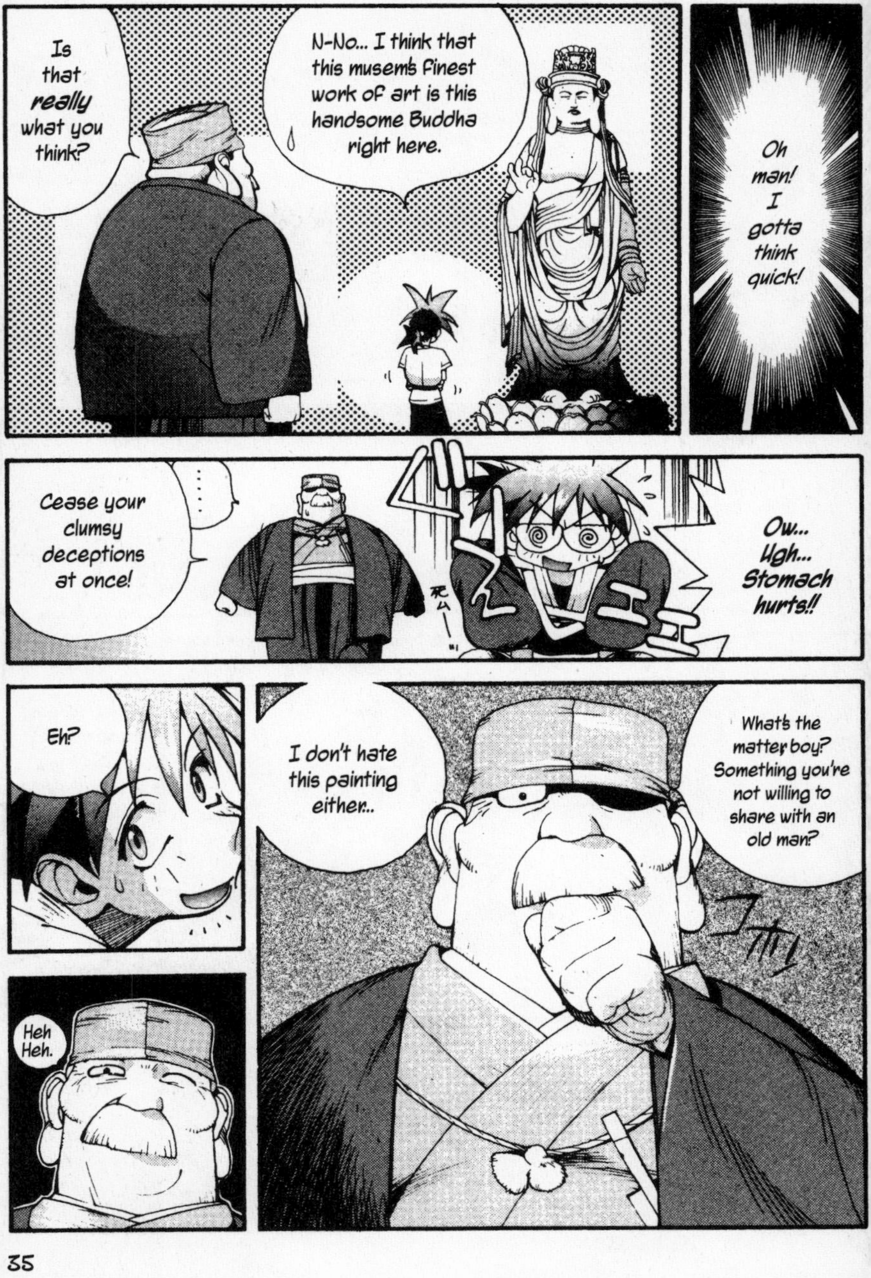
Oh man! I gotta think quick!
N-No... I think that this musem's finest work of art is this handsome Buddha right here.
Is that really what you think?
Ow... Ugh... Stomach hurts!!
...
Cease your clumsy deceptions at once!
What's the matter, boy? Something you're not willing to share with an old man?
I don't hate this painting either...
Eh?
Heh Heh.

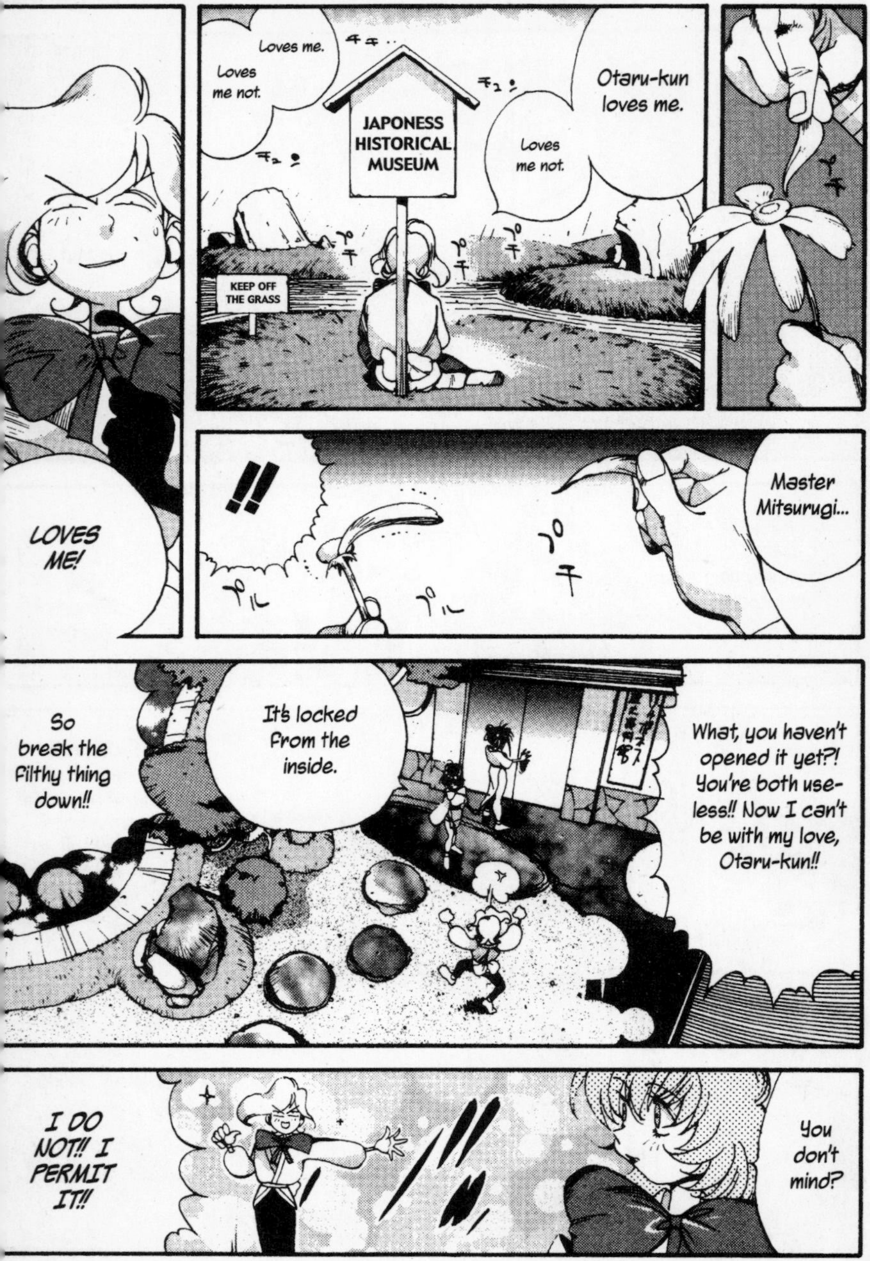
Otaru-kun loves me.
Loves me not.
JAPONESS HISTORICAL MUSEUM
Loves me.
Loves me not.
KEEP OFF THE GRASS
Master Mitsurugi...
!!
LOVES ME!
What, you haven't opened it yet?! You're both useless!! Now I can't be with my love, Otaru-kun!!
It's locked from the inside.
So break the filthy thing down!!
You don't mind?
I DO NOT!! I PERMIT IT!!

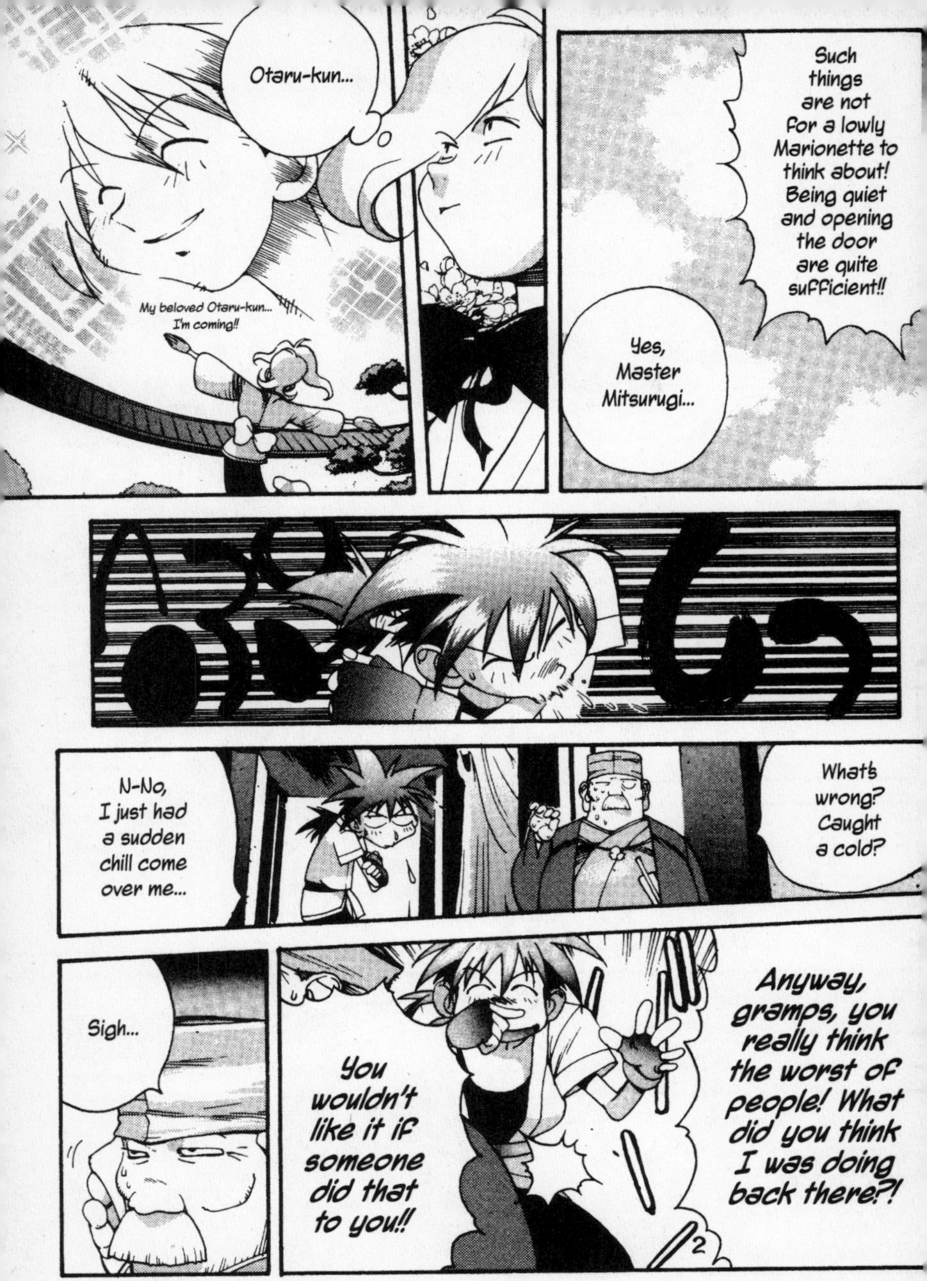

Such things are not for a lowly Marionette to think about! Being quiet and opening the door are quite sufficient!!
Yes, Master Mitsurugi...
Otaru-kun...
My beloved Otaru-kun... I'm coming!!
What's wrong? Caught a cold?
N-No, I just had a sudden chill come over me...
Anyway, gramps, you really think the worst of people! What did you think I was doing back there?!
You wouldn't like it if someone did that to you!!
Sigh...

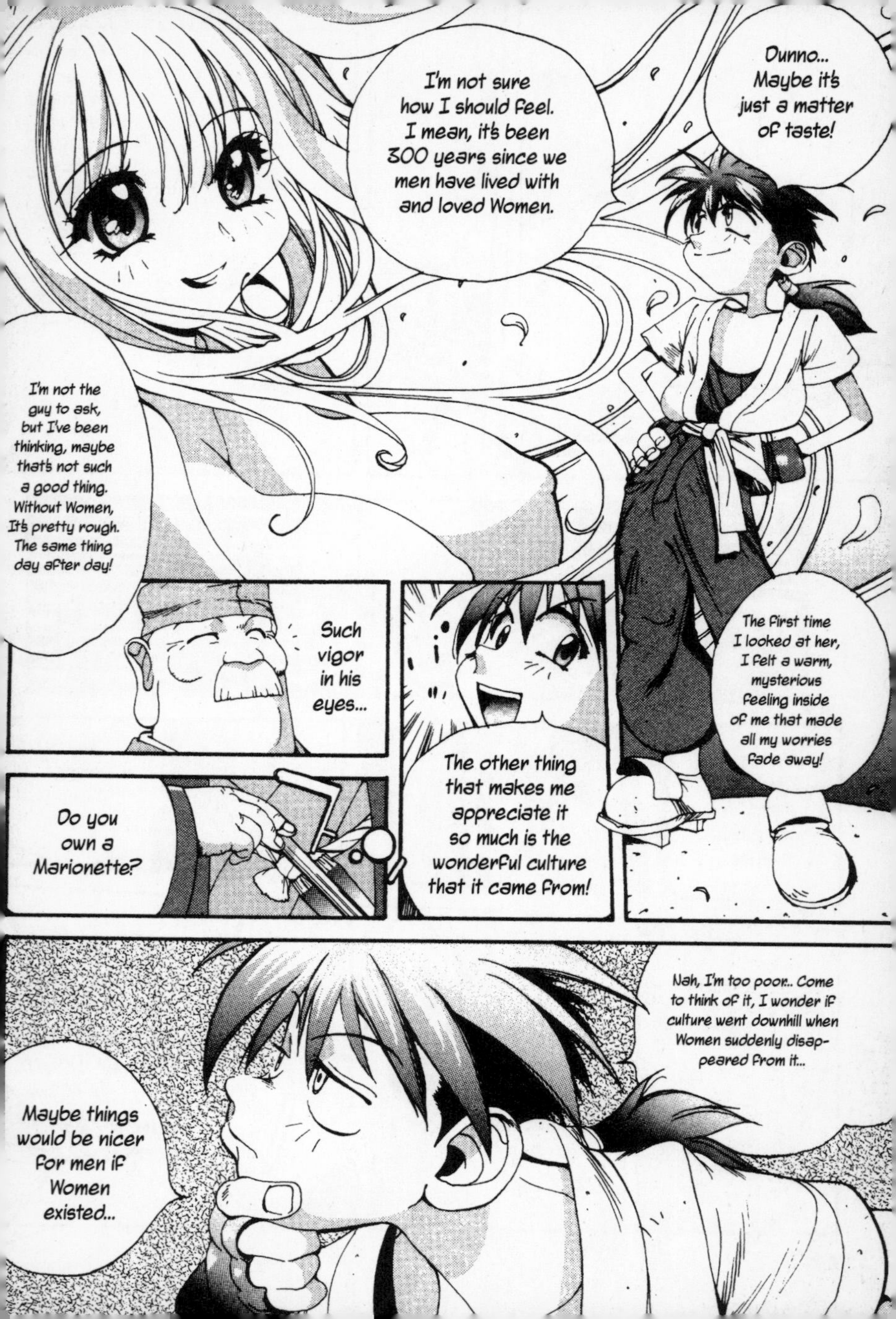
Dunno... Maybe it's just a matter of taste!
I'm not sure how I should feel. I mean, it's been 300 years since we men have lived with and loved Women.
I'm not the guy to ask, but I've been thinking, maybe that's not such a good thing. Without Women, It's pretty rough. The same thing day after day!
The first time I looked at her, I felt a warm, mysterious feeling inside of me that made all my worries fade away!
The other thing that makes me appreciate it so much is the wonderful culture that it came from!
Such vigor in his eyes...
Do you own a Marionette?
Nah, I'm too poor... Come to think of it, I wonder if culture went downhill when Women suddenly disappeared from it...
Maybe things would be nicer for men if Women existed...

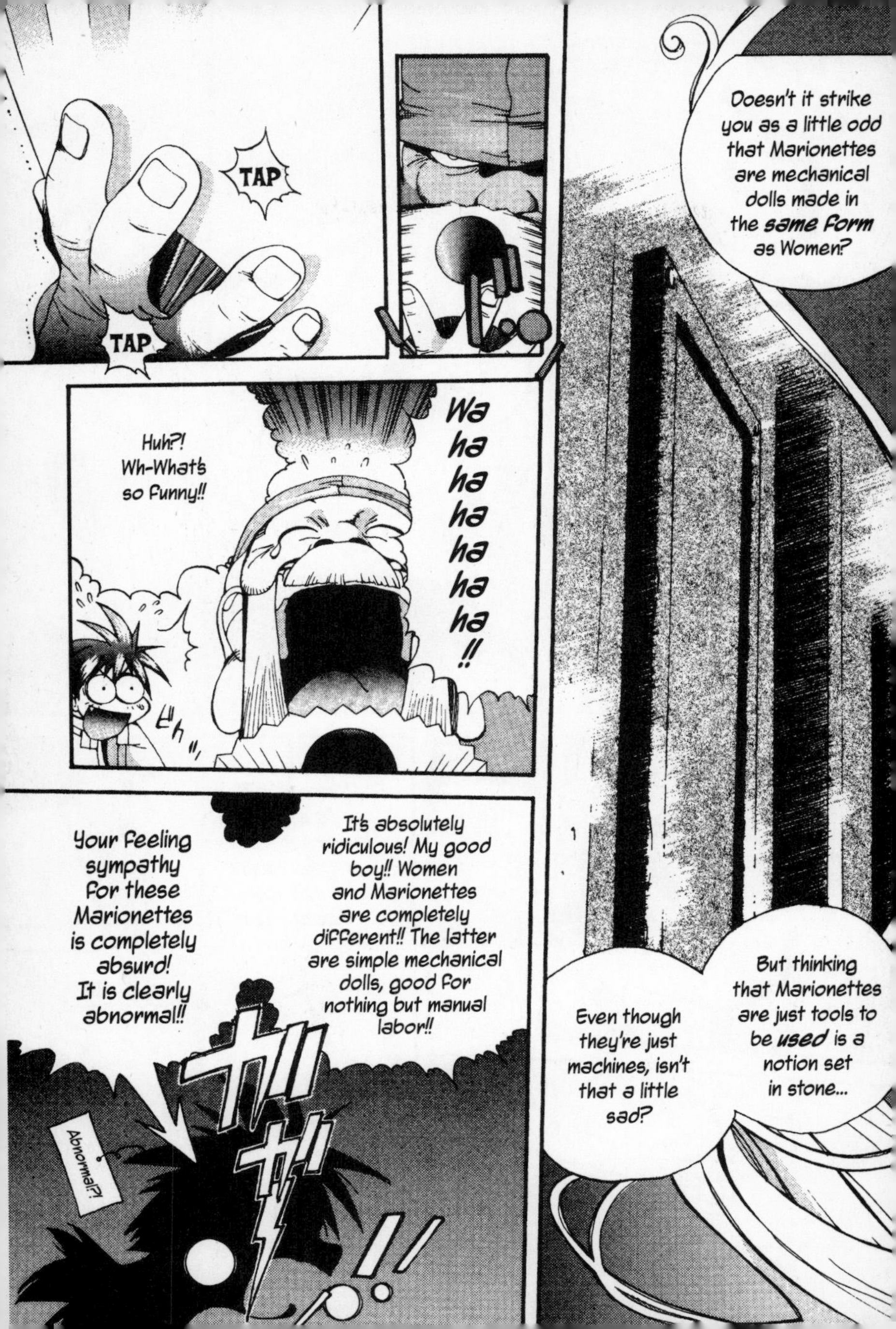

Doesn't it strike you as a little odd that Marionettes are mechanical dolls made in the ***same form*** as Women?
But thinking that Marionettes are just tools to be ***used*** is a notion set in stone...
Even though they're just machines, isn't that a little sad?
TAP
TAP
Wa ha ha ha ha ha ha!!
Huh?! Wh-What's so funny!!
It's absolutely ridiculous! My good boy!! Women and Marionettes are completely different!! The latter are simple mechanical dolls, good for nothing but manual labor!!
Your feeling sympathy for these Marionettes is completely absurd! It is clearly abnormal!!
Abnormal!?

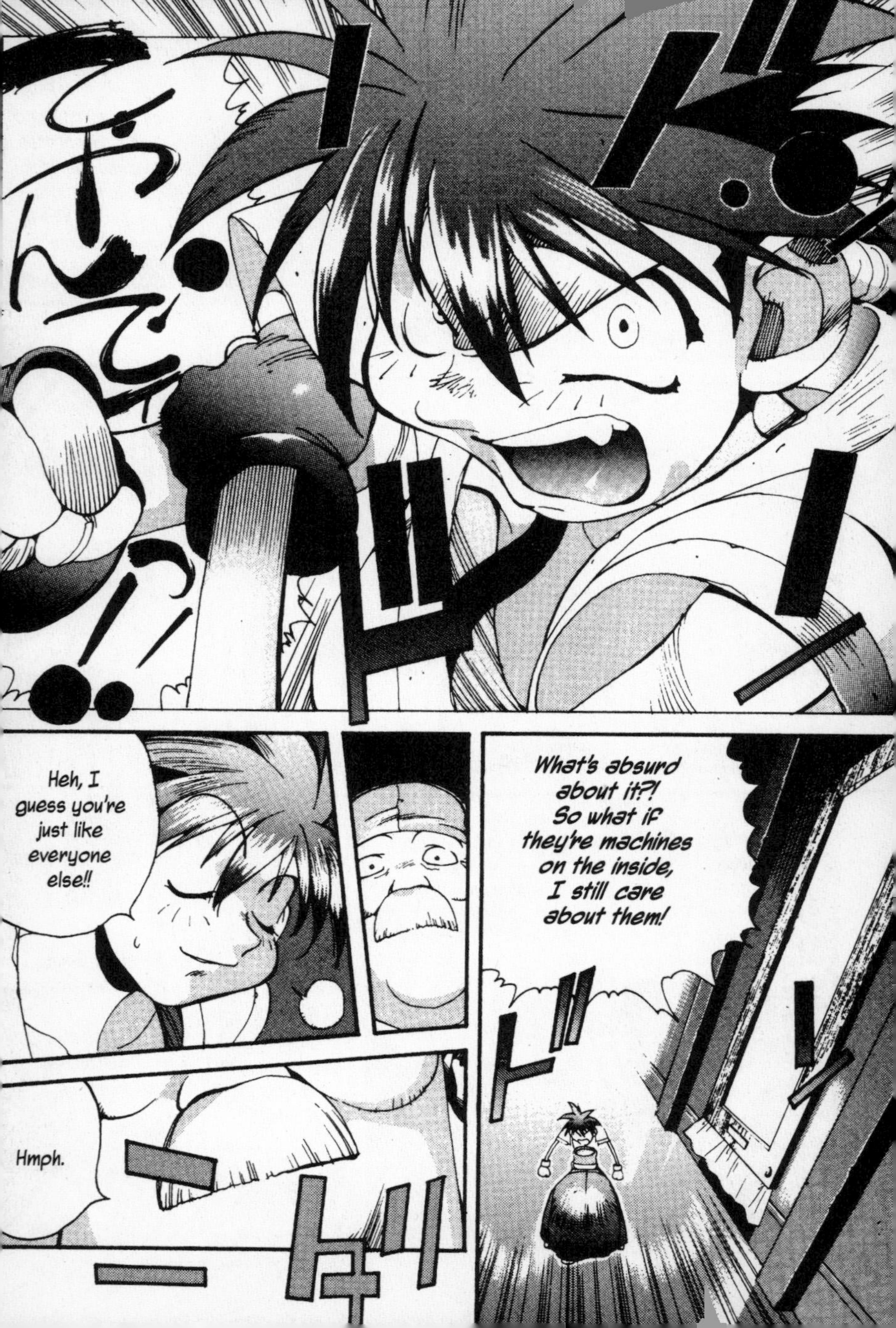
What's absurd about it?! So what if they're machines on the inside, I still care about them!
Heh, I guess you're just like everyone else!!
Hmph.

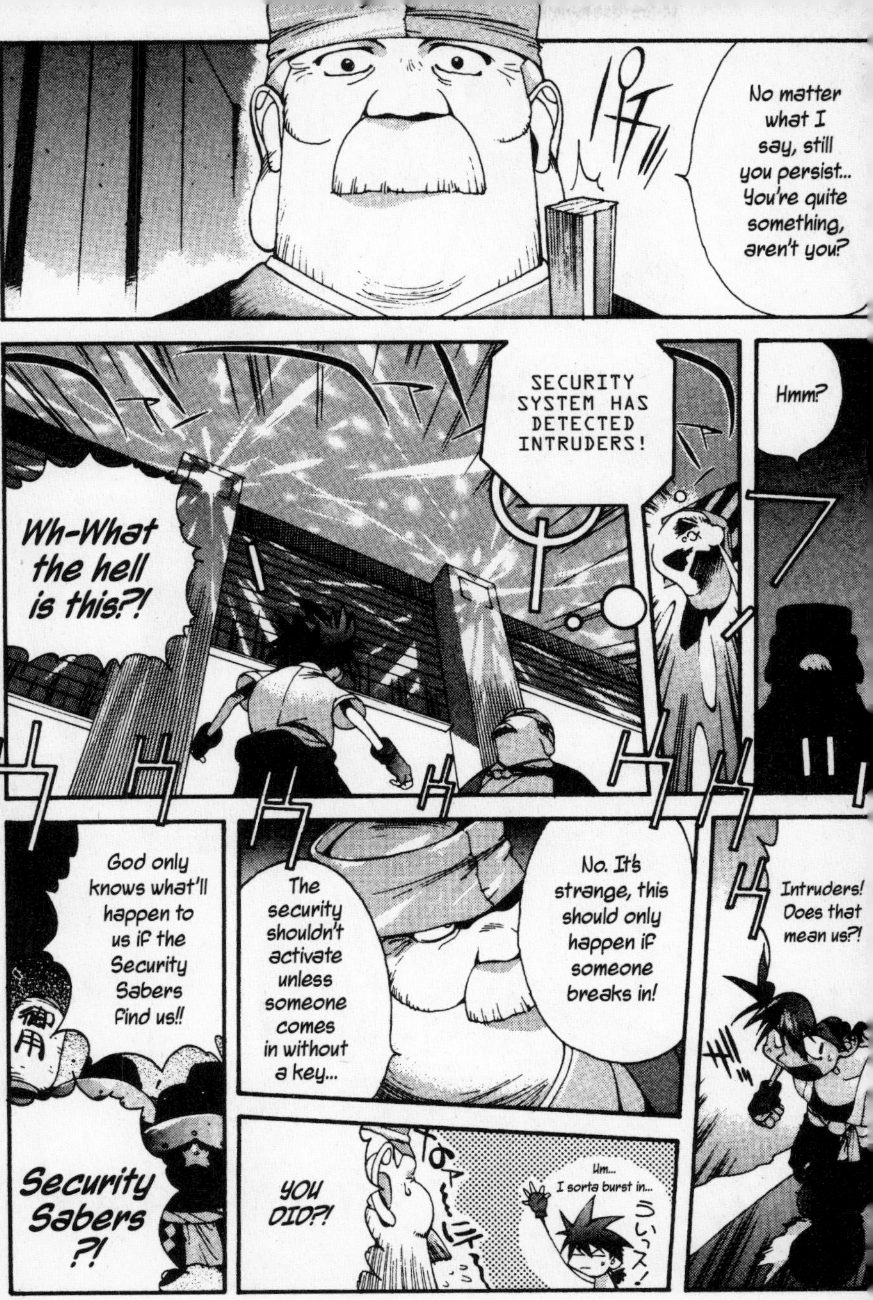
No matter what I say, still you persist... You're quite something, aren't you?
Hmm?
SECURITY SYSTEM HAS DETECTED INTRUDERS!
Wh-What the hell is this?!
Intruders! Does that mean us?!
No. It's strange, this should only happen if someone breaks in!
The security shouldn't activate unless someone comes in without a key...
Um... I sorta burst in...
YOU DID?!
God only knows what'll happen to us if the Security Sabers find us!!
Security Sabers?!

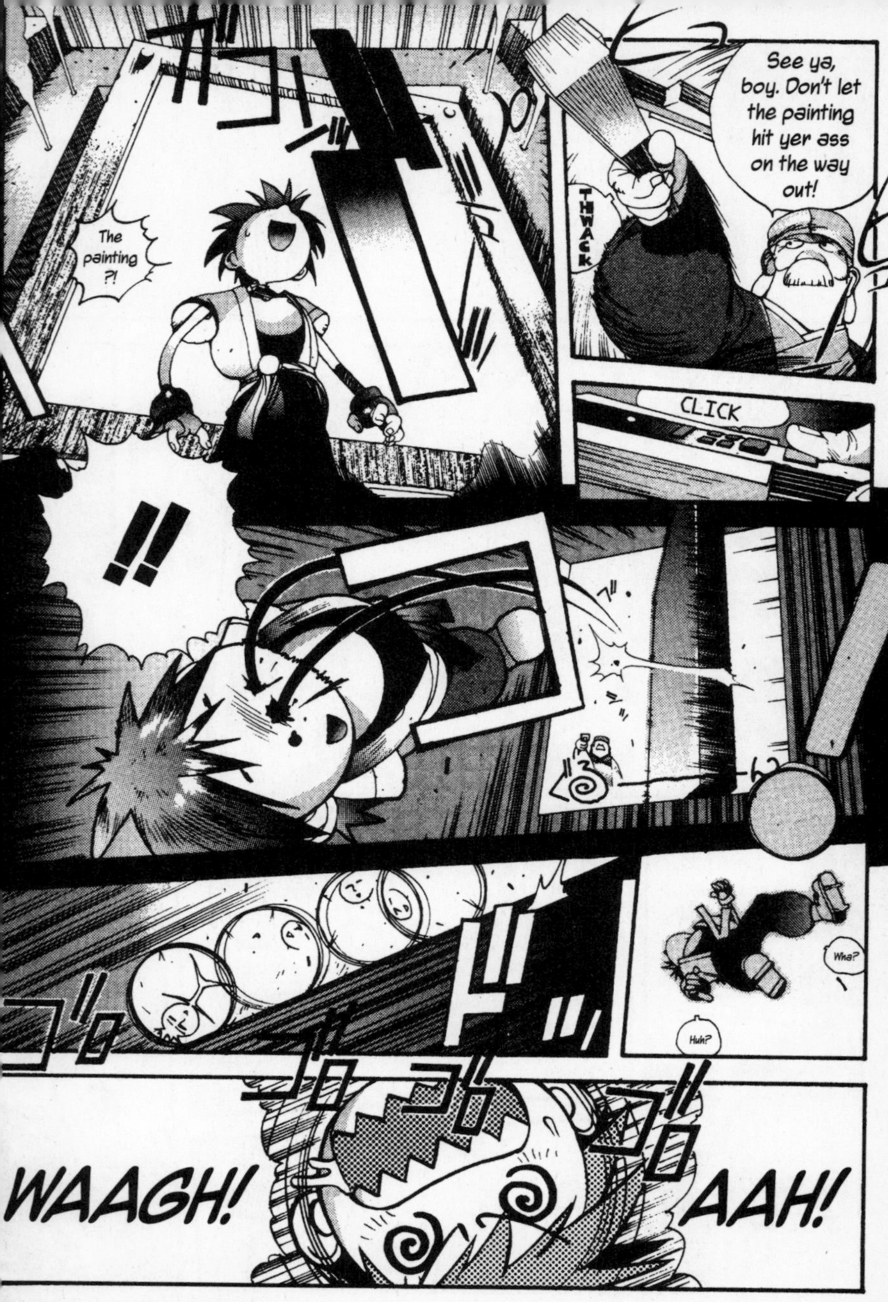
See ya, boy. Don't let the painting hit yer ass on the way out!
THWACK
CLICK
The painting ?!
!!
Wha?
Huh?
WAAGH!
AAH!

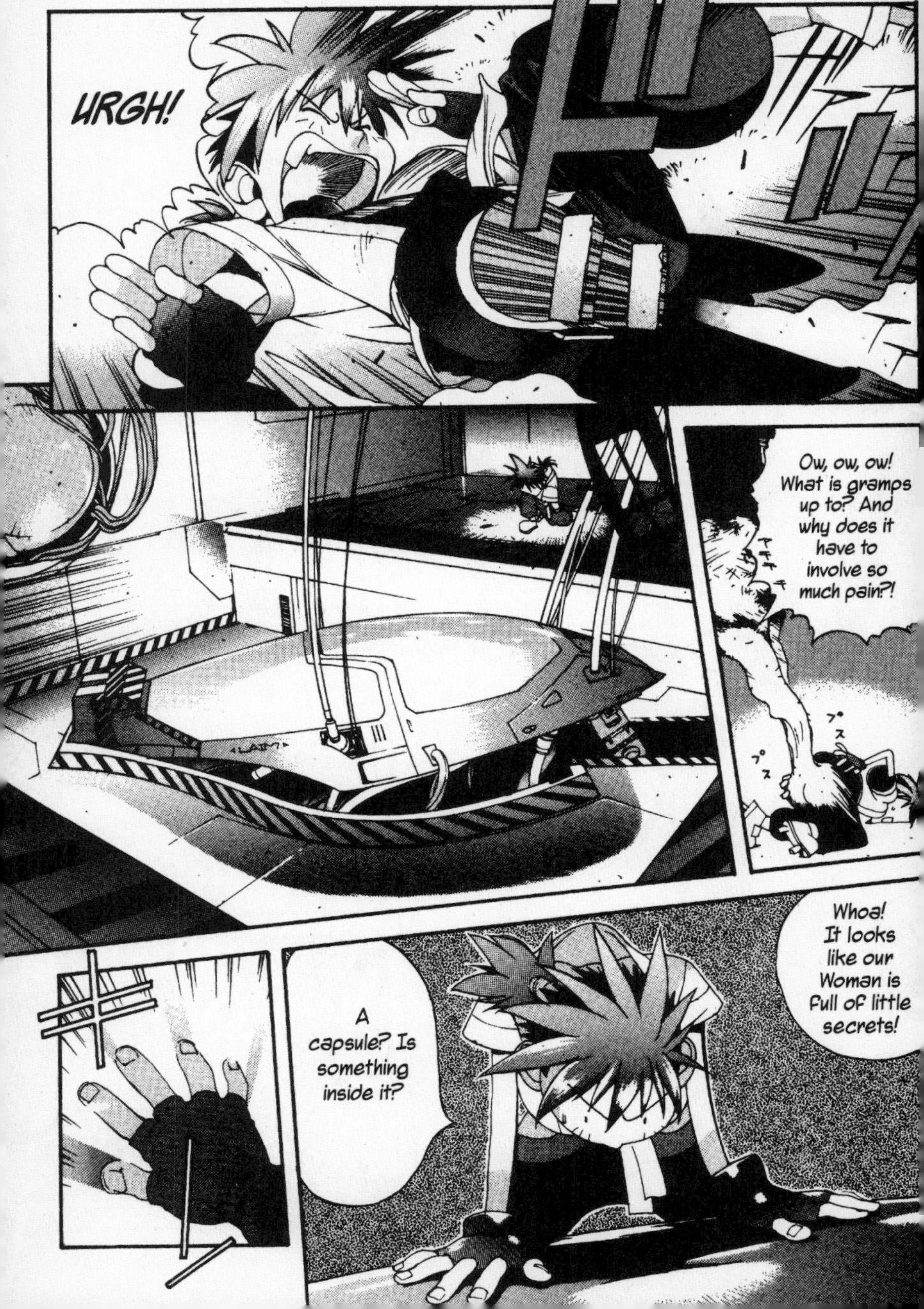
URGH!
Ow, ow, ow! What is gramps up to? And why does it have to involve so much pain?!
Whoa! It looks like our Woman is full of little secrets!
A capsule? Is something inside it?

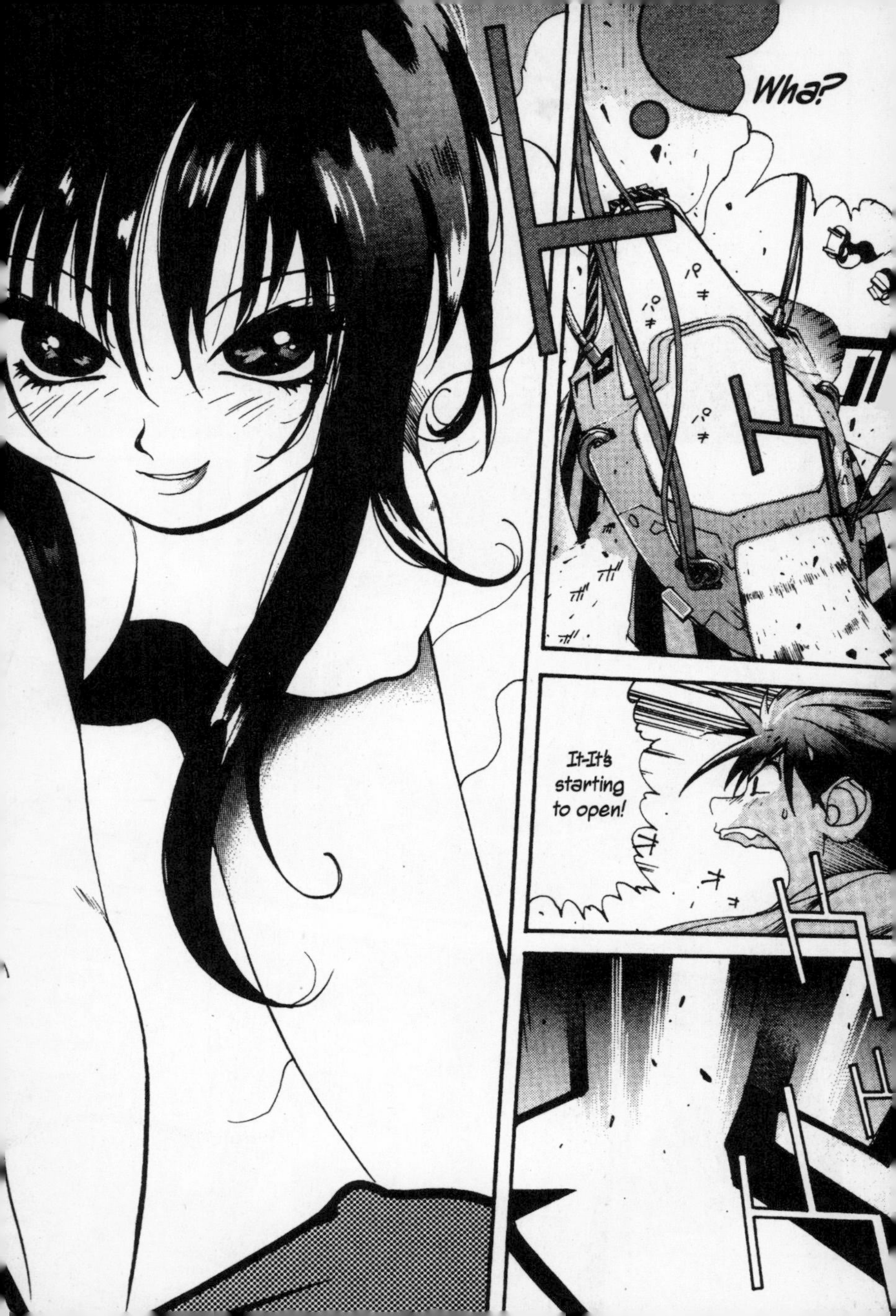
Wha?
It-It's starting to open!

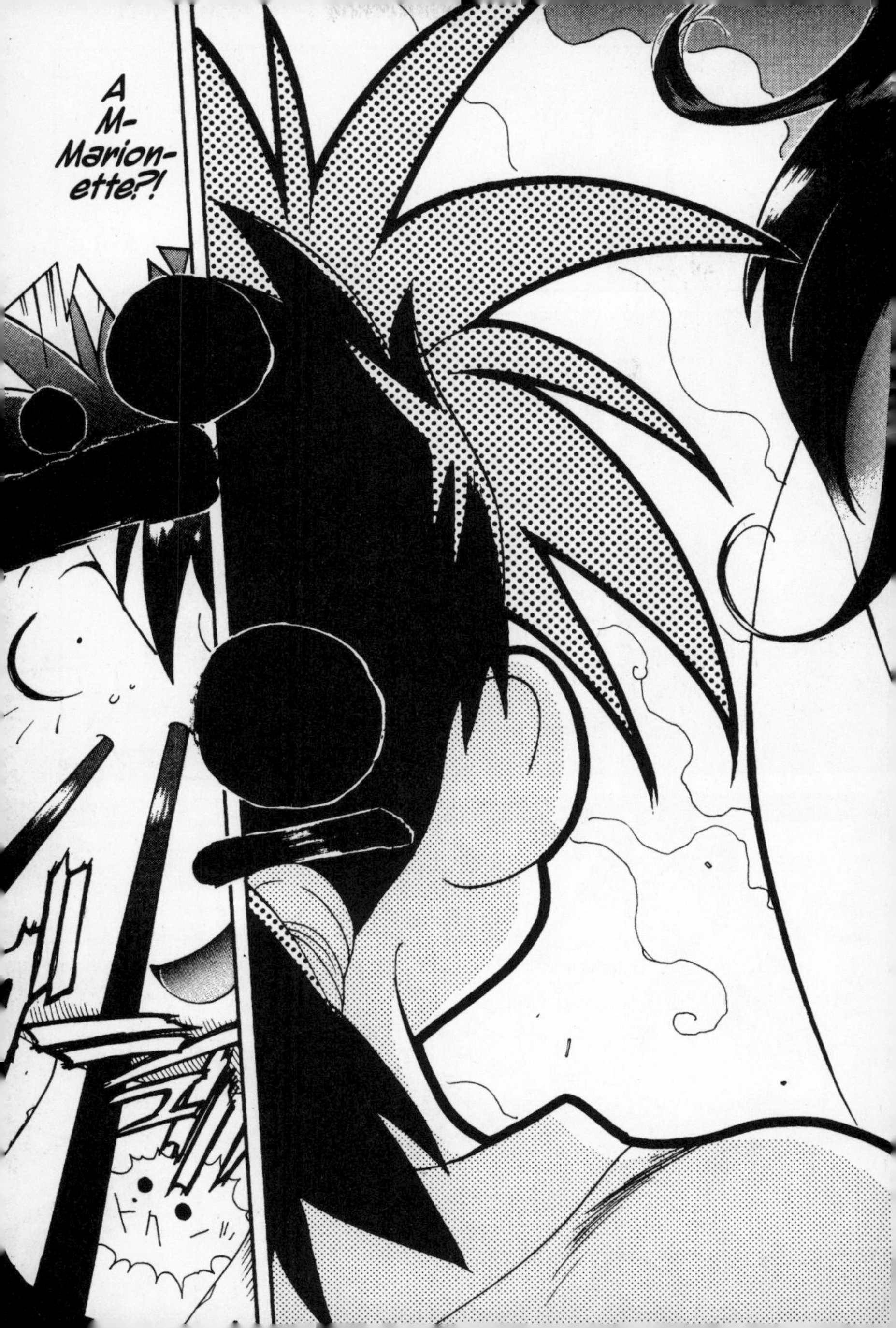
A M-Marion-ette?!

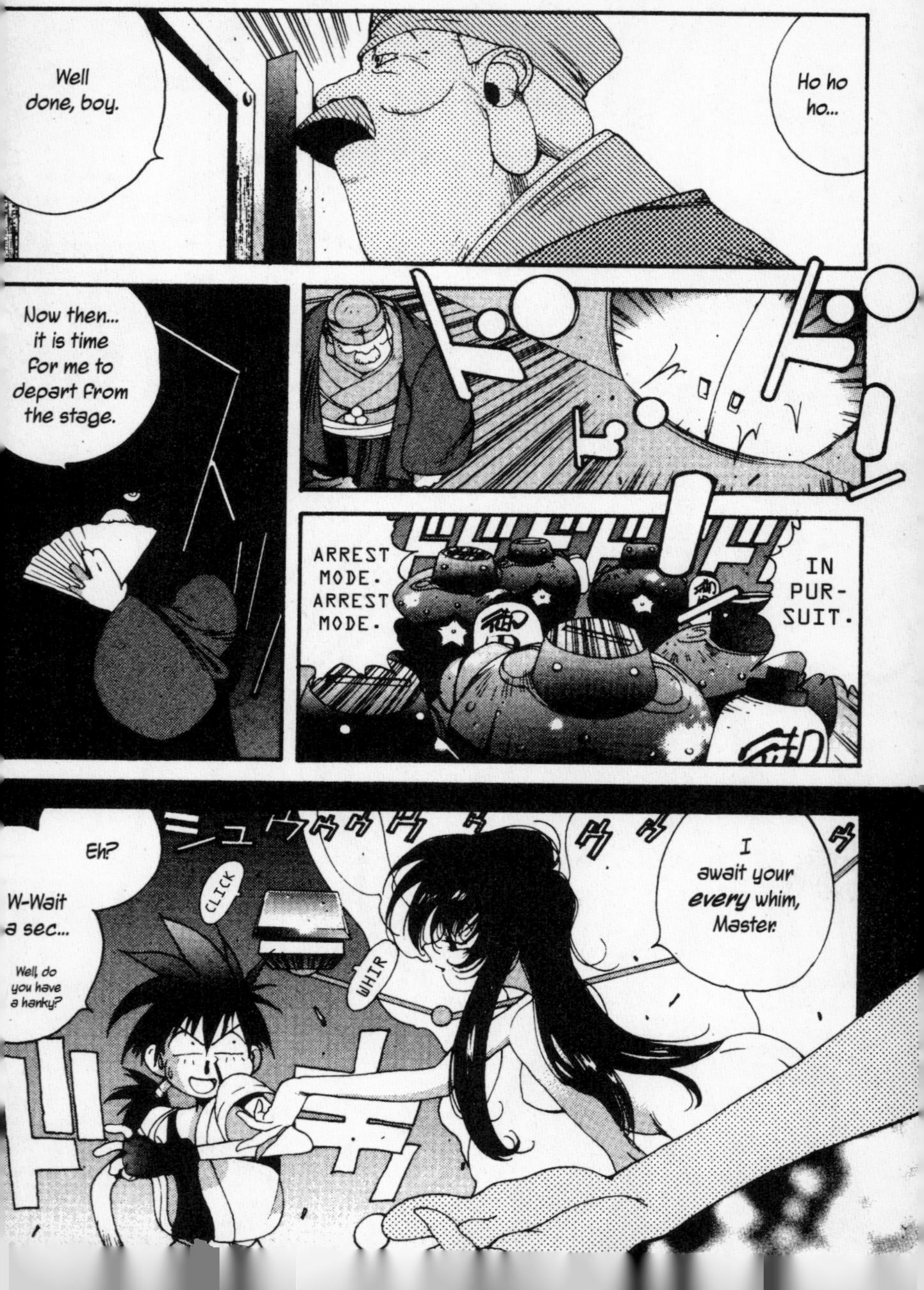
Ho ho ho...
Well done, boy.
IN PUR-SUIT.
ARREST MODE. ARREST MODE.
Now then... it is time for me to depart from the stage.
I await your *every* whim, Master.
Eh?
CLICK
WHIR
W-Wait a sec...
Well, do you have a hanky?

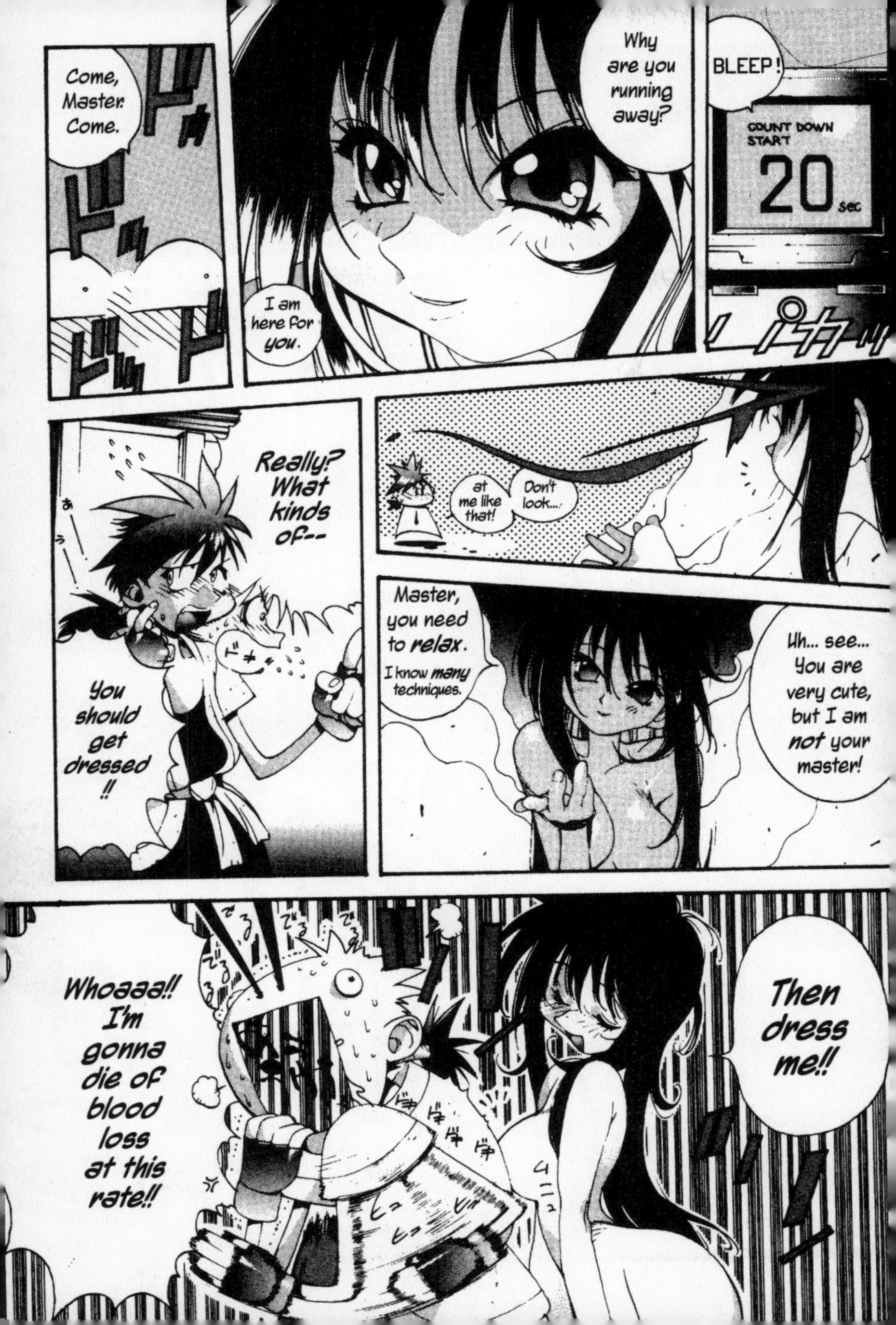
BLEEP!
COUNT DOWN START
20 sec
Why are you running away?
I am here for you.
Come, Master. Come.
Don't look...
at me like that!
Uh... see... You are very cute, but I am not your master!
Master, you need to relax.
I know many techniques.
Really? What kinds of--
You should get dressed!!
Then dress me!!
Whoaaa!! I'm gonna die of blood loss at this rate!!

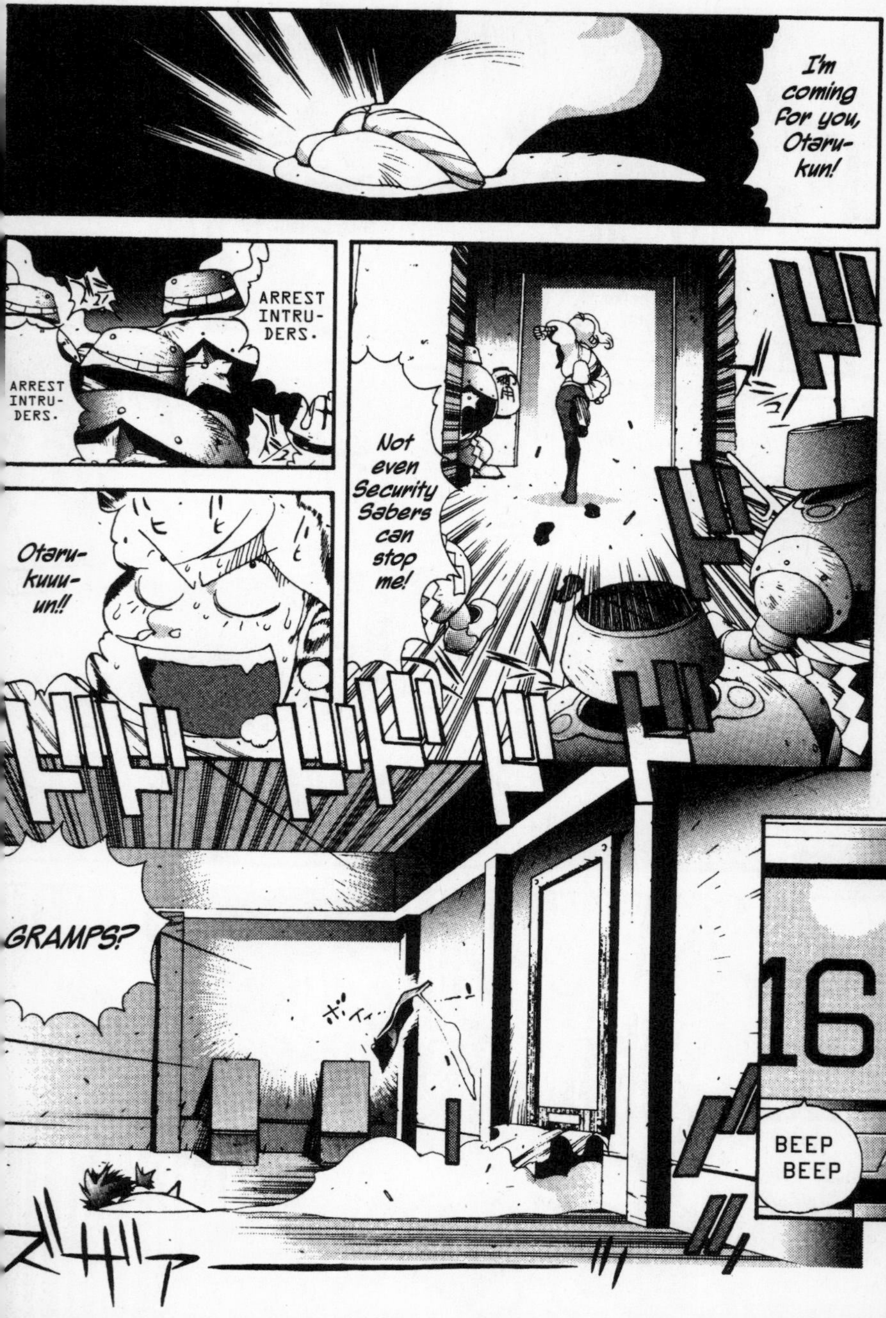
I'm coming for you, Otaru-kun!
Not even Security Sabers can stop me!
ARREST INTRUDERS.
ARREST INTRUDERS.
Otaru-kuuuun!!
BEEP BEEP
GRAMPS?

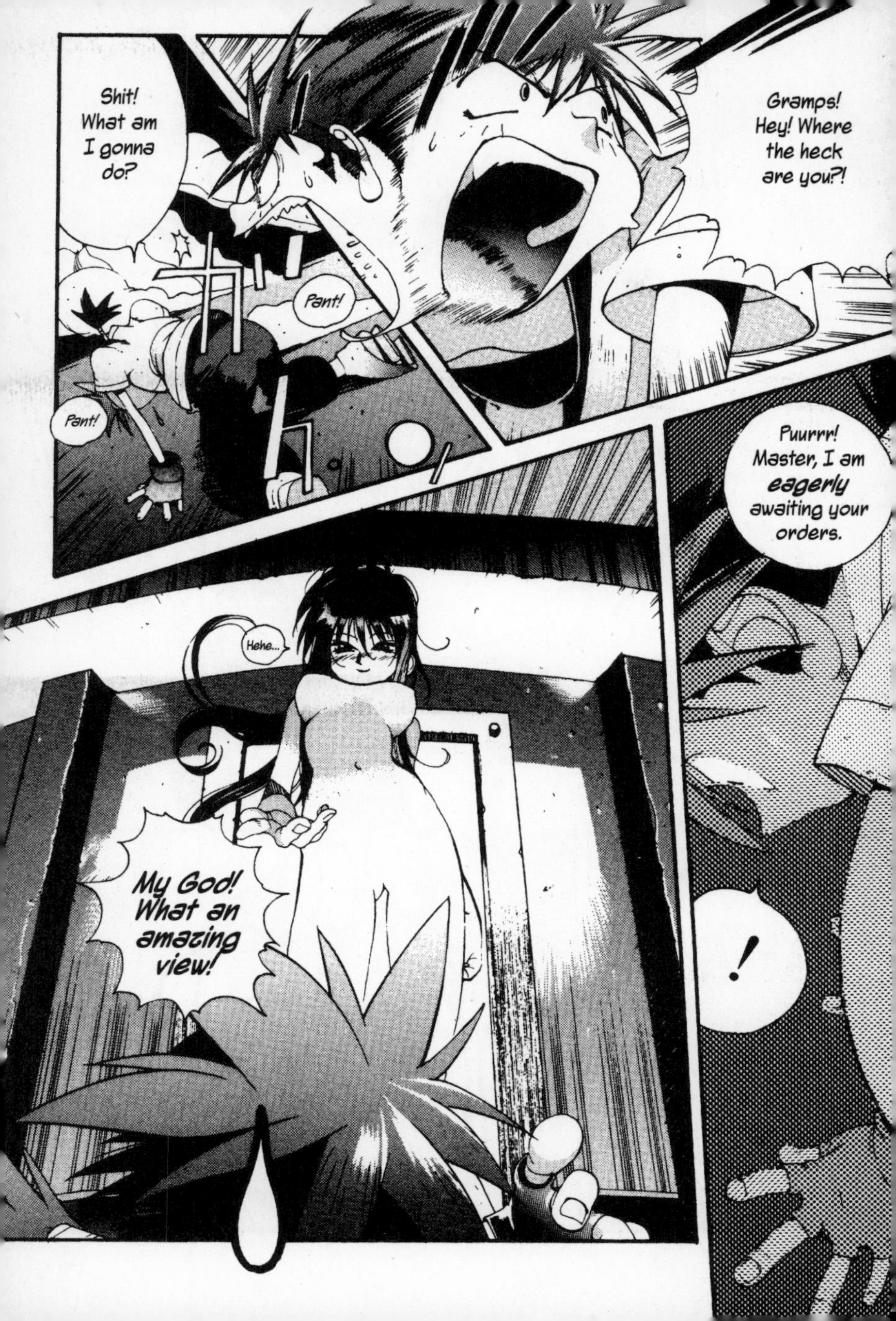
Gramps! Hey! Where the heck are you?!
Shit! What am I gonna do?
Pant!
Pant!
Puurrr! Master, I am eagerly awaiting your orders.
!
Hehe...
My God! What an amazing view!

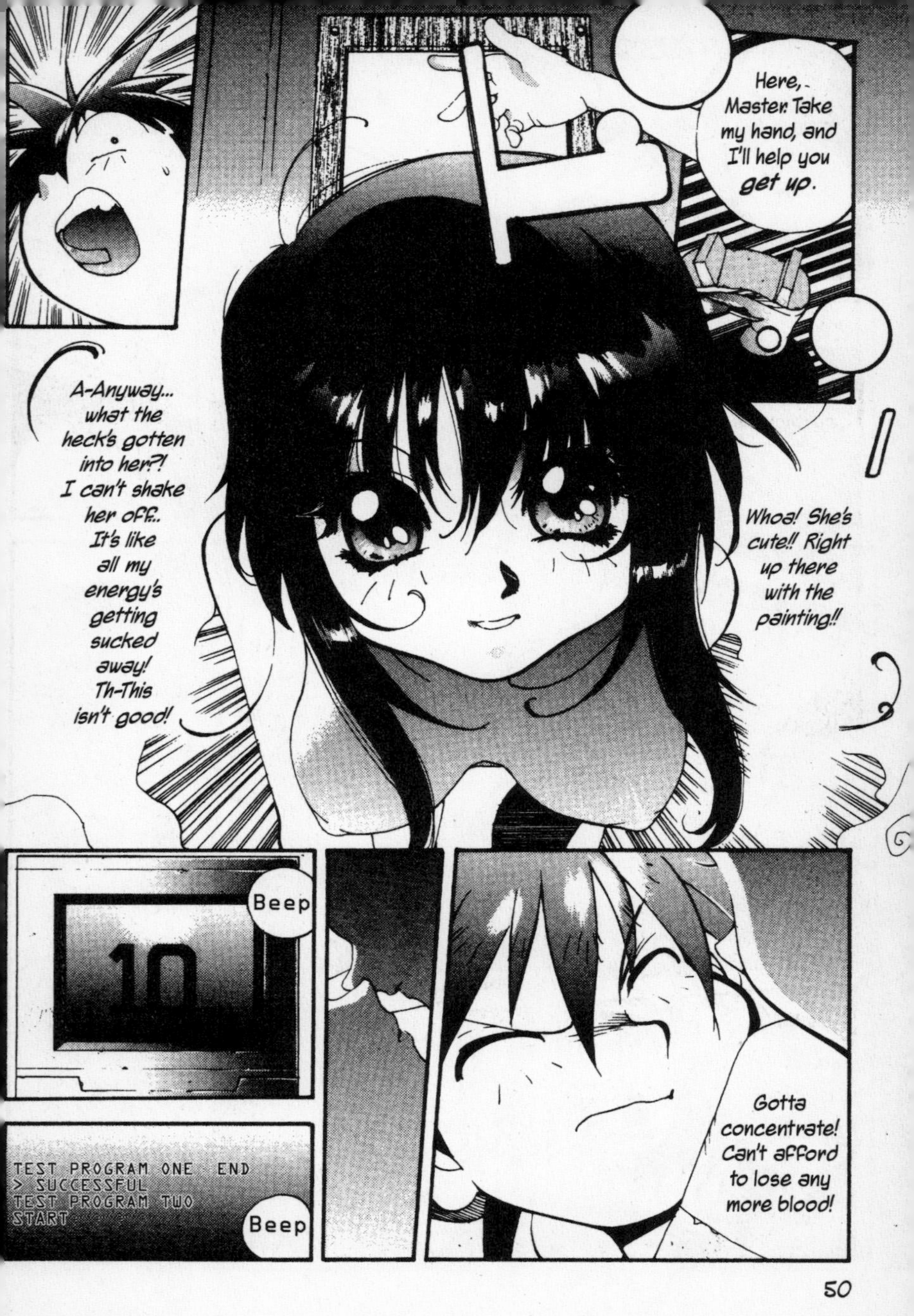
Here, Master. Take my hand, and I'll help you get up.
Whoa! She's cute!! Right up there with the painting!!
A-Anyway... what the heck's gotten into her?! I can't shake her off.. It's like all my energy's getting sucked away! Th-This isn't good!
Gotta concentrate! Can't afford to lose any more blood!
Beep
10
TEST PROGRAM ONE END
> SUCCESSFUL
TEST PROGRAM TWO
START
Beep

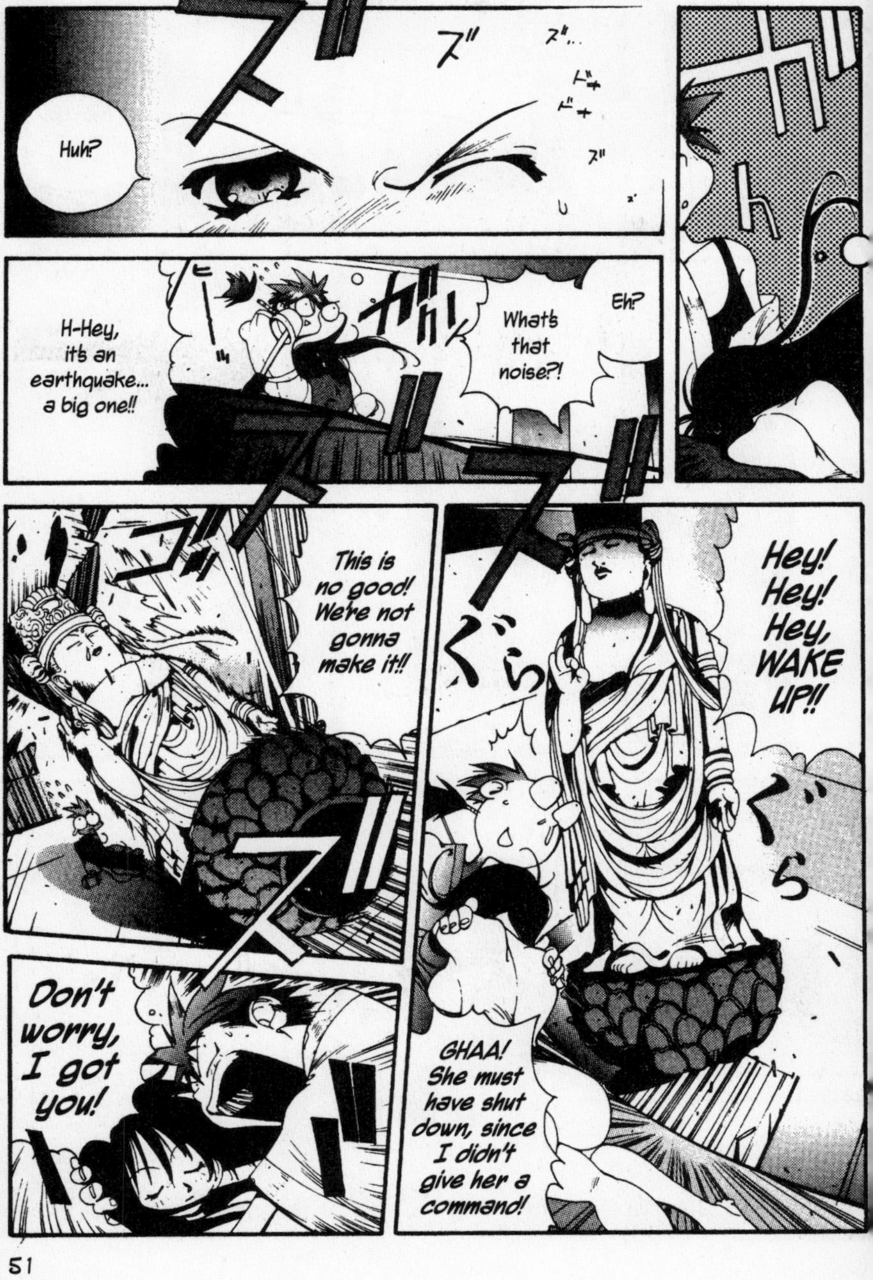

Huh?
Eh?
What's that noise?!
H-Hey, it's an earthquake... a big one!!
Hey! Hey! Hey, WAKE UP!!
GHAA! She must have shut down, since I didn't give her a command!
This is no good! We're not gonna make it!!
Don't worry, I got you!

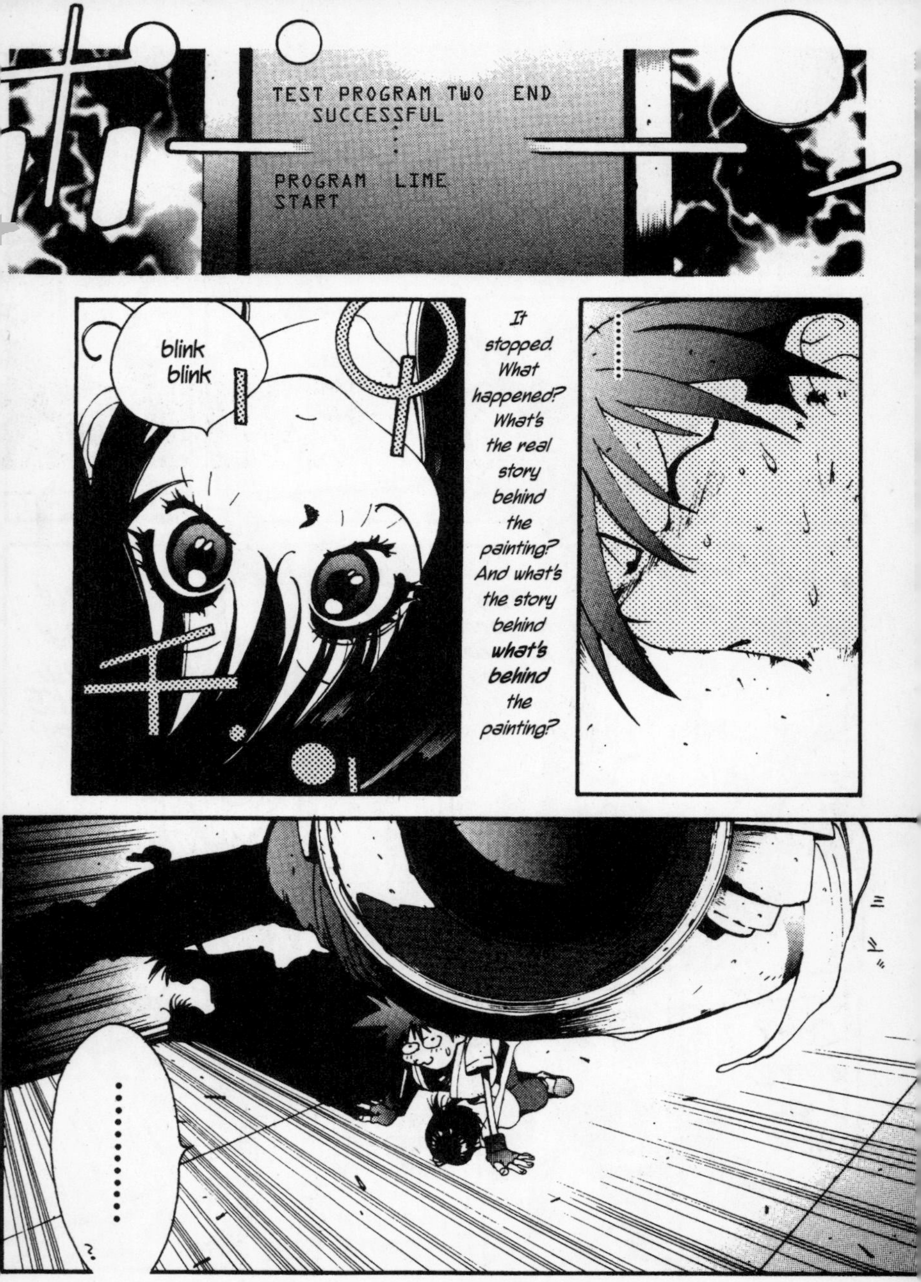
TEST PROGRAM TWO END
SUCCESSFUL
:
PROGRAM LIME
START
......
It stopped. What happened? What's the real story behind the painting? And what's the story behind what's behind the painting?
blink blink
..........?

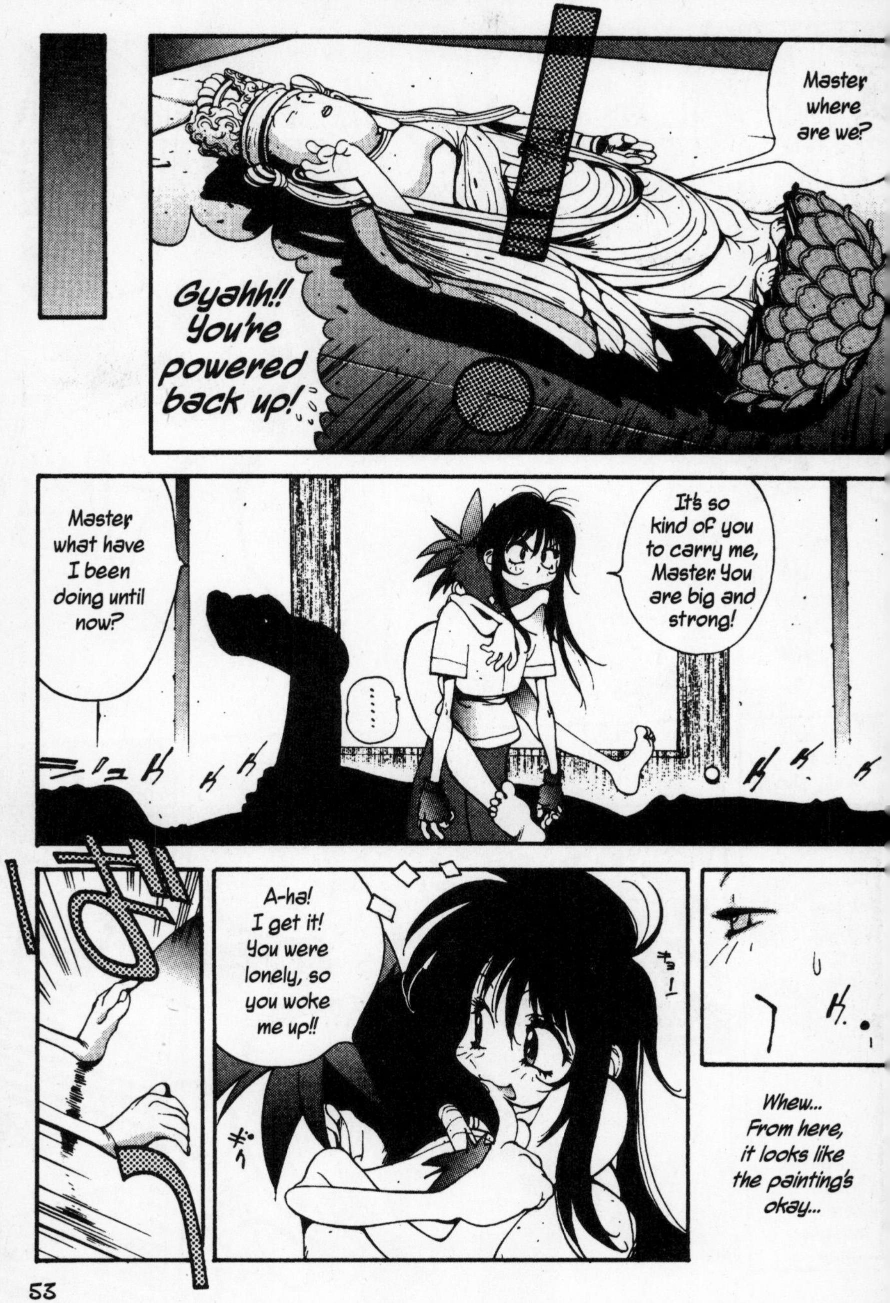
Master, where are we?
Gyahh!! You're powered back up!
It's so kind of you to carry me, Master. You are big and strong!
......
Master, what have I been doing until now?
Whew... From here, it looks like the painting's okay...
A-ha! I get it! You were lonely, so you woke me up!!

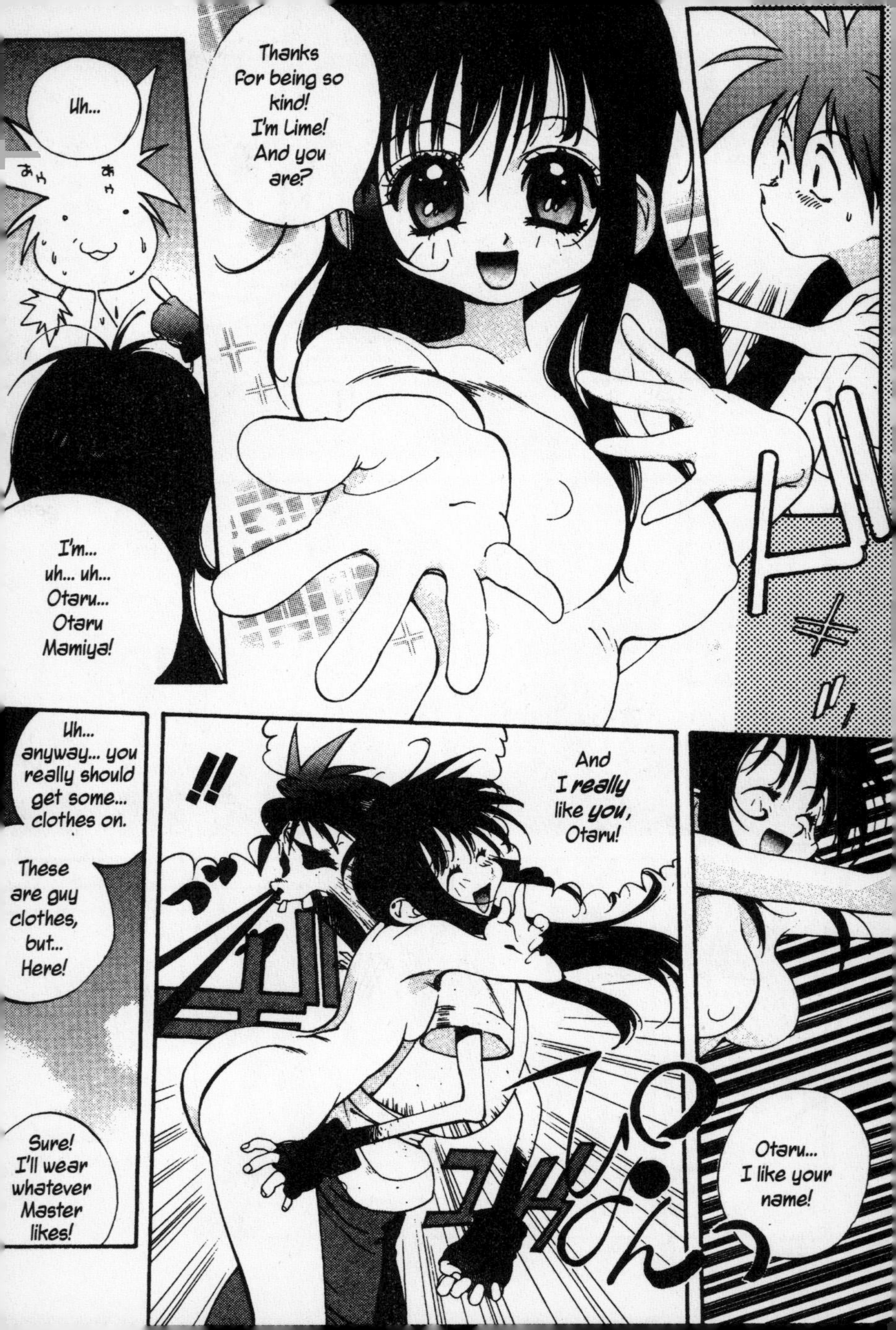
Thanks for being so kind! I'm Lime! And you are?
Uh...
I'm... uh... uh... Otaru... Otaru Mamiya!
Otaru... I like your name!
And I *really* like *you*, Otaru!
Uh... anyway... you really should get some... clothes on.
These are guy clothes, but... Here!
Sure! I'll wear whatever Master likes!

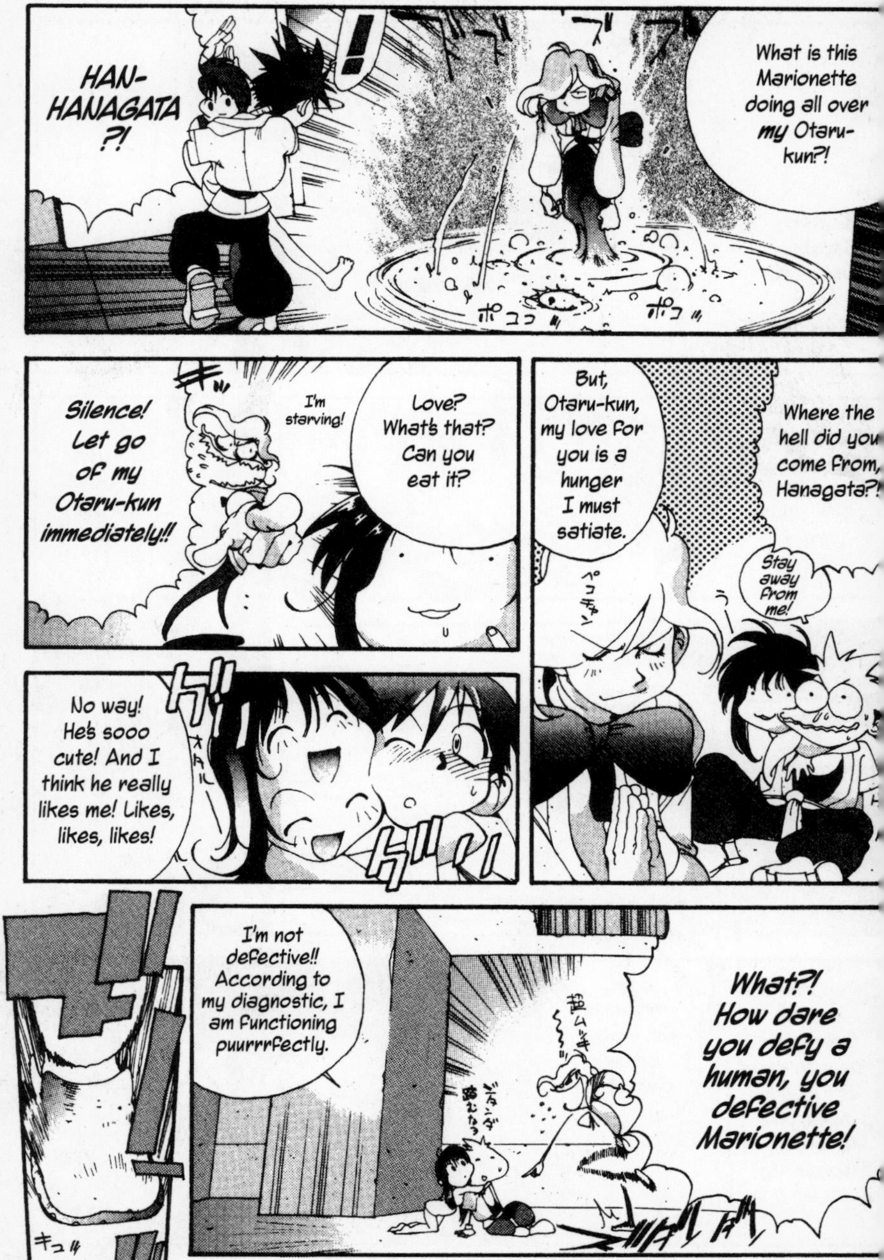
What is this Marionette doing all over my Otaru-kun?!
HAN-HANAGATA?!
Where the hell did you come from, Hanagata?!
But, Otaru-kun, my love for you is a hunger I must satiate.
Stay away from me!
Love? What's that? Can you eat it?
I'm starving!
Silence! Let go of my Otaru-kun immediately!!
No way! He's sooo cute! And I think he really likes me! Likes, likes, likes!
What?! How dare you defy a human, you defective Marionette!
I'm not defective!! According to my diagnostic, I am functioning puurrrfectly.

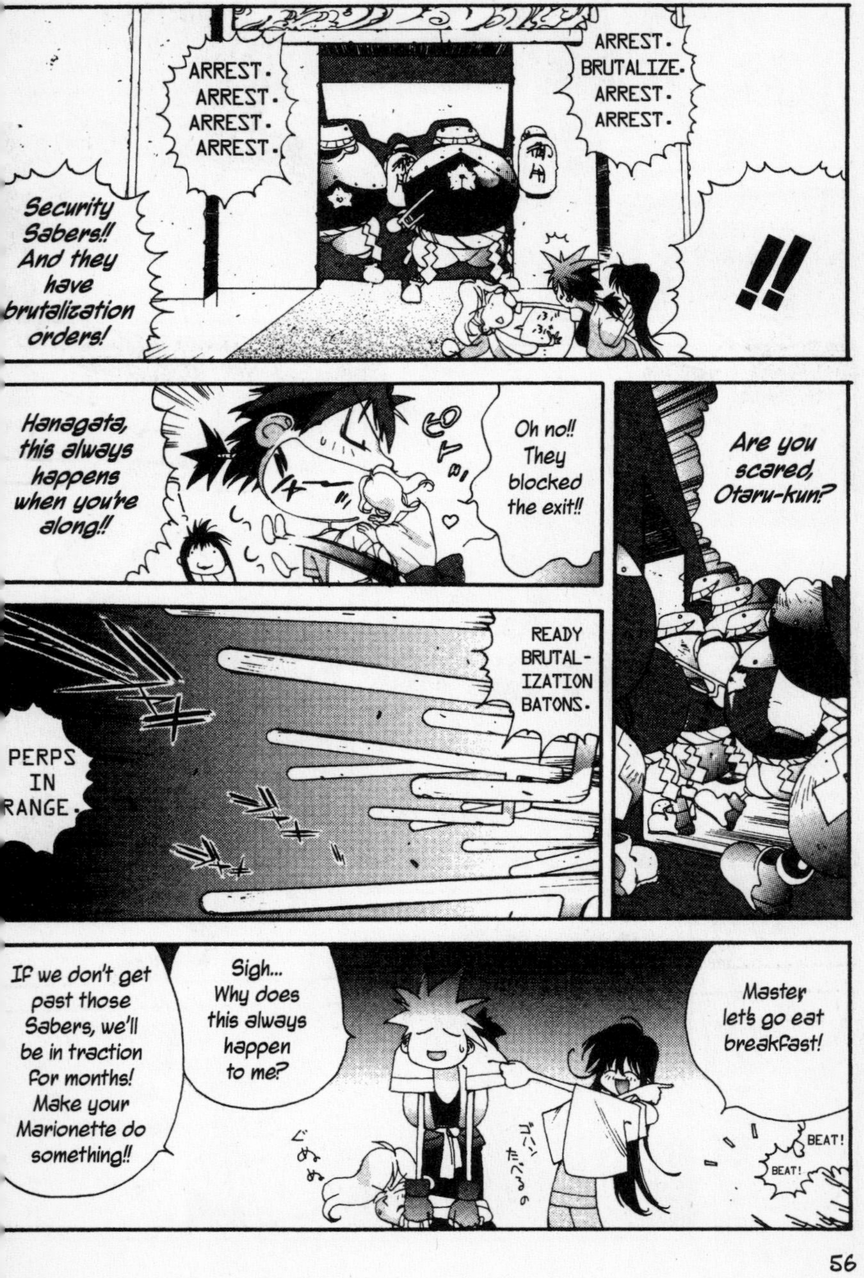
ARREST. BRUTALIZE. ARREST. ARREST.
!!
ARREST. ARREST. ARREST. ARREST.
Security Sabers!! And they have brutalization orders!
Are you scared, Otaru-kun?
Oh no!! They blocked the exit!!
Hanagata, this always happens when you're along!!
READY BRUTALIZATION BATONS.
PERPS IN RANGE.
Master, let's go eat breakfast!
BEAT!
BEAT!
Sigh... Why does this always happen to me?
If we don't get past those Sabers, we'll be in traction for months! Make your Marionette do something!!

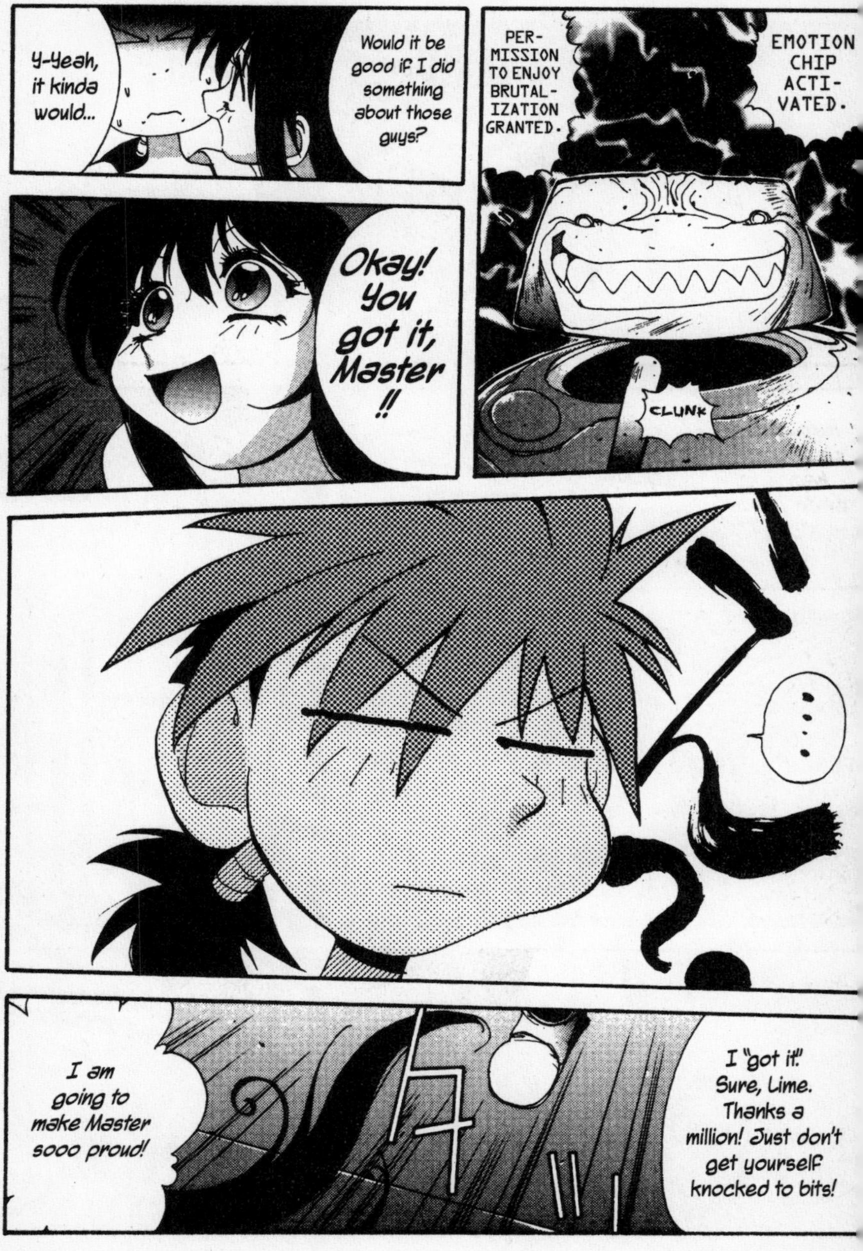
EMOTION CHIP ACTIVATED.
PERMISSION TO ENJOY BRUTALIZATION GRANTED.
Would it be good if I did something about those guys?
Y-Yeah, it kinda would...
CLUNK
Okay! You got it, Master!!
...
I "got it." Sure, Lime. Thanks a million! Just don't get yourself knocked to bits!
I am going to make Master sooo proud!

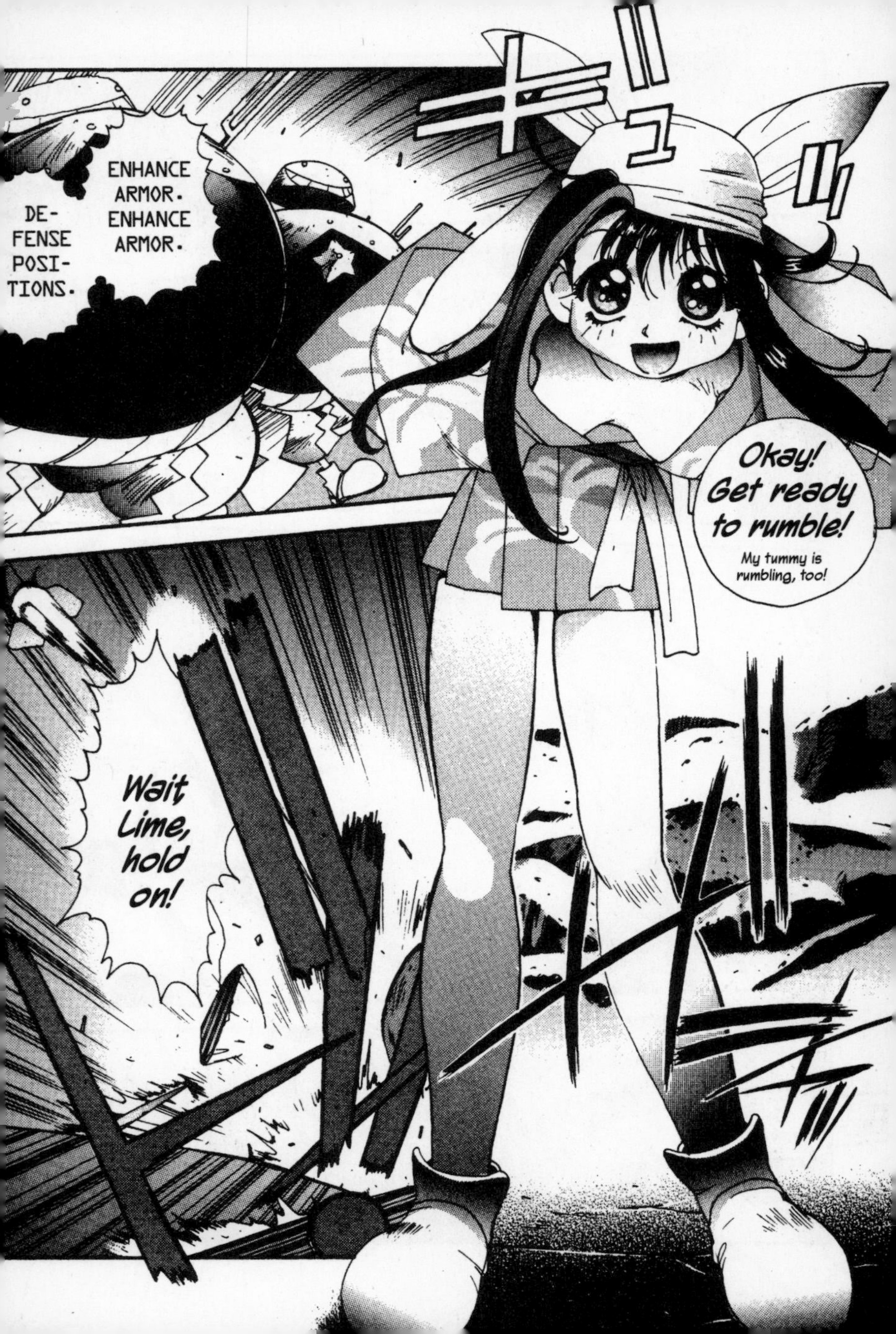
ギュッ
Okay! Get ready to rumble!
My tummy is rumbling, too!
ENHANCE ARMOR. ENHANCE ARMOR.
DEFENSE POSITIONS.
Wait Lime, hold on!

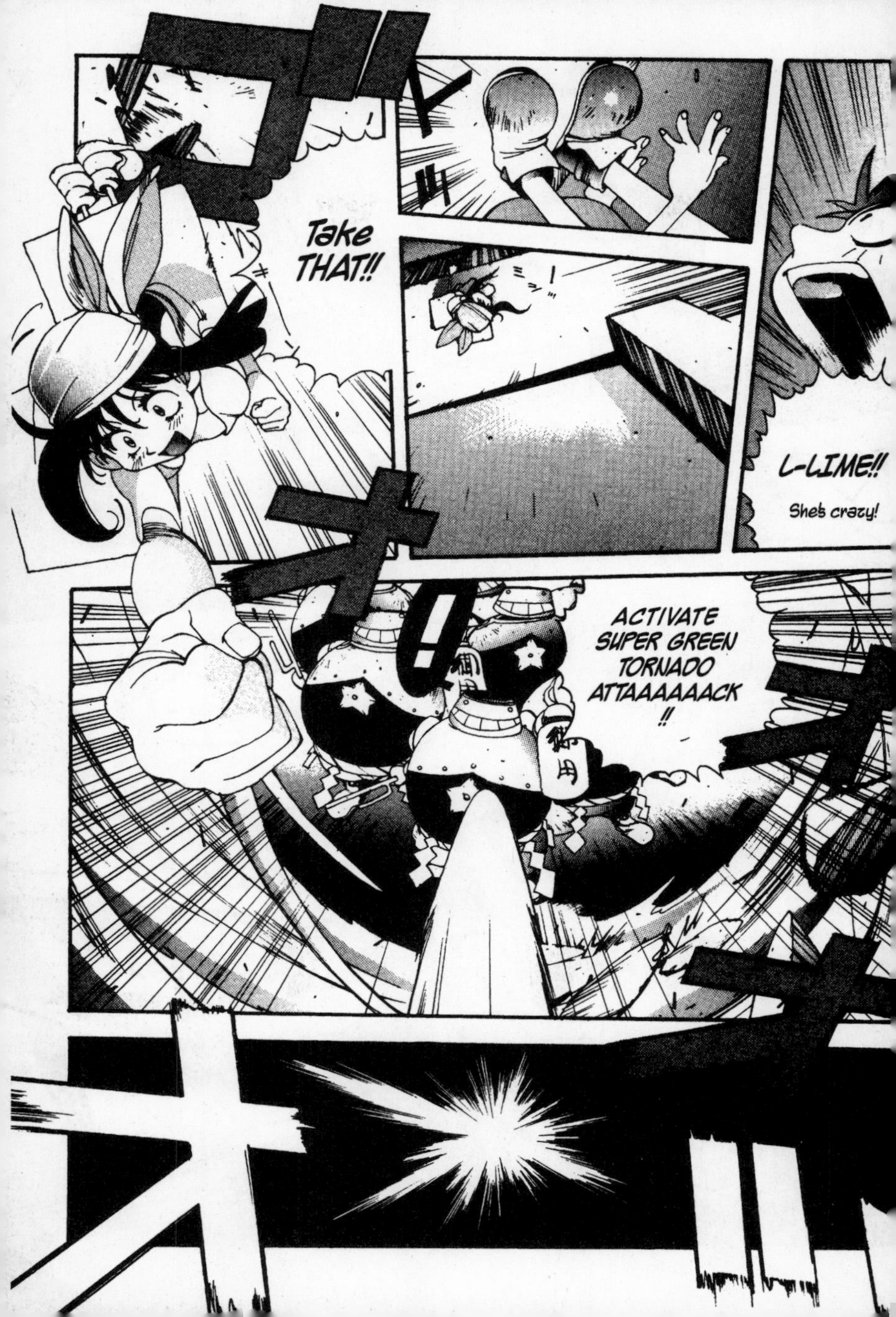
L-LIME!!
She's crazy!
Take THAT!!
ACTIVATE SUPER GREEN TORNADO ATTAAAAAACK !!

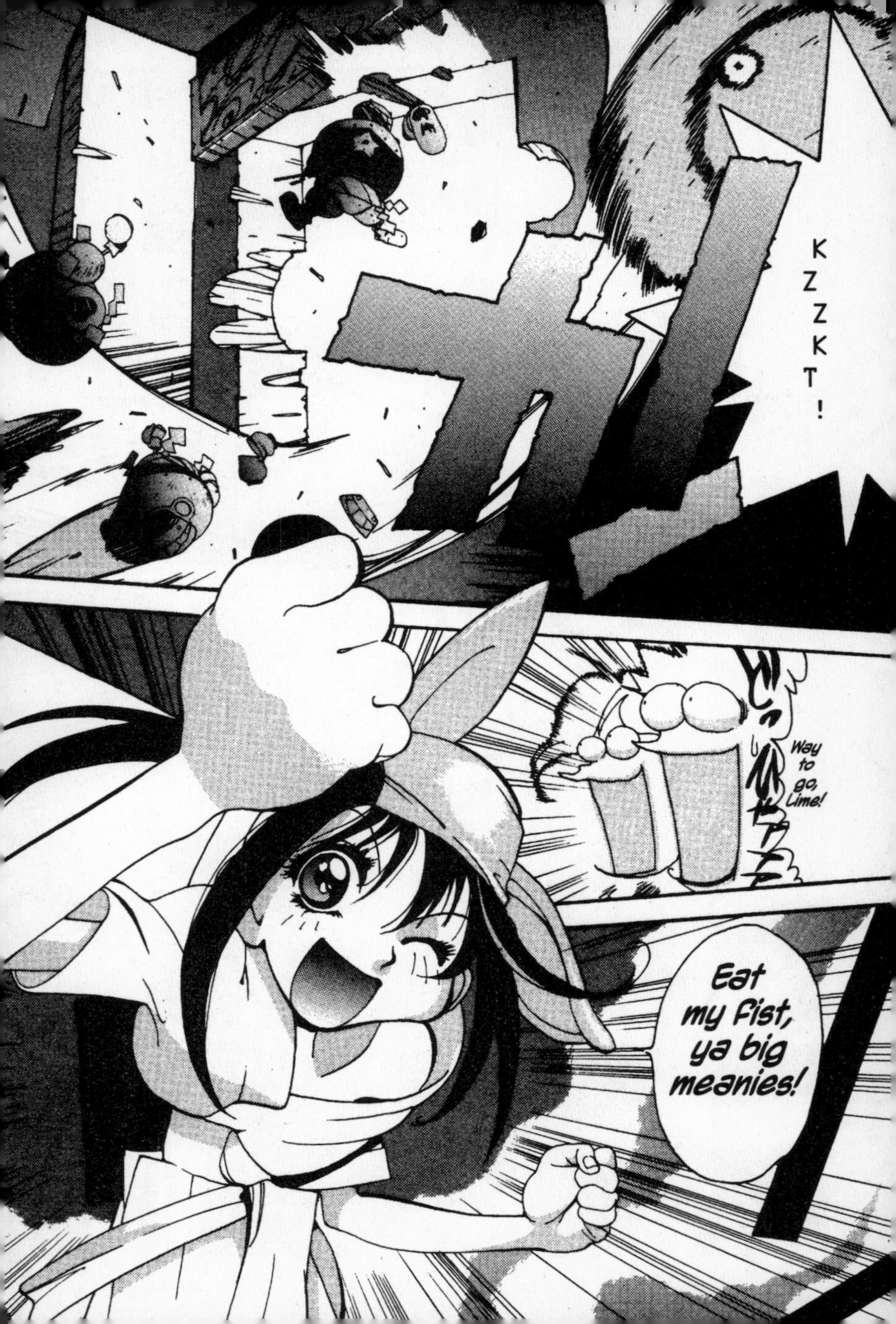
KZZKT!
Way to go, Lime!
Eat my fist, ya big meanies!

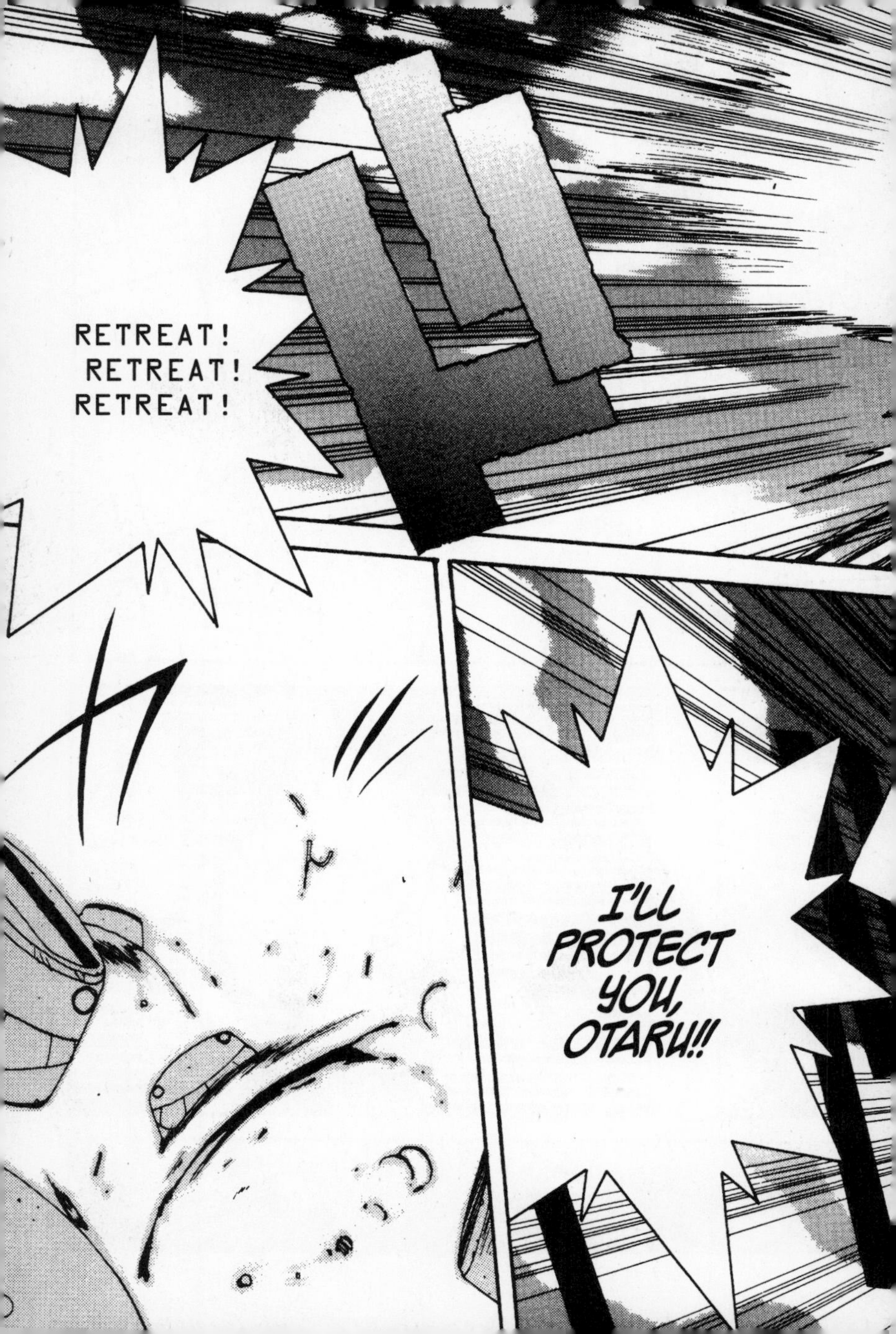
RETREAT! RETREAT! RETREAT!
I'LL PROTECT YOU, OTARU!!

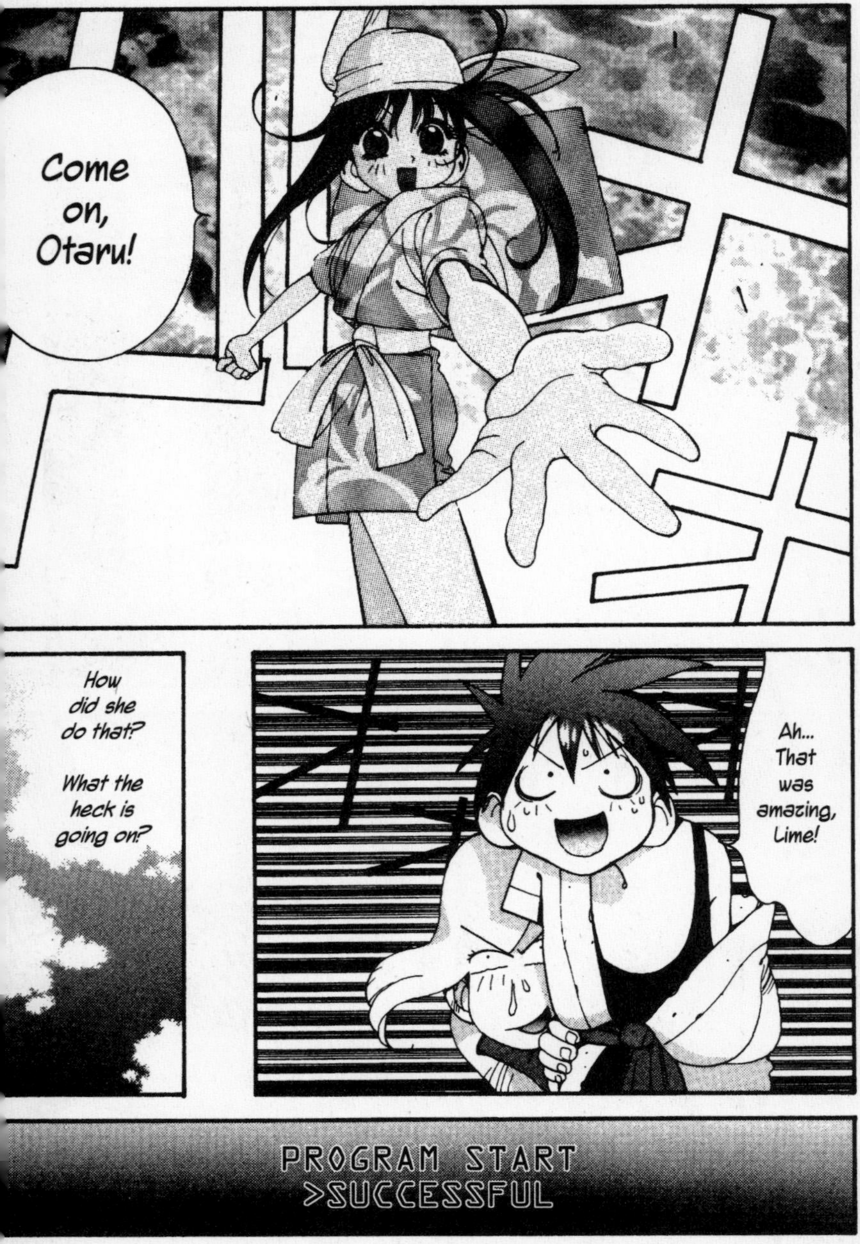
Come on, Otaru!
Ah... That was amazing, Lime!
How did she do that?
What the heck is going on?
PROGRAM START
>SUCCESSFUL

Mmm... I feel so cozy and warm here in Lime's lap.
Otaru...
Girls feel so good... So warm... So soft...
Otaru...
Master, I will **never** leave your side.
Oh, sweet Lime...
Otaru... Otaru...
OTARU!

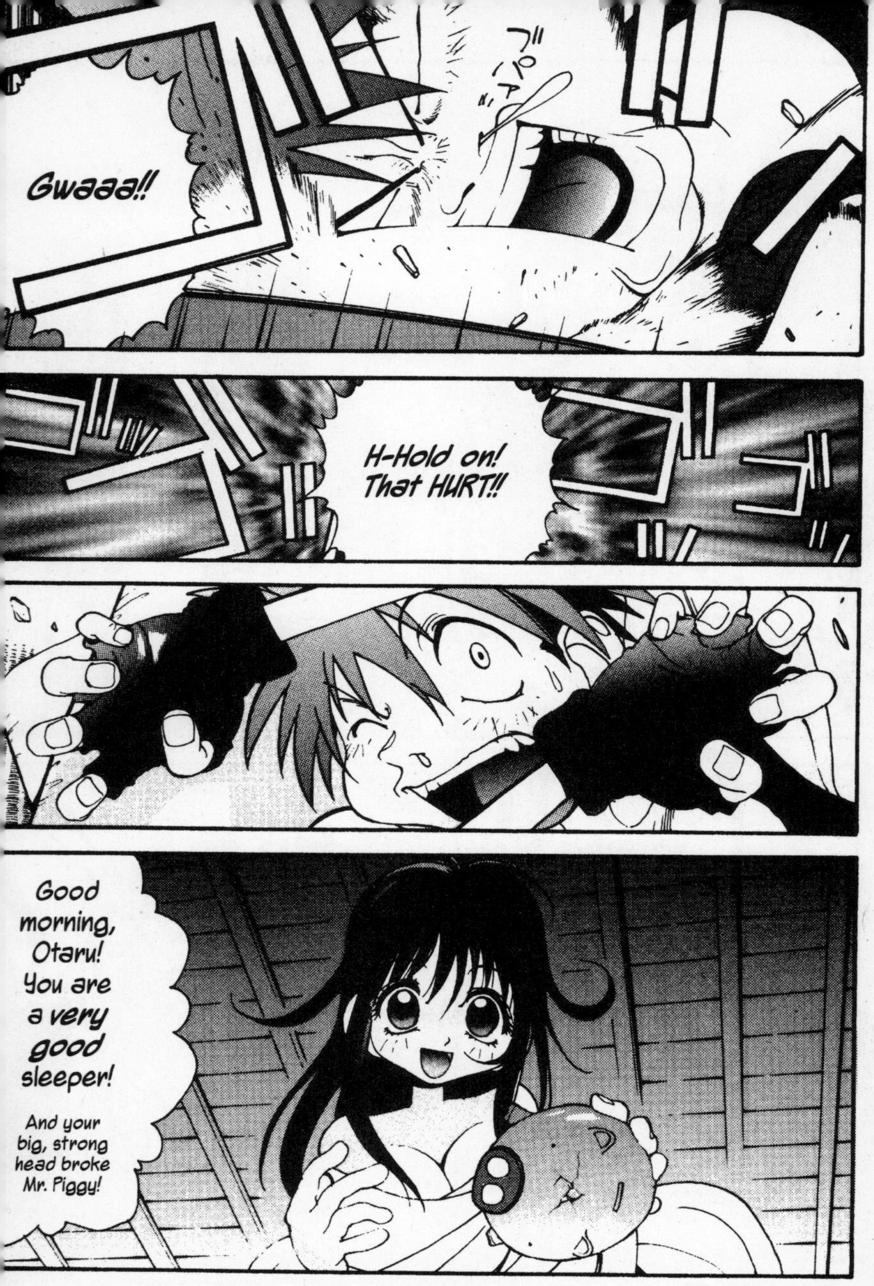
Gwaaa!!
H-Hold on! That HURT!!
Good morning, Otaru! You are a very good sleeper!
And your big, strong head broke Mr. Piggy!

Chapter 3 - The Fearsome Dictator Appears

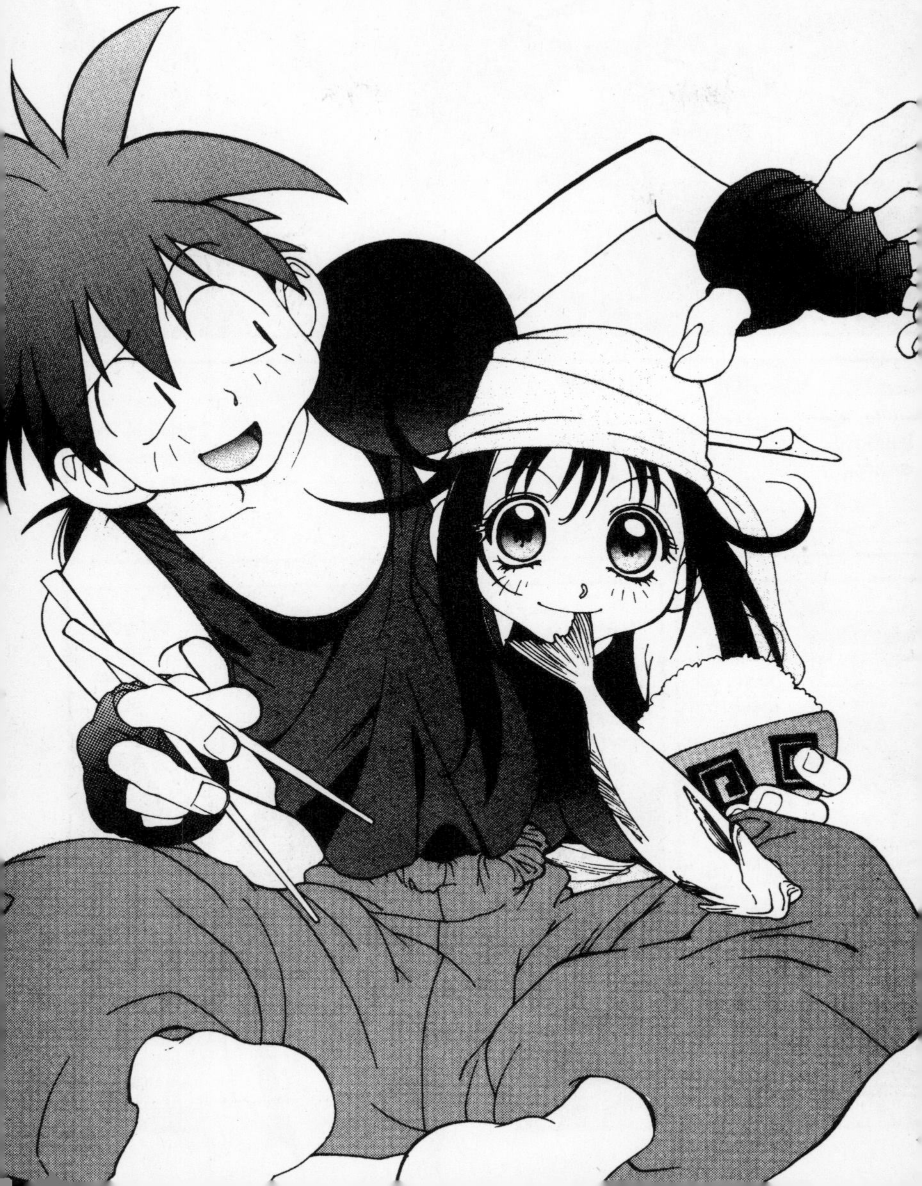

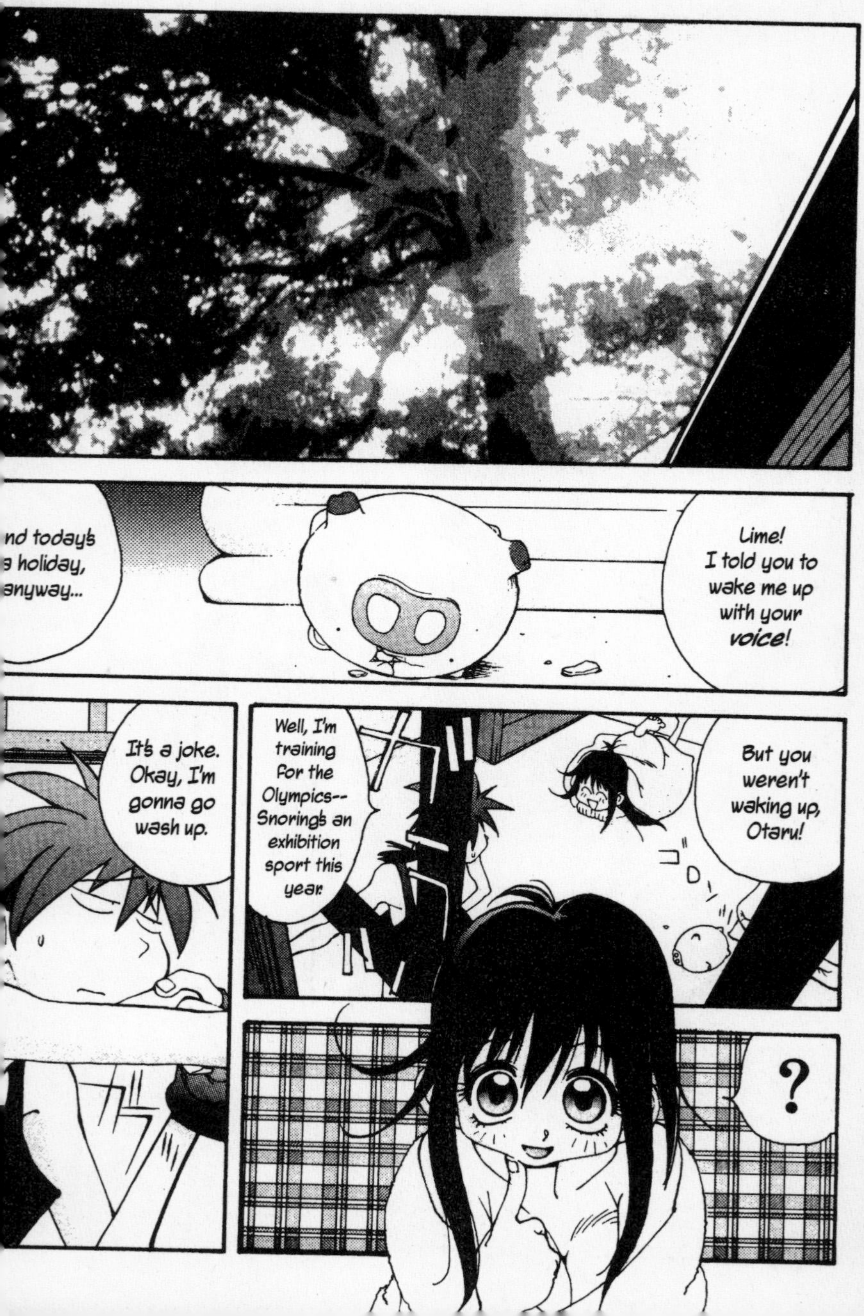

Lime! I told you to wake me up with your voice!
nd today's a holiday, anyway...
But you weren't waking up, Otaru!
Well, I'm training for the Olympics-- Snoring's an exhibition sport this year.
It's a joke. Okay, I'm gonna go wash up.
?

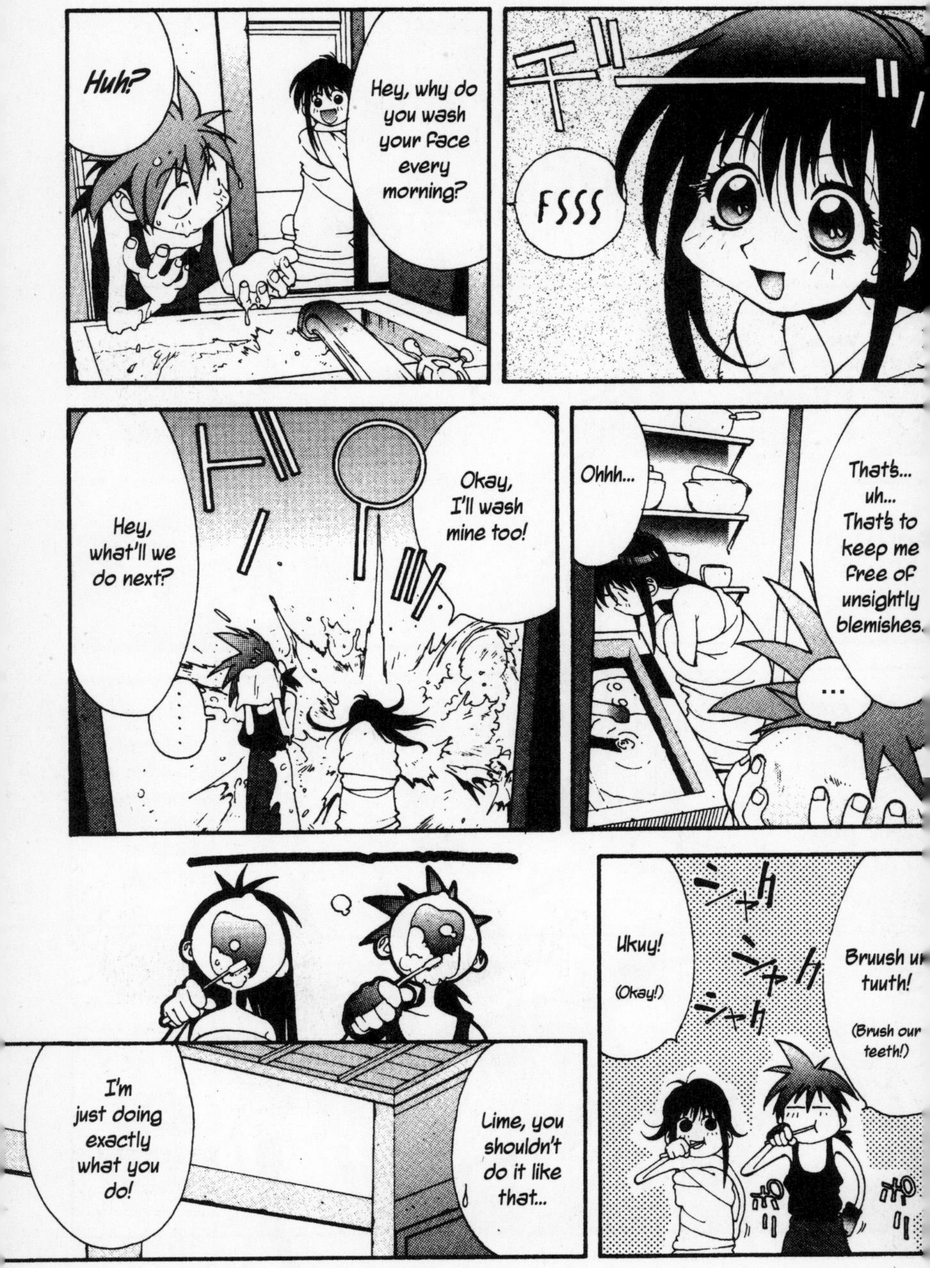
FSSS
Hey, why do you wash your face every morning?
Huh?
That's... uh... That's to keep me free of unsightly blemishes.
...
Ohhh...
Okay, I'll wash mine too!
Hey, what'll we do next?
...
Bruush u tuuth!
(Brush our teeth!)
Ukuy!
(Okay!)
Lime, you shouldn't do it like that...
I'm just doing exactly what you do!

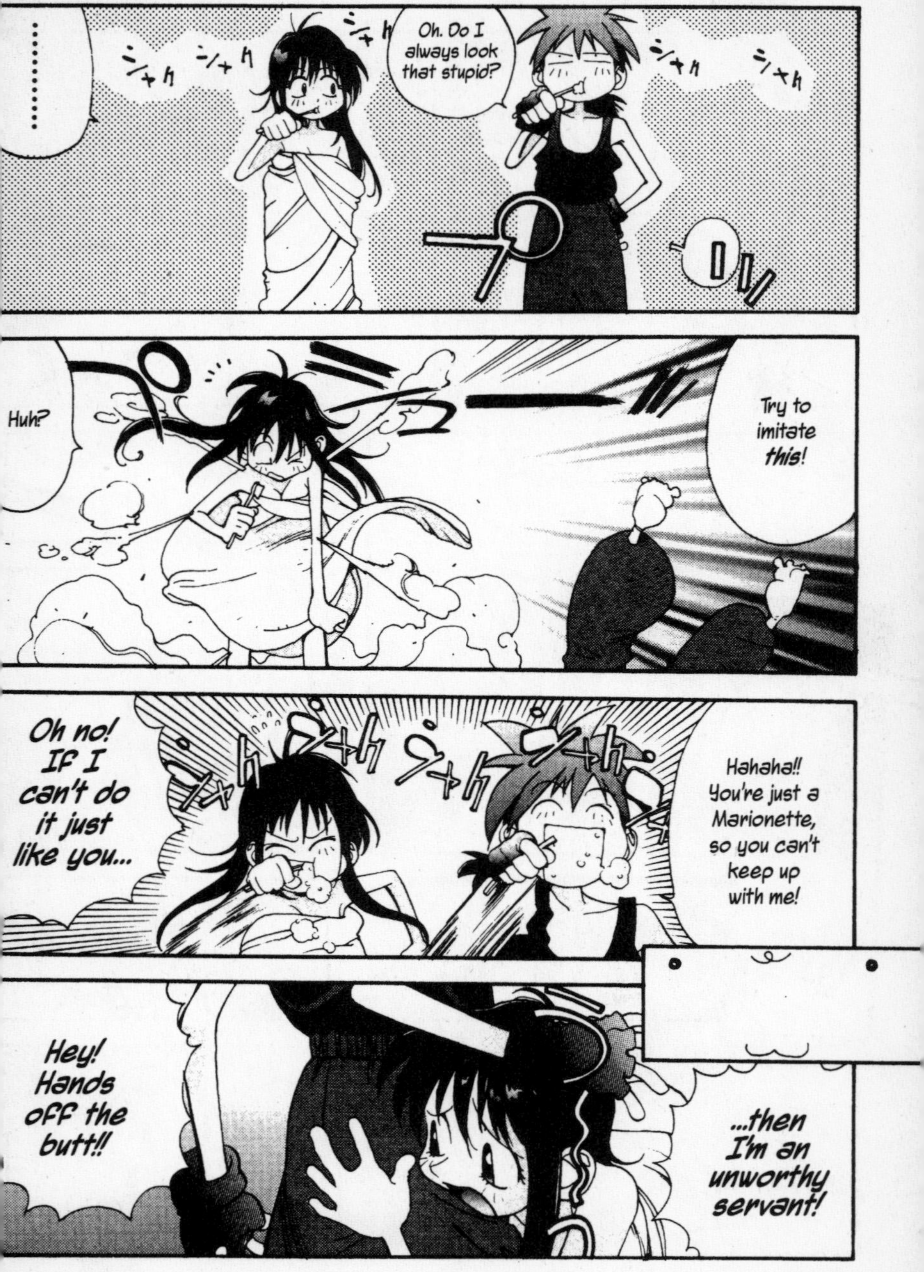
Oh. Do I always look that stupid?
......
Try to imitate this!
Huh?
Hahaha!! You're just a Marionette, so you can't keep up with me!
Oh no! If I can't do it just like you...
...then I'm an unworthy servant!
Hey! Hands off the butt!!

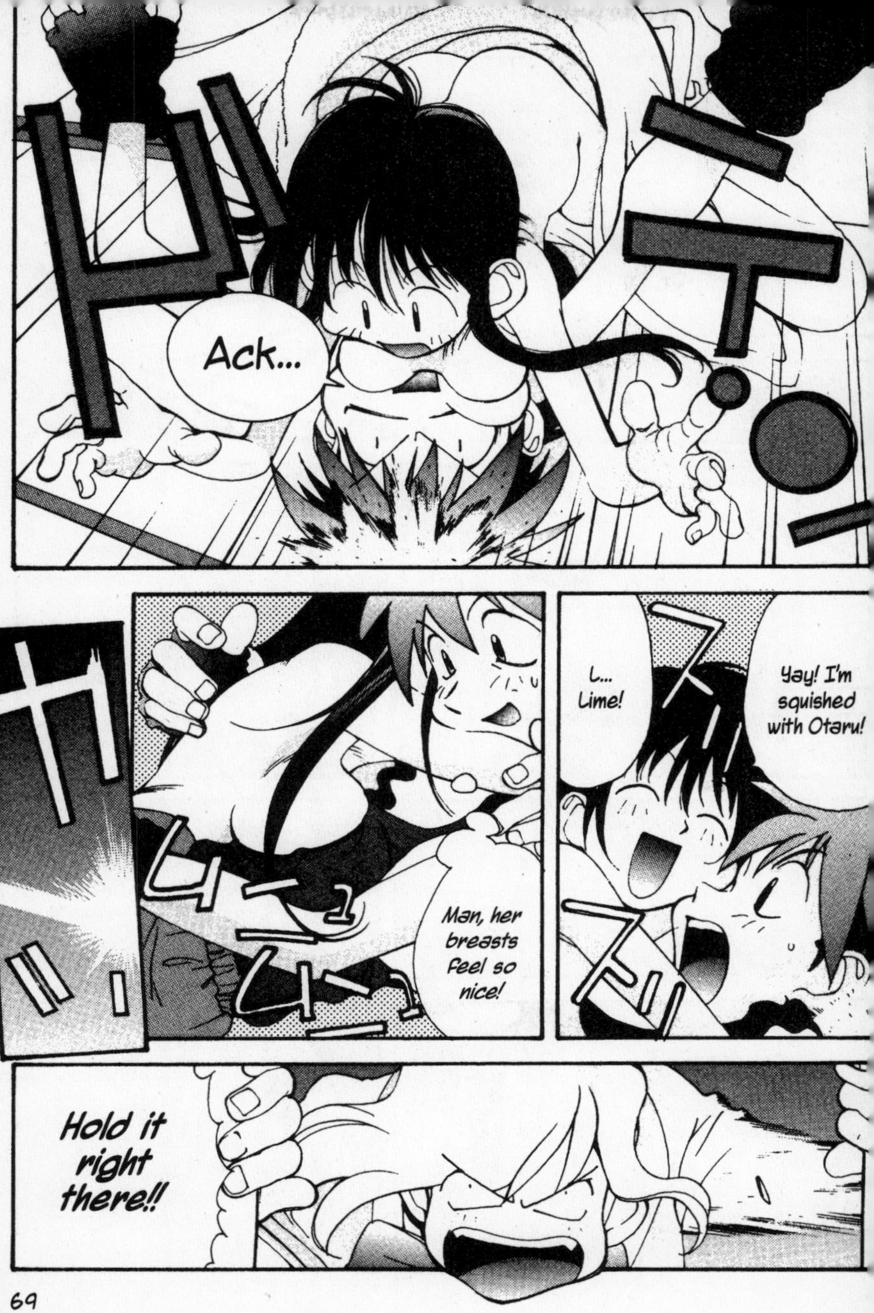
Ack...
Yay! I'm squished with Otaru!
L... Lime!
Man, her breasts feel so nice!
Hold it right there!!

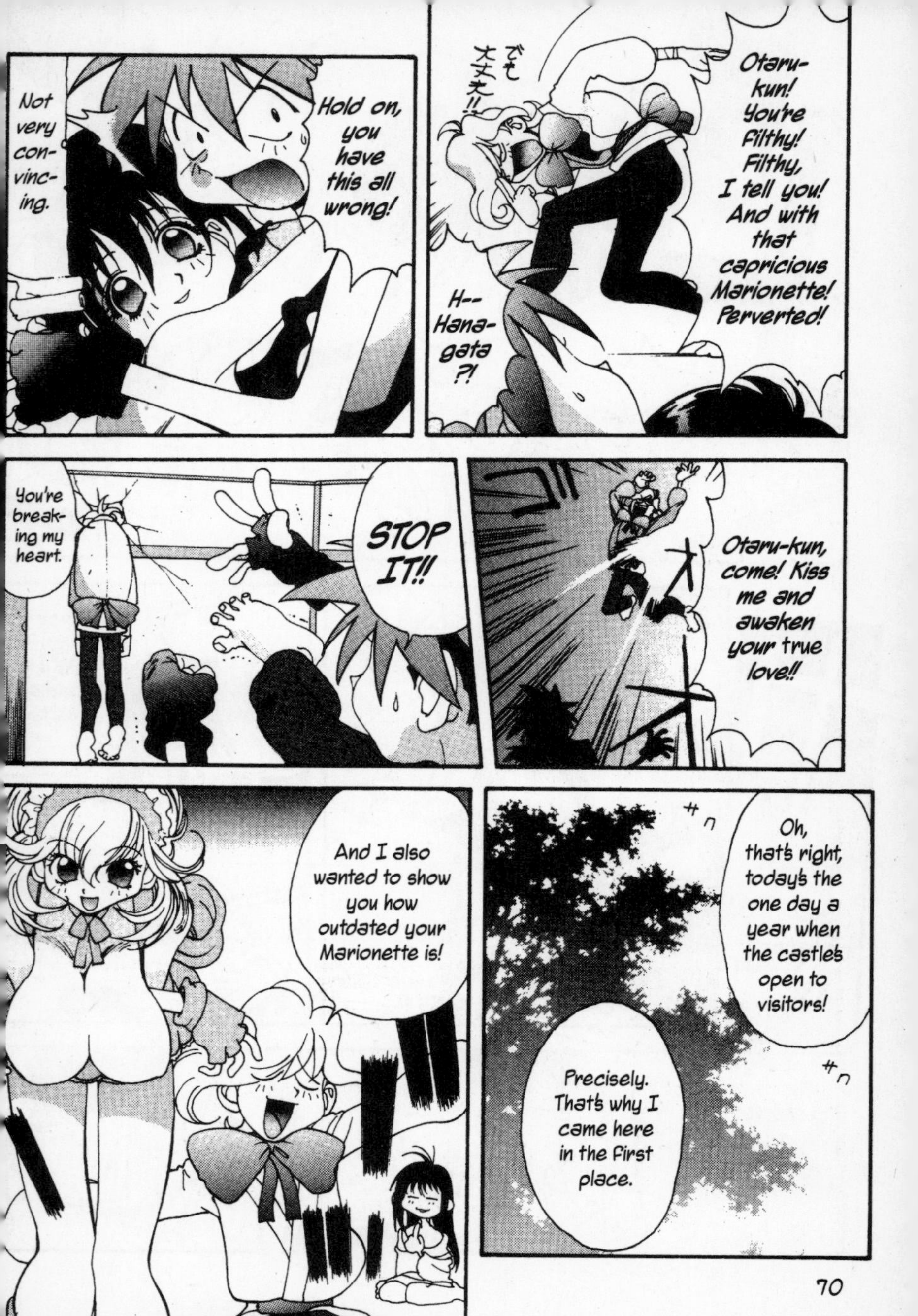
Otaru-kun! You're filthy! Filthy, I tell you! And with that capricious Marionette! Perverted!
でも大丈夫!!
H-- Hanagata?!
Hold on, you have this all wrong!
Not very con-vinc-ing.
Otaru-kun, come! Kiss me and awaken your true love!!
STOP IT!!
You're break-ing my heart.
Oh, that's right, today's the one day a year when the castle's open to visitors!
Precisely. That's why I came here in the first place.
And I also wanted to show you how outdated your Marionette is!

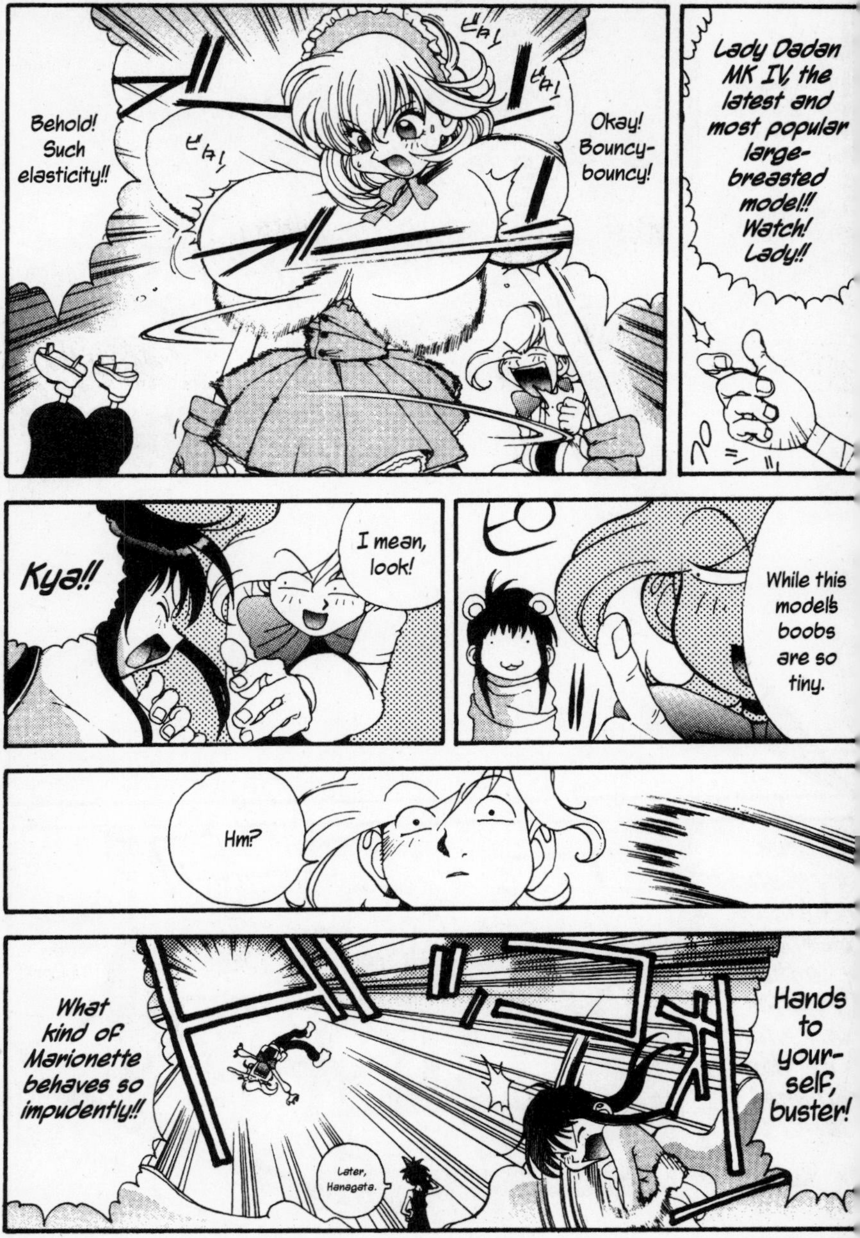
Lady Odadan MK IV, the latest and most popular large-breasted model!! Watch! Lady!!
Okay! Bouncy-bouncy!
Behold! Such elasticity!!
While this model's boobs are so tiny.
I mean, look!
Kya!!
Hm?
Hands to your-self, buster!
What kind of Marionette behaves so impudently!!
Later, Hanagata.

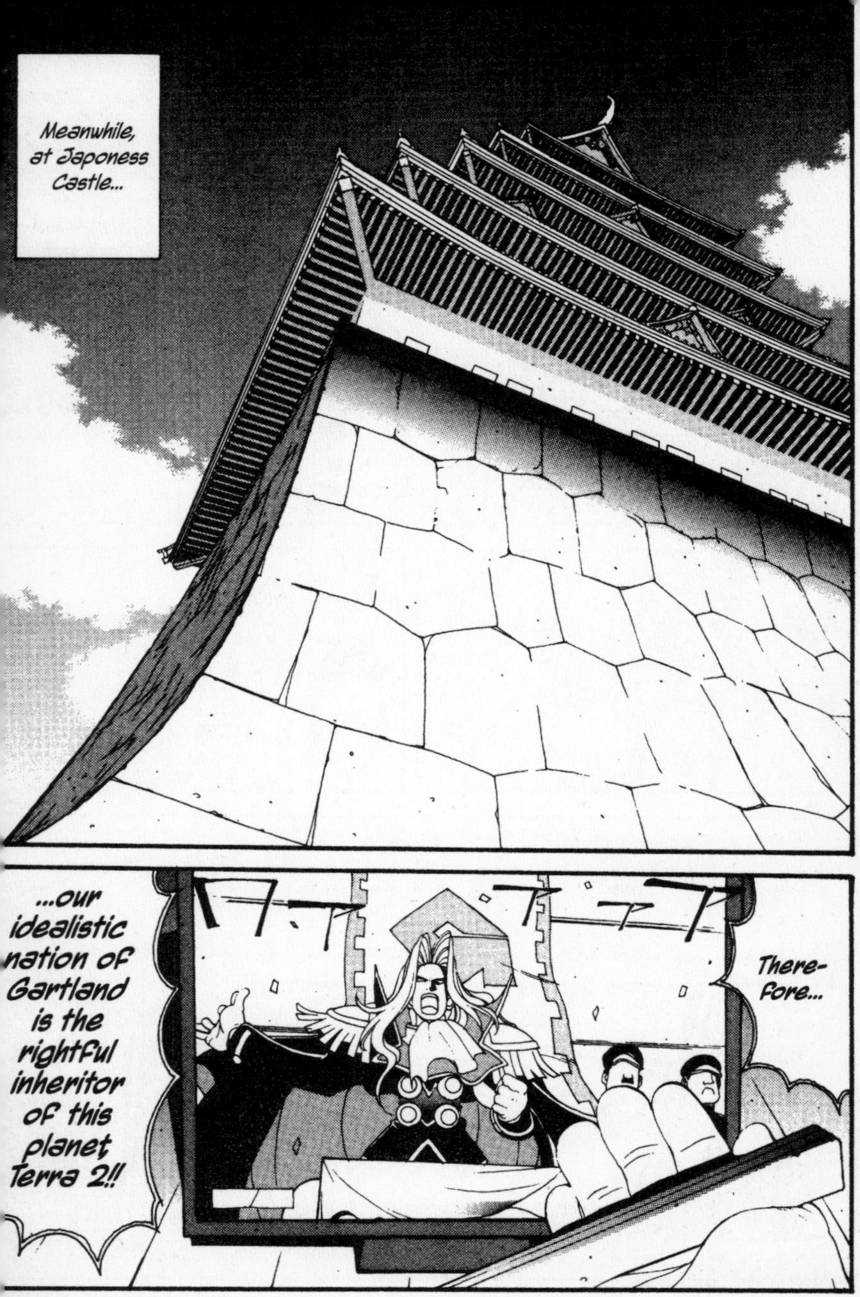
Meanwhile, at Japoness Castle...
There-fore...
...our idealistic nation of Gartland is the rightful inheritor of this planet Terra 2!!

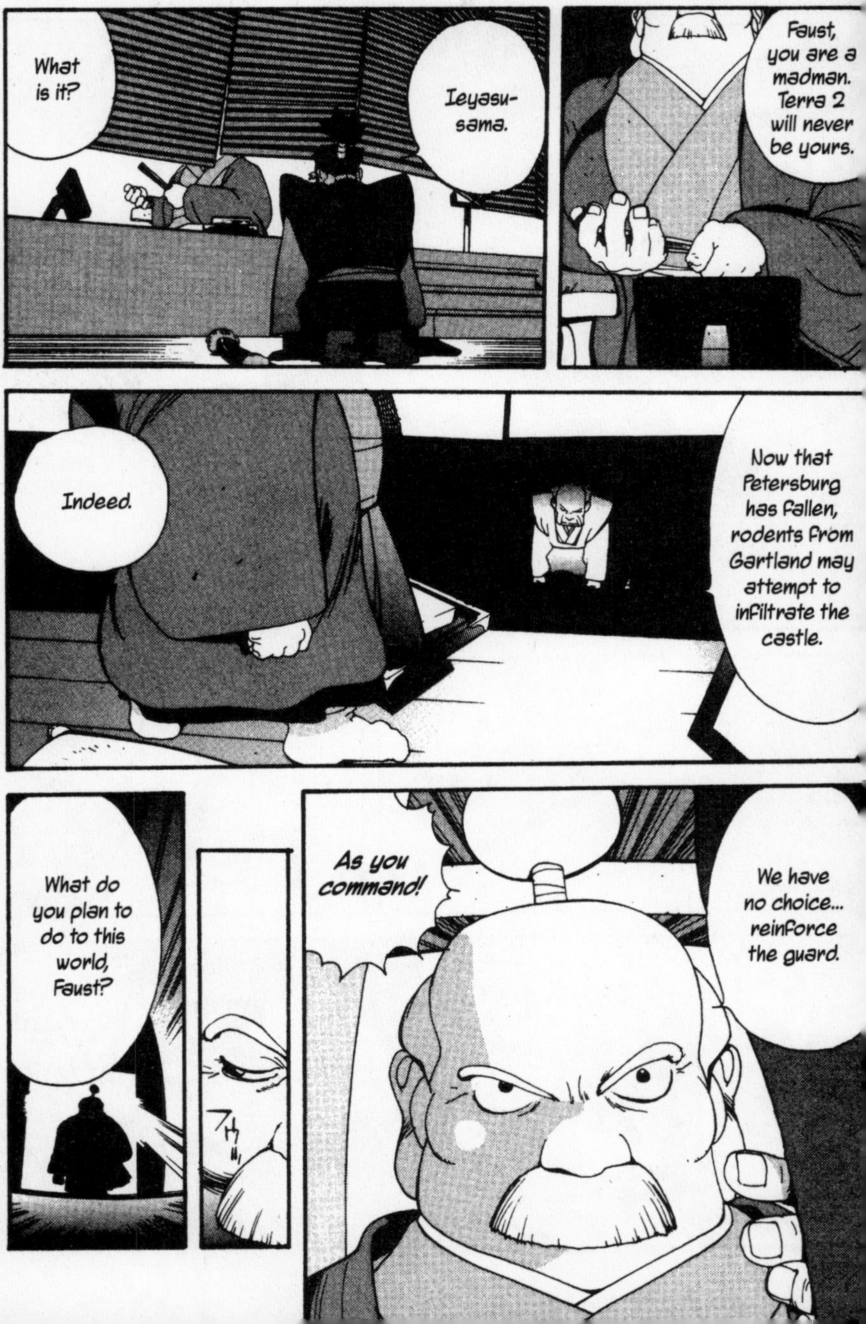
Faust, you are a madman. Terra 2 will never be yours.
Ieyasu-sama.
What is it?
Now that Petersburg has fallen, rodents from Gartland may attempt to infiltrate the castle.
Indeed.
We have no choice... reinforce the guard.
As you command!
What do you plan to do to this world, Faust?

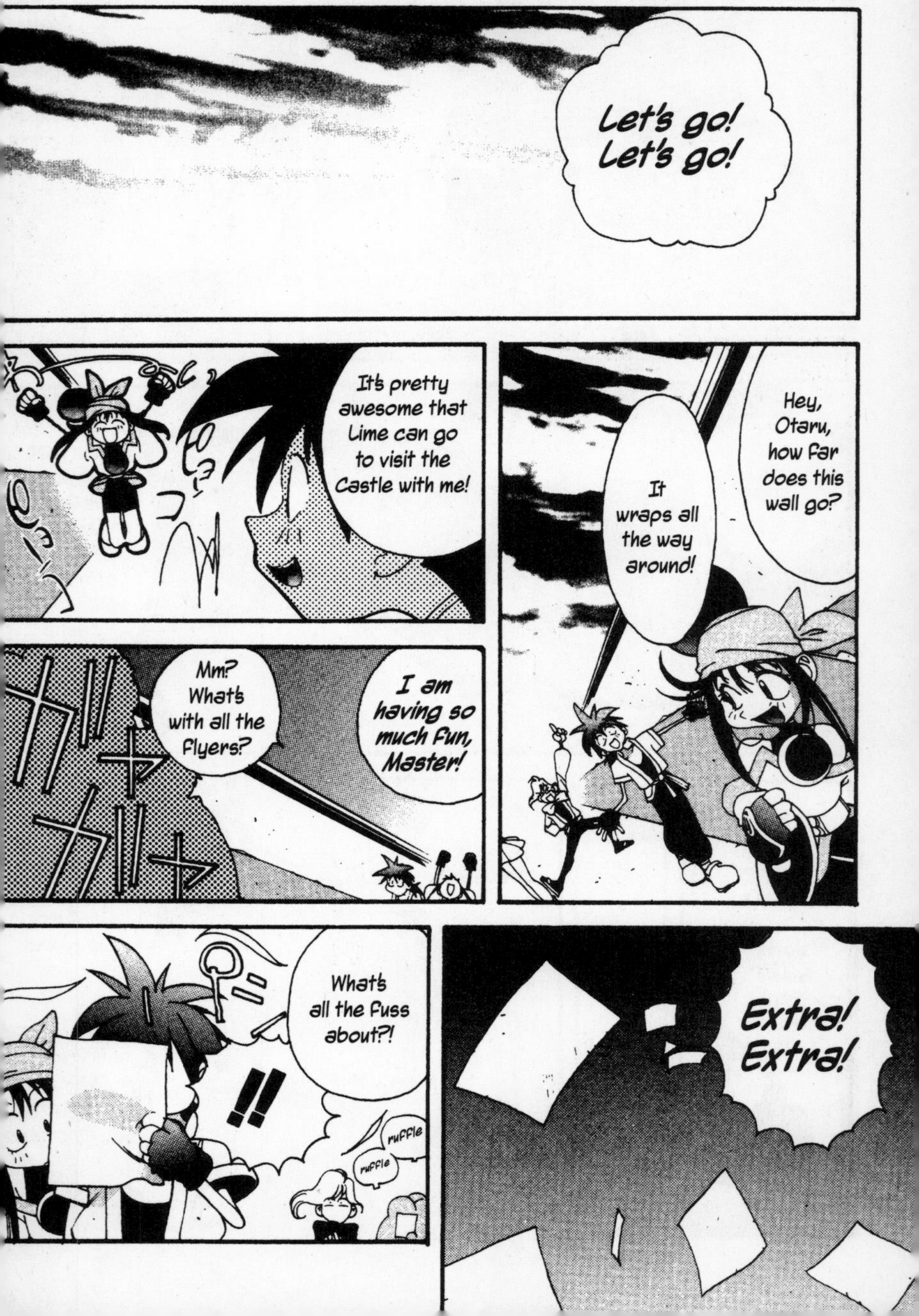
Let's go! Let's go!
Hey, Otaru, how far does this wall go?
It wraps all the way around!
It's pretty awesome that Lime can go to visit the Castle with me!
I am having so much fun, Master!
Mm? What's with all the flyers?
Extra! Extra!
What's all the fuss about?!
!!
ruffle
ruffle

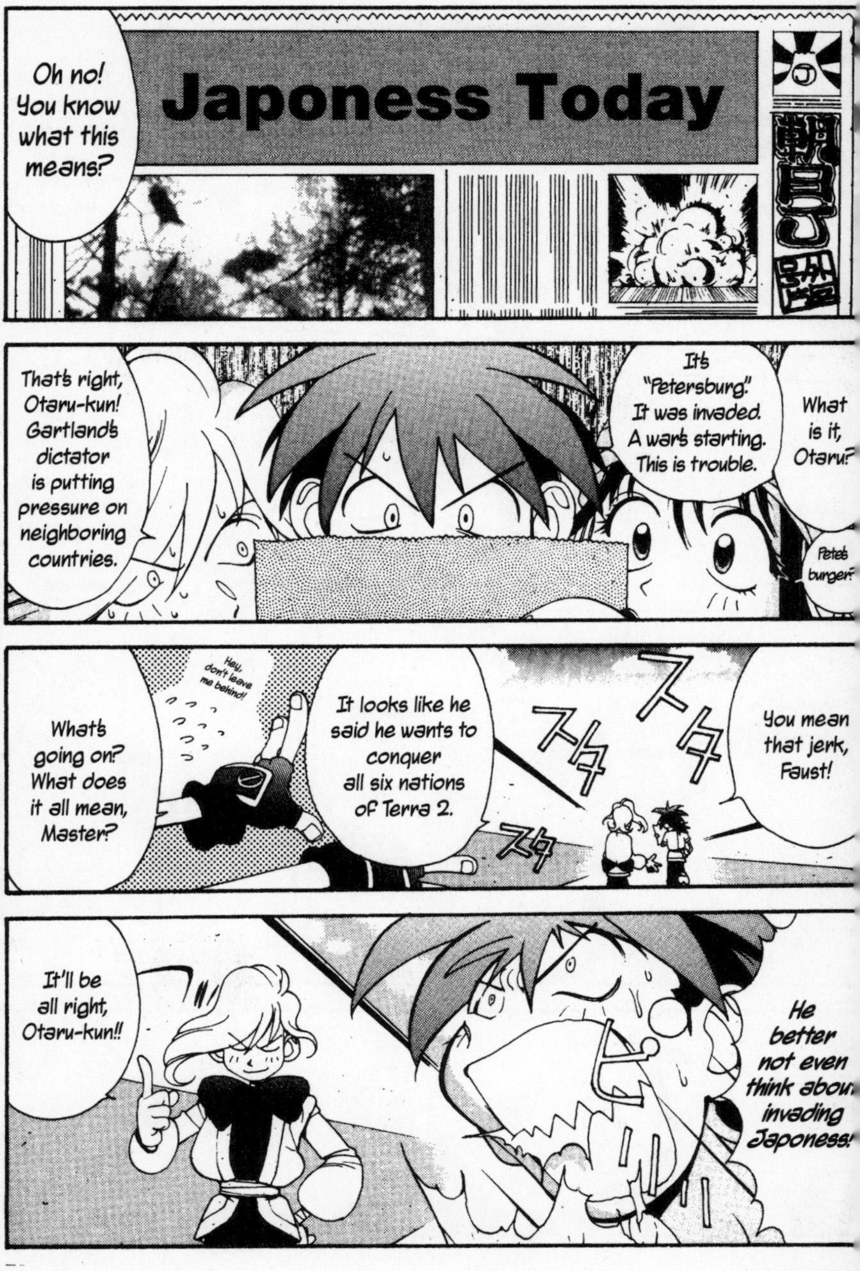
Japoness Today
Oh no! You know what this means?
What is it, Otaru?
Pete's burger?
It's "Petersburg." It was invaded. A war's starting. This is trouble.
That's right, Otaru-kun! Gartland's dictator is putting pressure on neighboring countries.
You mean that jerk, Faust!
スタ スタ スタ
It looks like he said he wants to conquer all six nations of Terra 2.
Hey, don't leave me behind!
What's going on? What does it all mean, Master?
He better not even think abou invading Japoness!
It'll be all right, Otaru-kun!!

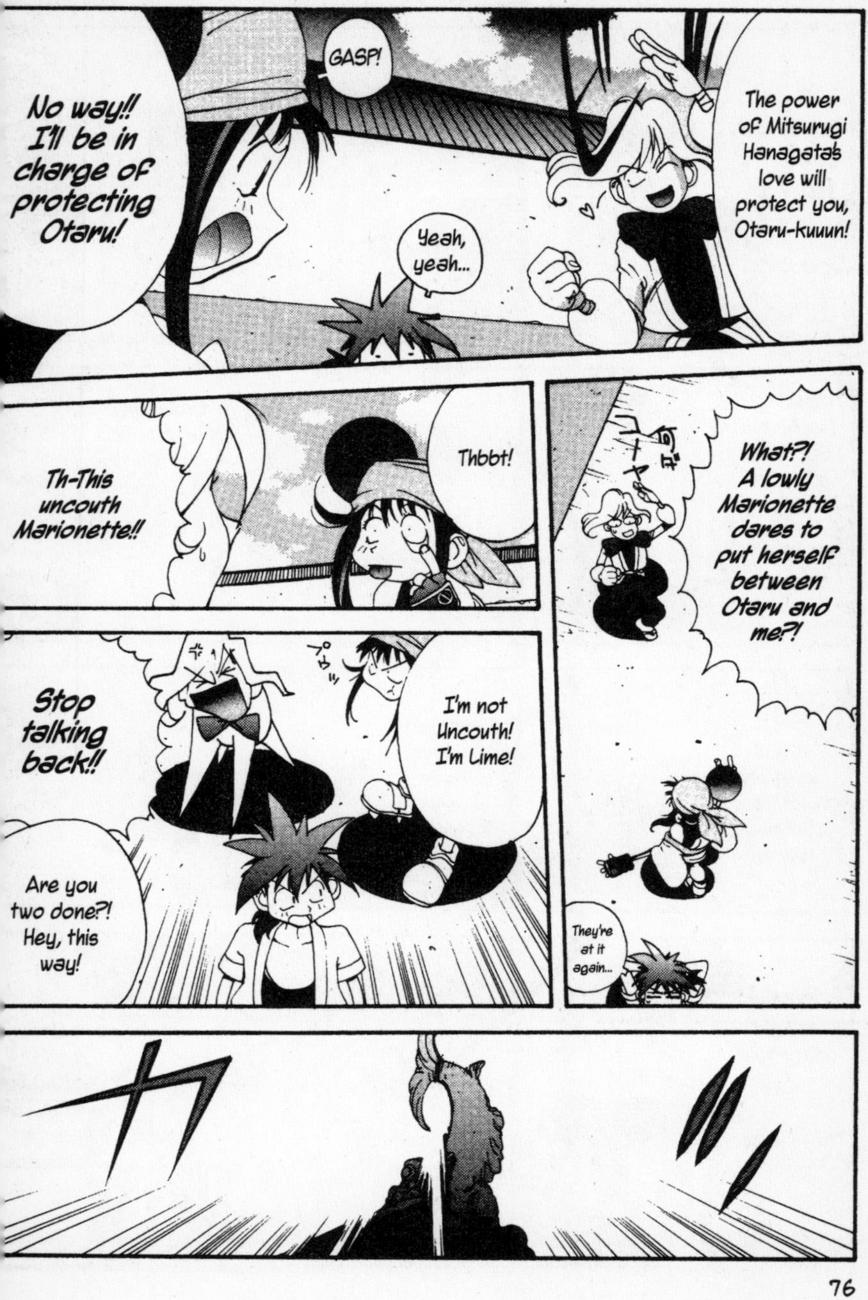
The power of Mitsurugi Hanagata's love will protect you, Otaru-kuuun!
GASP!
No way!! I'll be in charge of protecting Otaru!
Yeah, yeah...
What?! A lowly Marionette dares to put herself between Otaru and me?!
They're at it again...
Thbbt!
Th-This uncouth Marionette!!
I'm not Uncouth! I'm Lime!
Stop talking back!!
Are you two done?! Hey, this way!

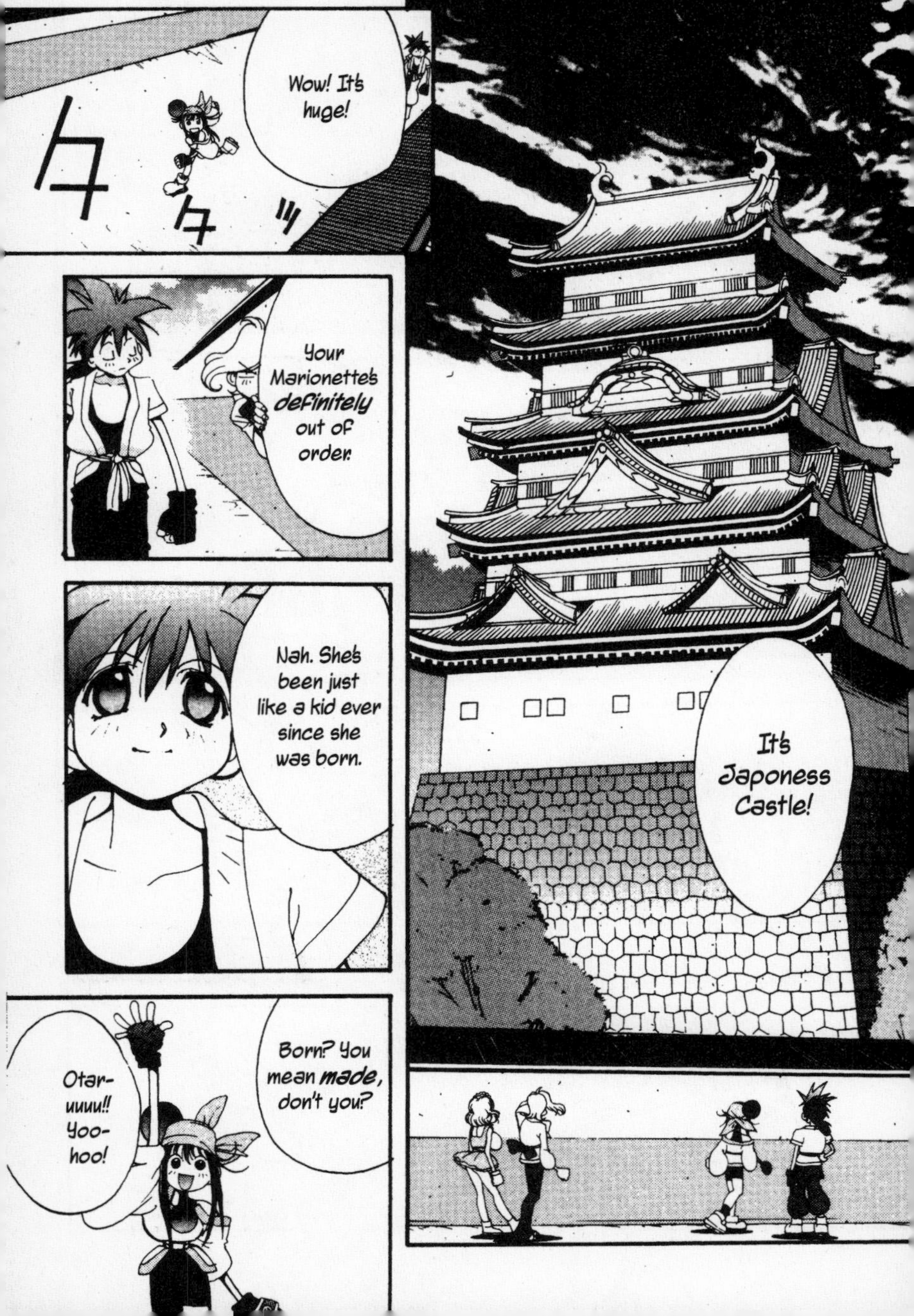
It's Japoness Castle!
Wow! It's huge!
タタッ
Your Marionette's definitely out of order.
Nah. She's been just like a kid ever since she was born.
Born? You mean made, don't you?
Otar-uuuu!! Yoo-hoo!

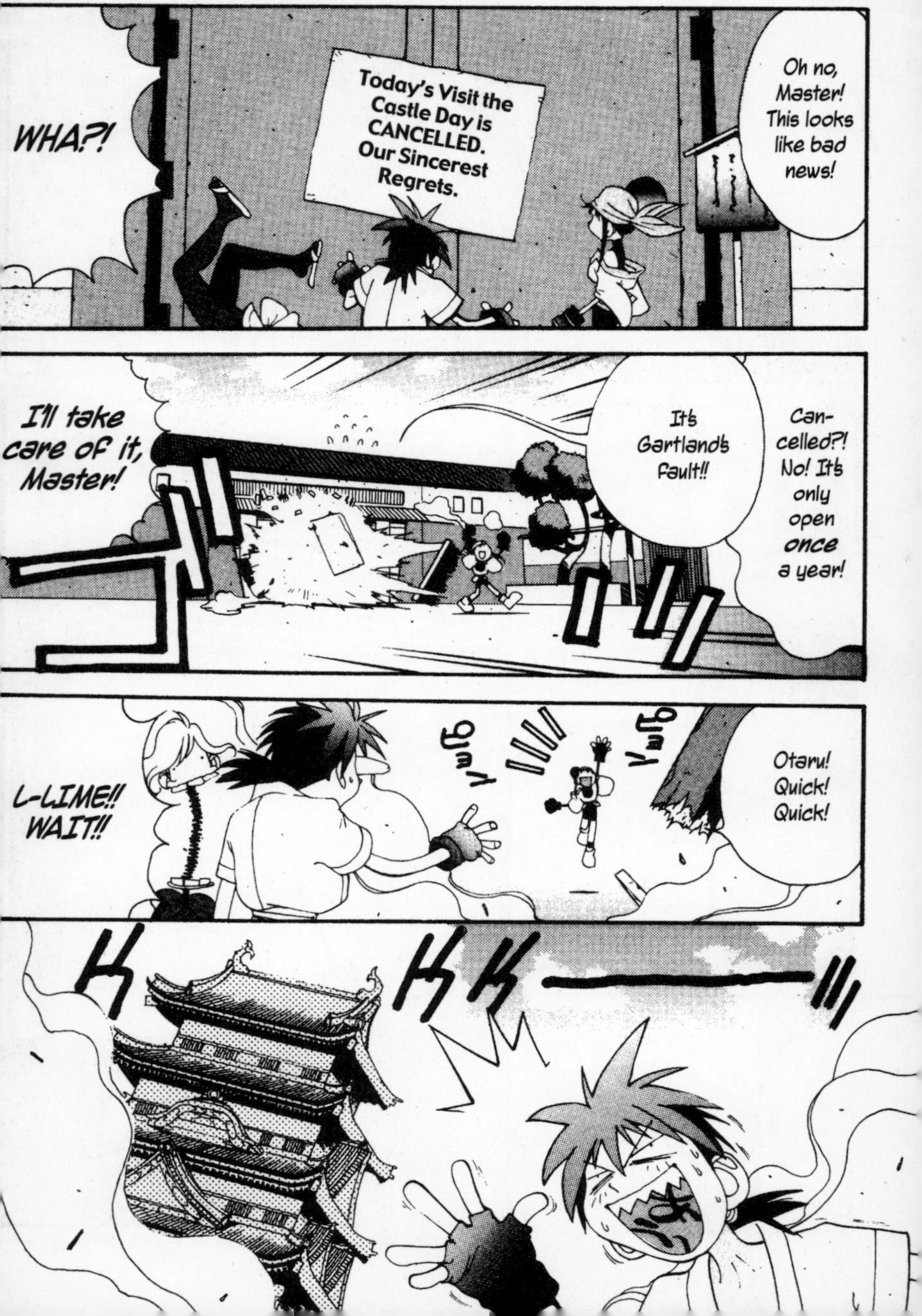
Oh no, Master! This looks like bad news!
Today's Visit the Castle Day is CANCELLED. Our Sincerest Regrets.
WHA?!
Can-celled?! No! It's only open once a year!
It's Gartland's fault!!
I'll take care of it, Master!
Otaru! Quick! Quick!
L-LIME!! WAIT!!
K KK—!!!

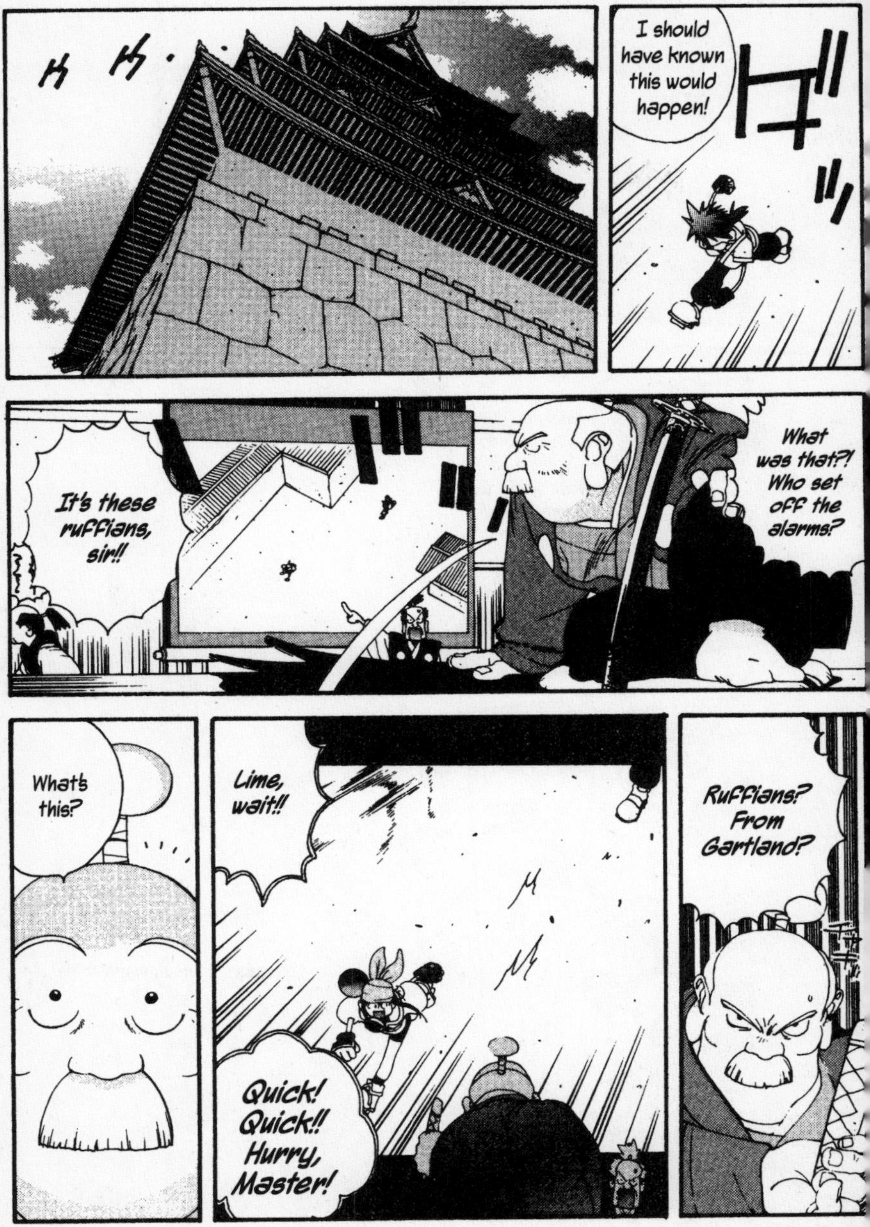
I should have known this would happen!
What was that?! Who set off the alarms?
It's these ruffians, sir!!
Ruffians? From Gartland?
Lime, wait!!
Quick! Quick!! Hurry, Master!
What's this?

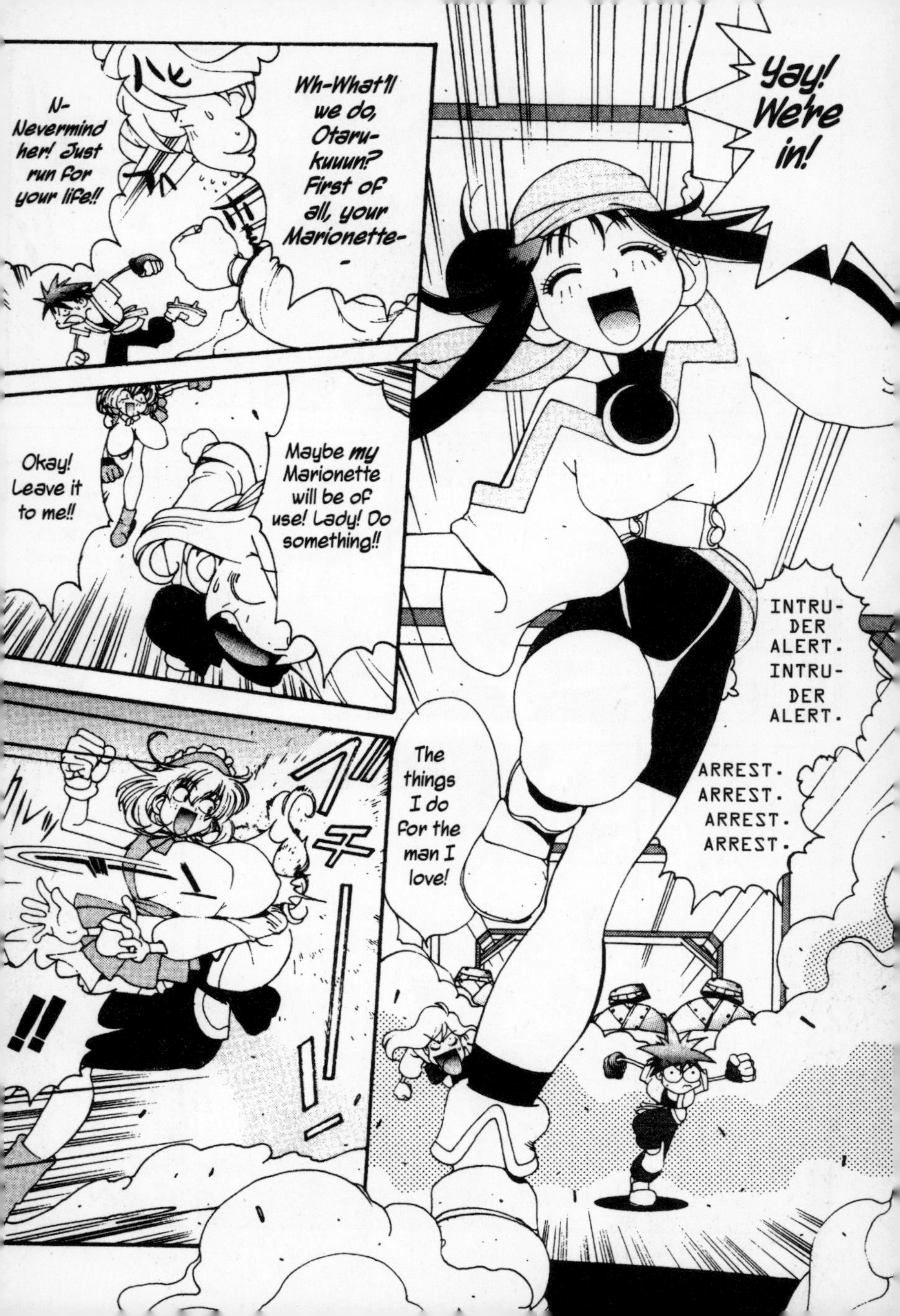
Yay! We're in!
INTRU- DER ALERT. INTRU- DER ALERT.
ARREST. ARREST. ARREST. ARREST.
The things I do for the man I love!
Wh-What'll we do, Otaru- kuuun? First of all, your Marionette- -
N- Nevermind her! Just run for your life!!
Maybe my Marionette will be of use! Lady! Do something!!
Okay! Leave it to me!!
!!

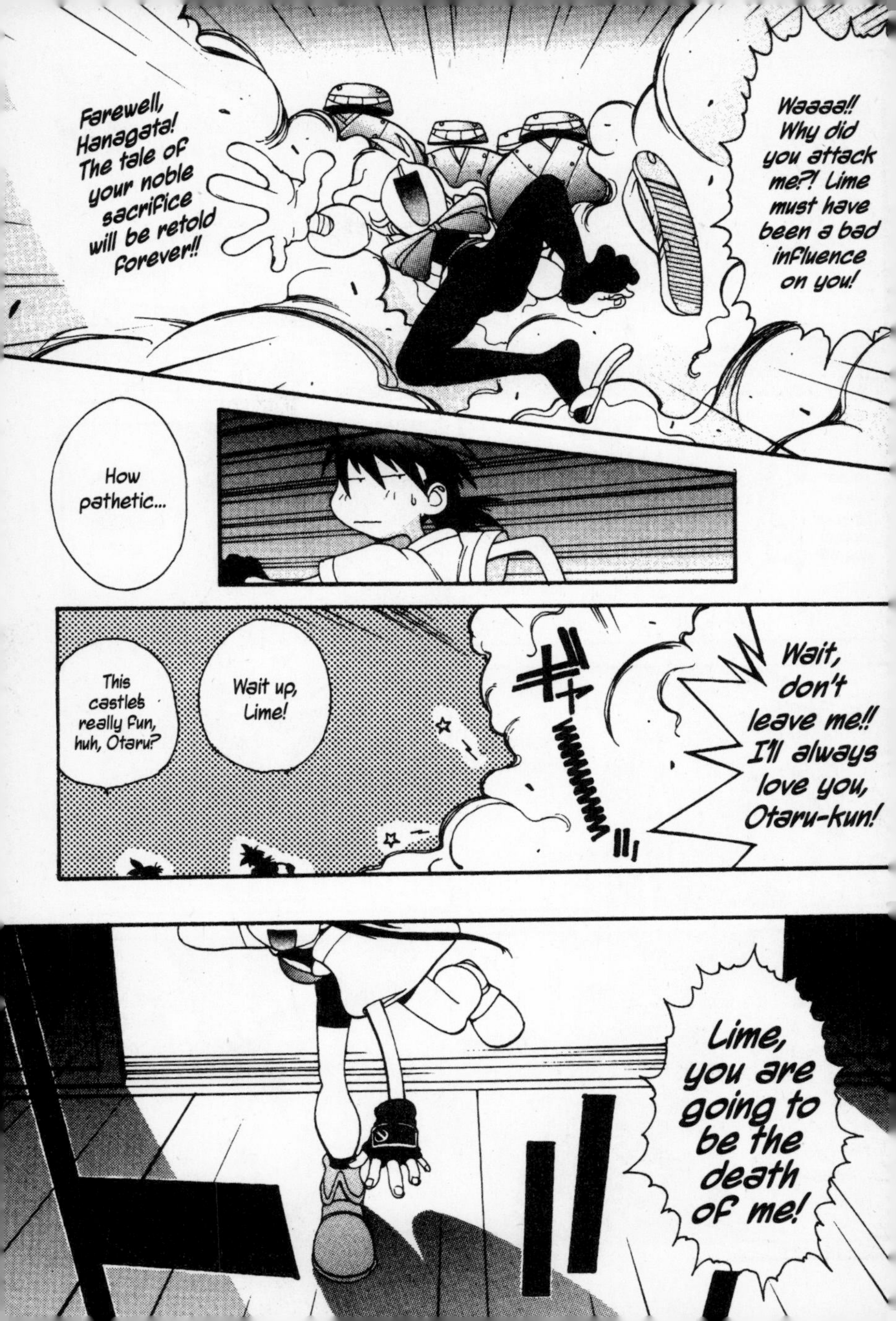
Waaaa!! Why did you attack me?! Lime must have been a bad influence on you!
Farewell, Hanagata! The tale of your noble sacrifice will be retold forever!!
How pathetic...
Wait, don't leave me!! I'll always love you, Otaru-kun!
Wait up, Lime!
This castle's really fun, huh, Otaru?
Lime, you are going to be the death of me!

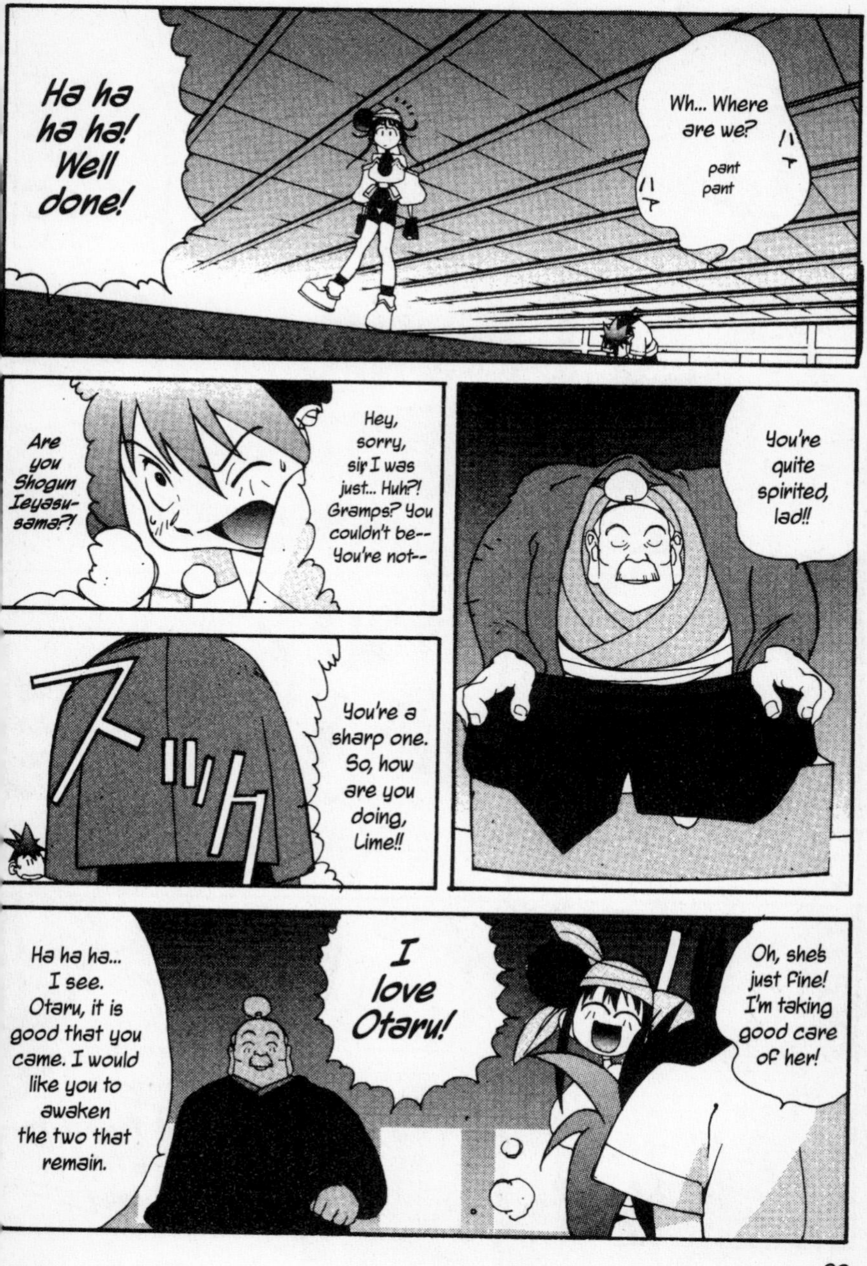
Wh... Where are we?
pant pant
Ha ha ha ha! Well done!
You're quite spirited, lad!!
Hey, sorry, sir, I was just... Huh?! Gramps? You couldn't be-- You're not--
Are you Shogun Ieyasu-sama?!
You're a sharp one. So, how are you doing, Lime!!
Oh, she's just fine! I'm taking good care of her!
I love Otaru!
Ha ha ha... I see. Otaru, it is good that you came. I would like you to awaken the two that remain.

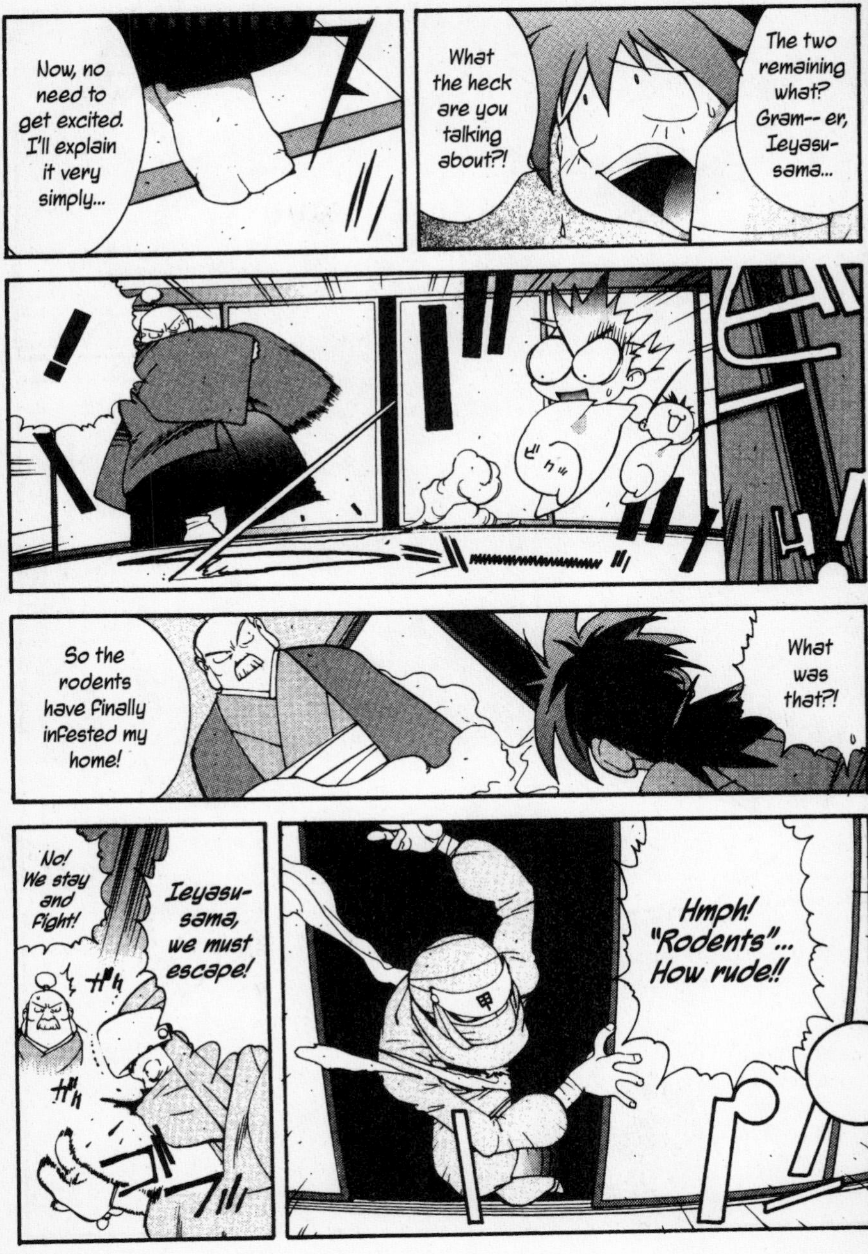
The two remaining what? Gram-- er, Ieyasu-sama...
What the heck are you talking about?!
Now, no need to get excited. I'll explain it very simply...
!
What was that?!
So the rodents have finally infested my home!
Hmph! "Rodents"... How rude!!
Ieyasu-sama, we must escape!
No! We stay and fight!

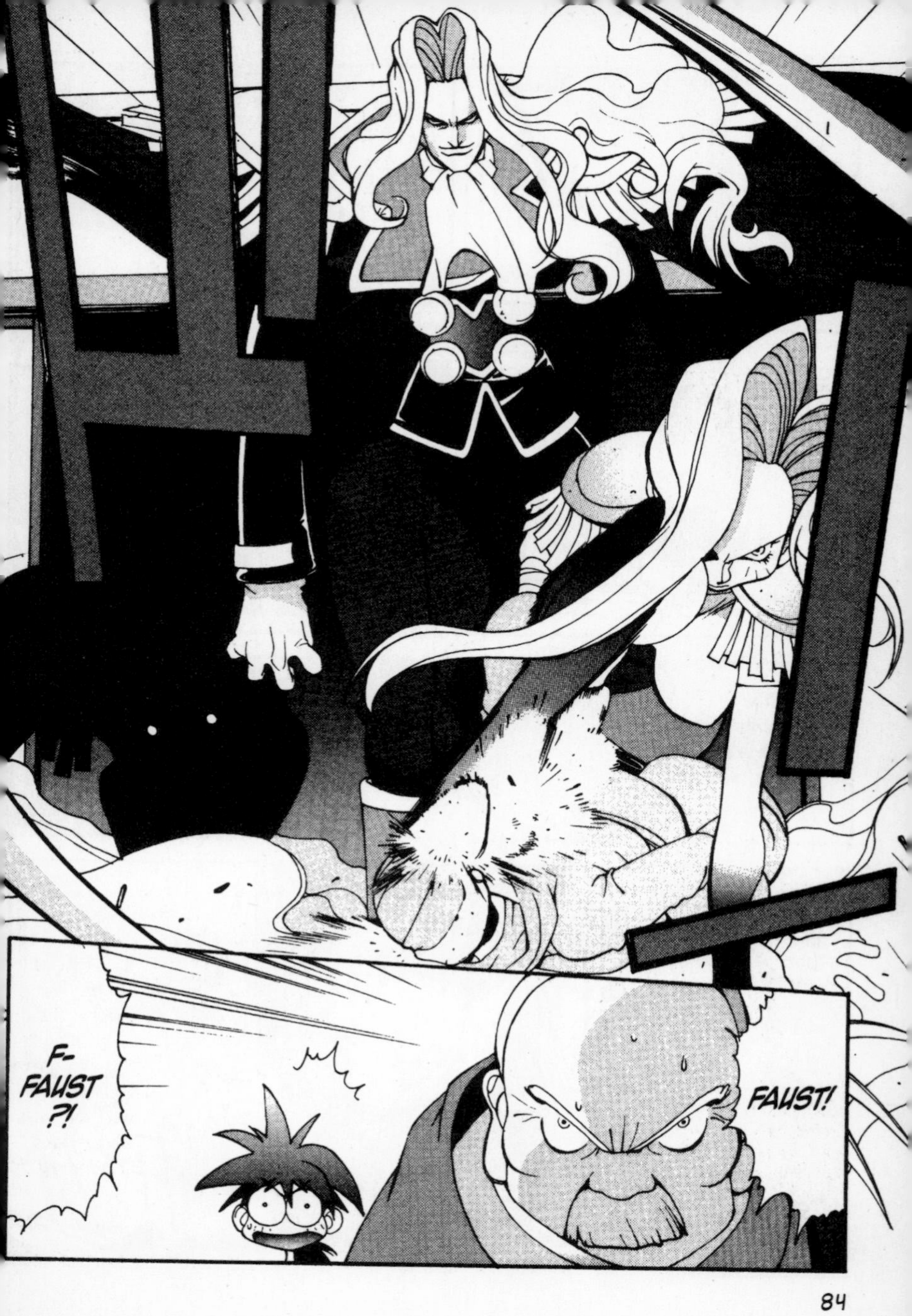
FAUST!
F- FAUST ?!

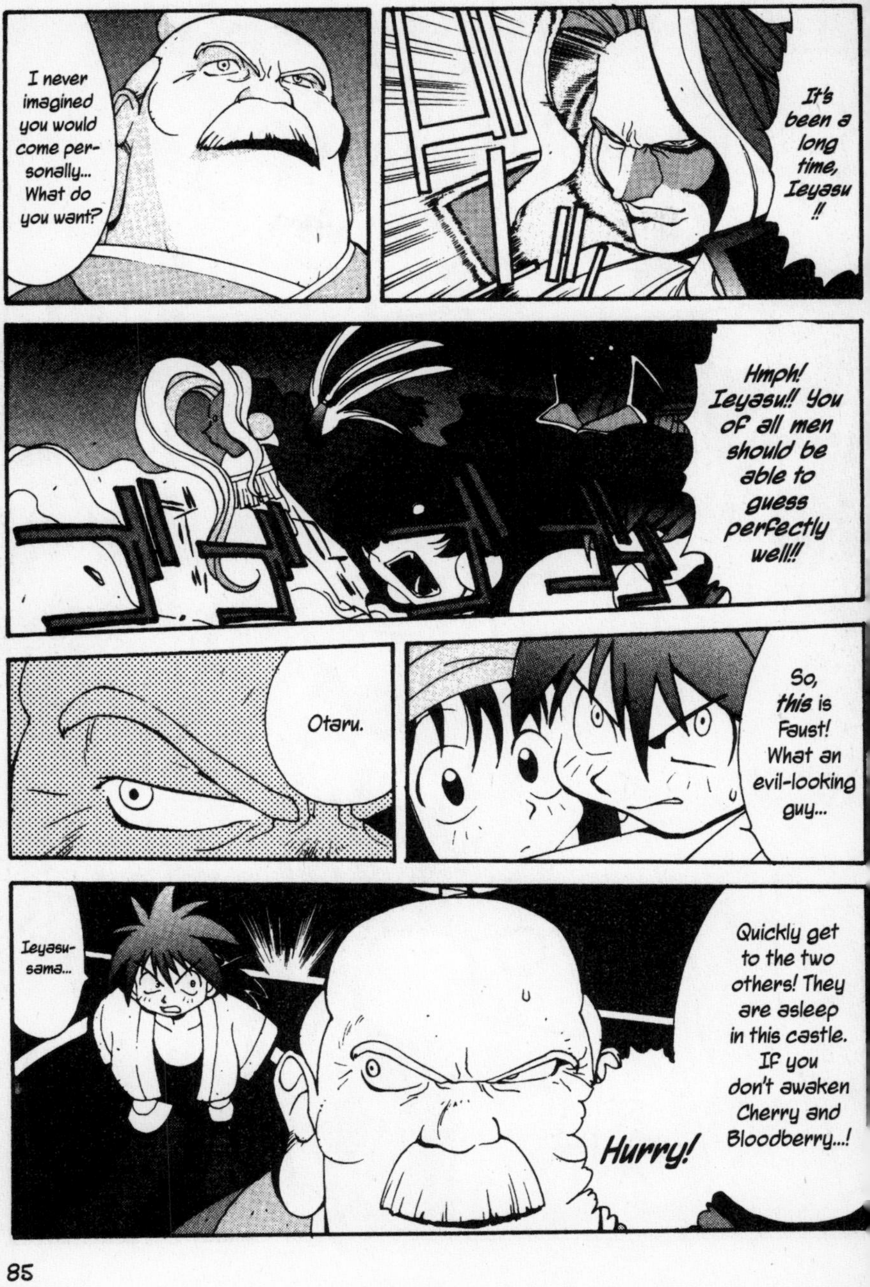
It's been a long time, Ieyasu!!
I never imagined you would come per-sonally... What do you want?
Hmph! Ieyasu!! You of all men should be able to guess perfectly well!!
So, this is Faust! What an evil-looking guy...
Otaru.
Quickly get to the two others! They are asleep in this castle. If you don't awaken Cherry and Bloodberry...!
Hurry!
Ieyasu-sama...

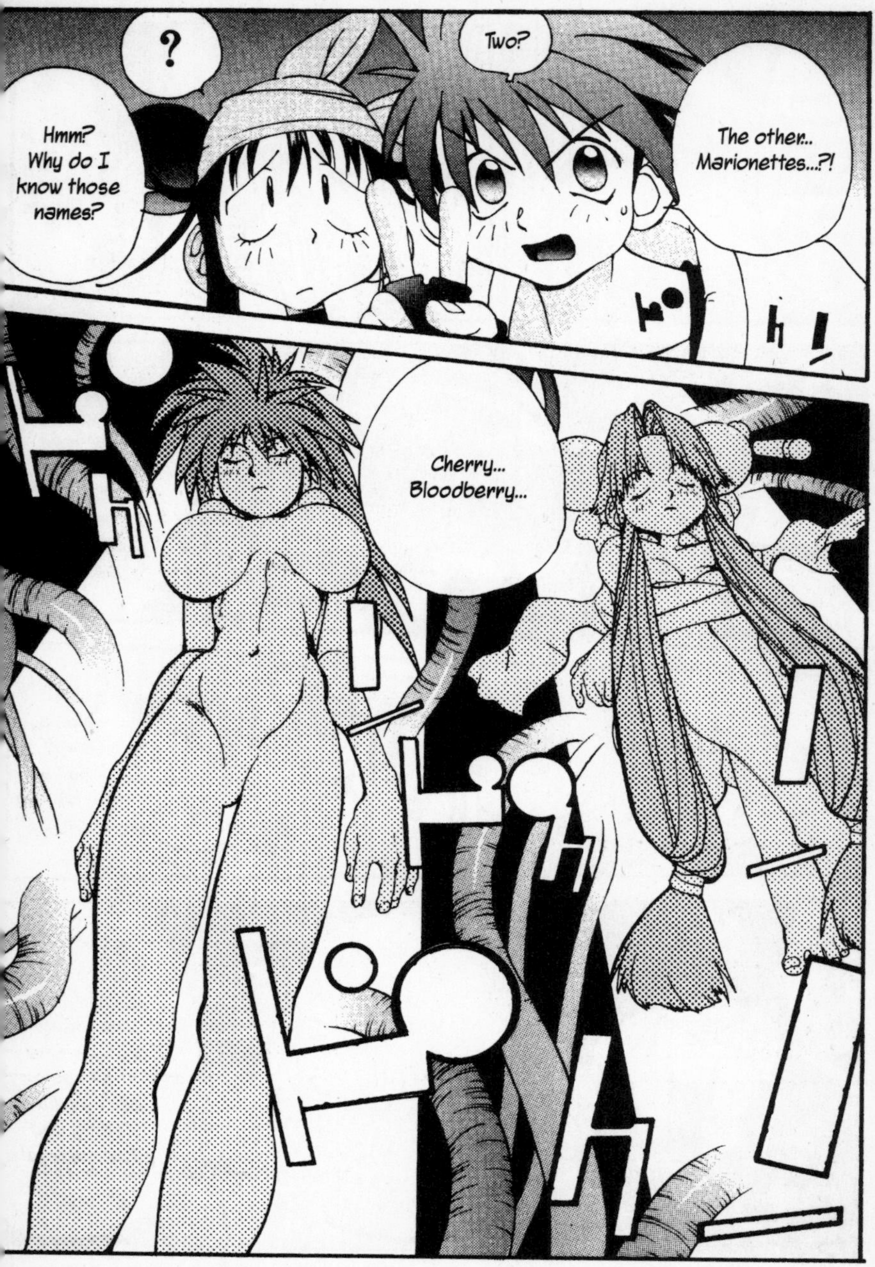
Two?
The other... Marionettes...?!
?
Hmm? Why do I know those names?
Cherry... Bloodberry...

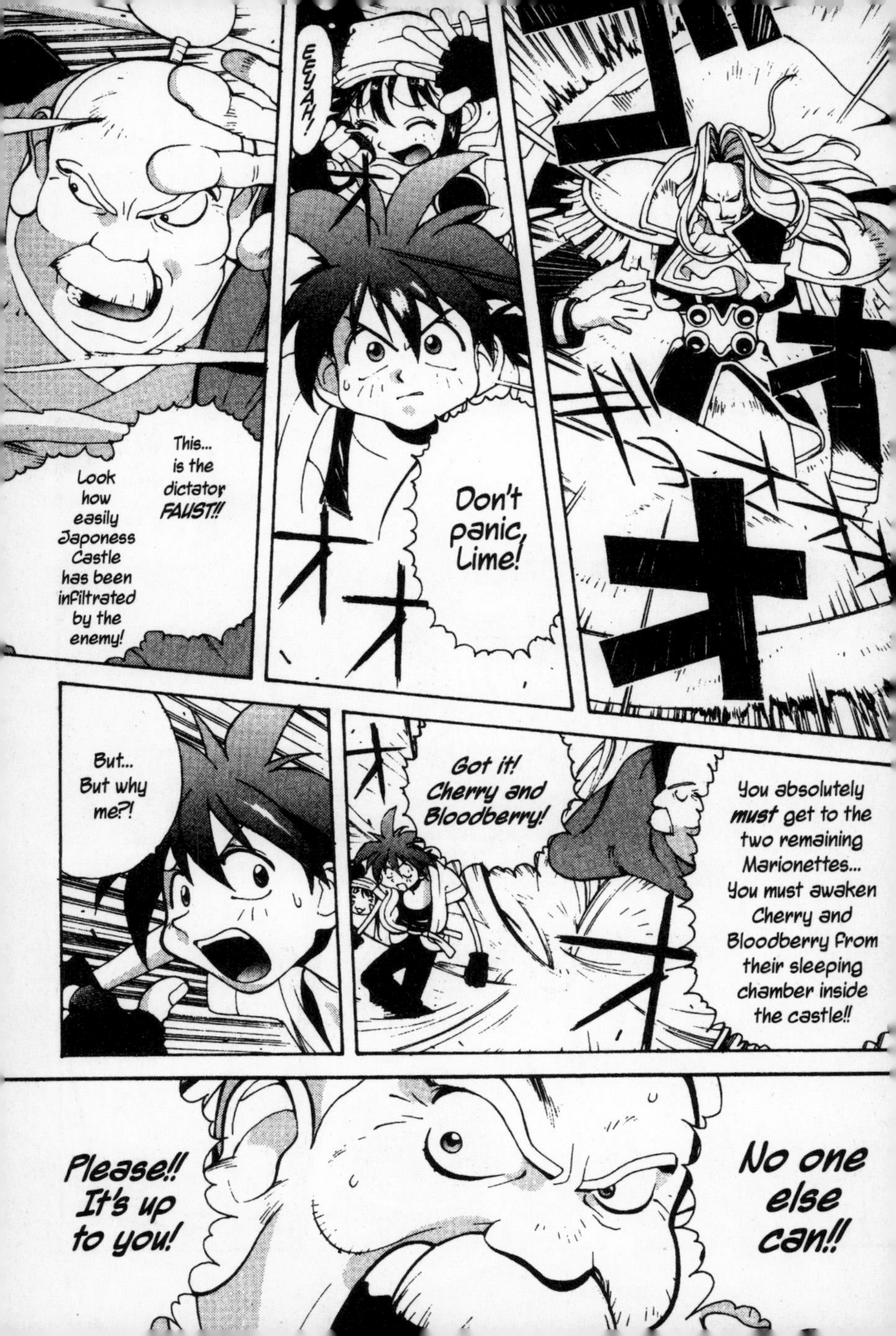
EEYAH!
Don't panic, Lime!
This... is the dictator FAUST!!
Look how easily Japoness Castle has been infiltrated by the enemy!
You absolutely must get to the two remaining Marionettes... You must awaken Cherry and Bloodberry from their sleeping chamber inside the castle!!
Got it! Cherry and Bloodberry!
But... But why me?!
No one else can!!
Please!! It's up to you!

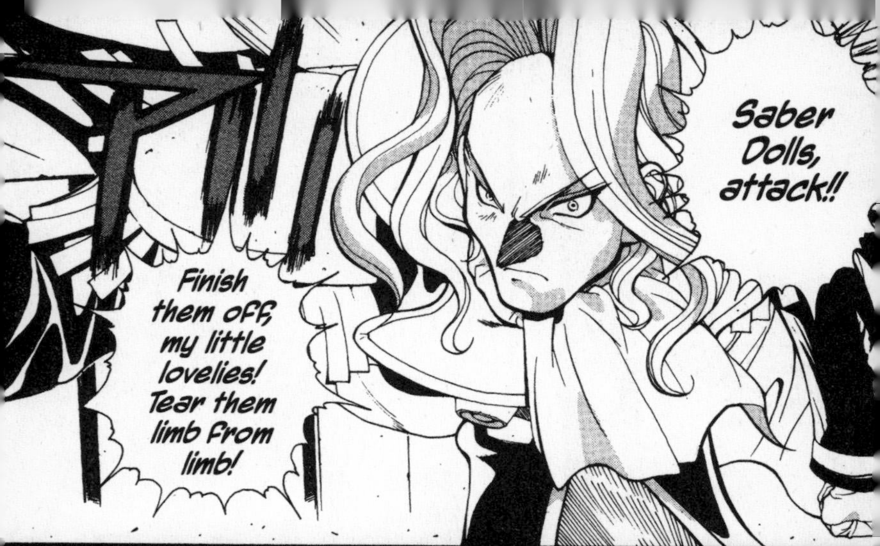
Saber Dolls, attack!!
Finish them off, my little lovelies! Tear them limb from limb!

Chapter 4 -
Finally, All 3 Maidens Activated

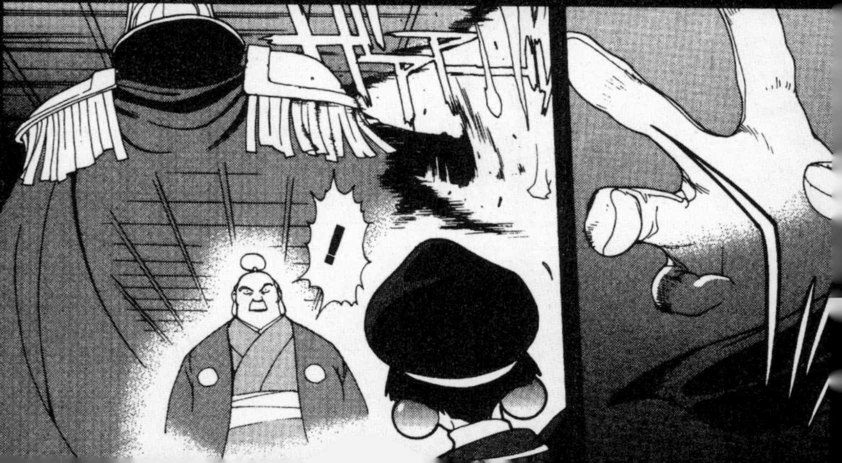
!

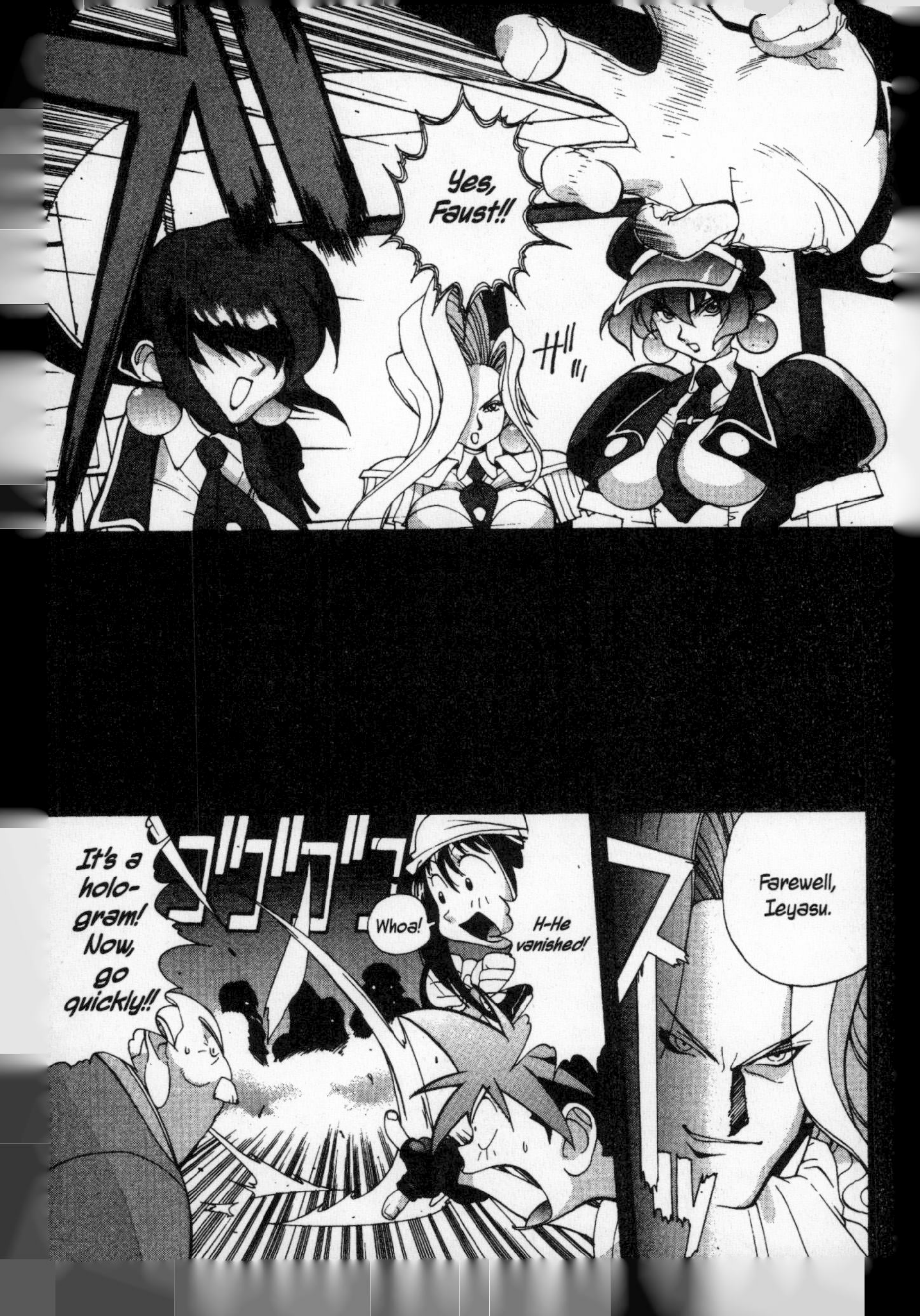
Yes, Faust!!
Farewell, Ieyasu.
H-He vanished!
Whoa!
It's a holo-gram! Now, go quickly!!

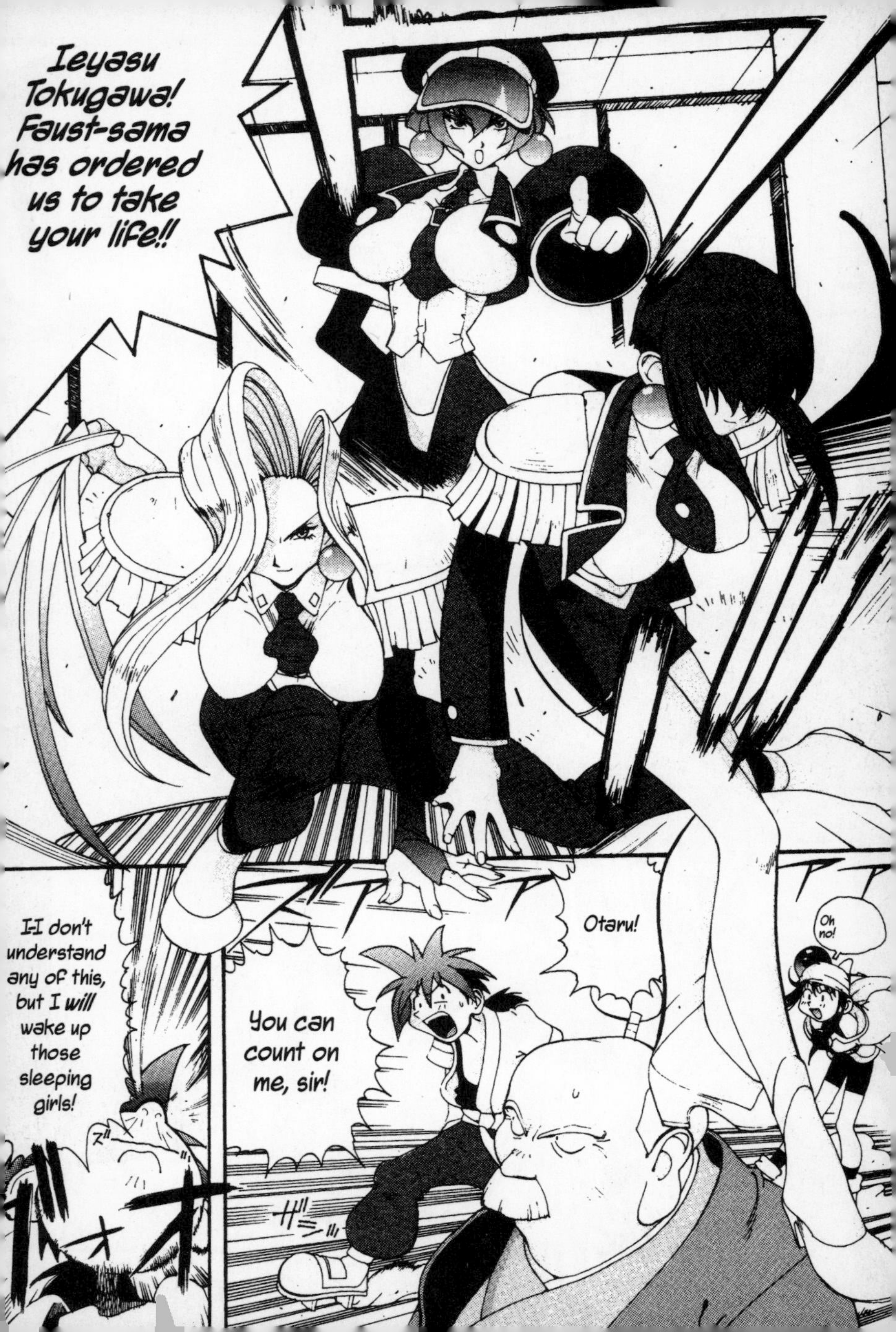
Ieyasu Tokugawa! Faust-sama has ordered us to take your life!!
Oh no!
Otaru!
You can count on me, sir!
I-I don't understand any of this, but I *will* wake up those sleeping girls!

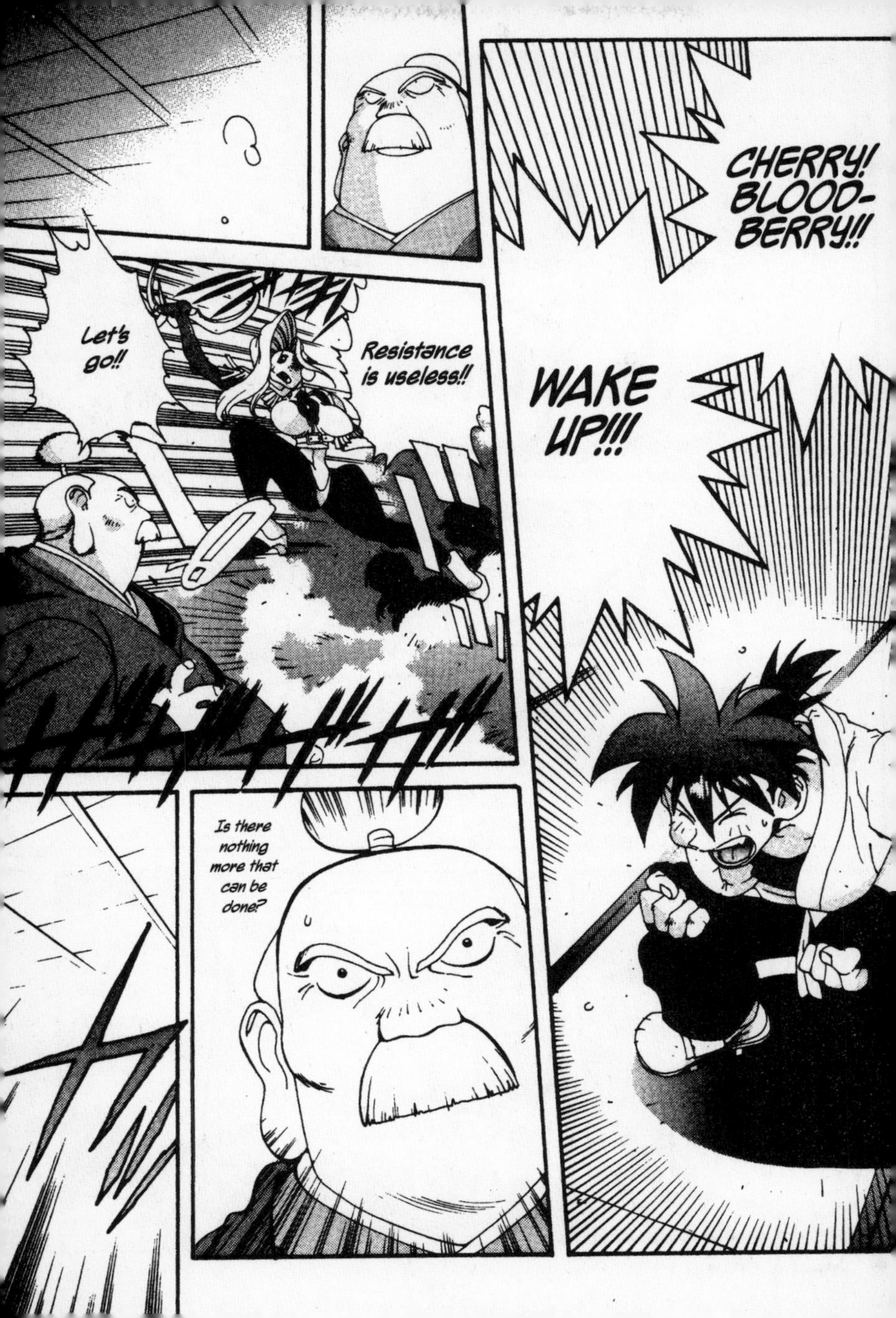
CHERRY! BLOOD-BERRY!!
WAKE UP!!!
Resistance is useless!!
Let's go!!
Is there nothing more that can be done?

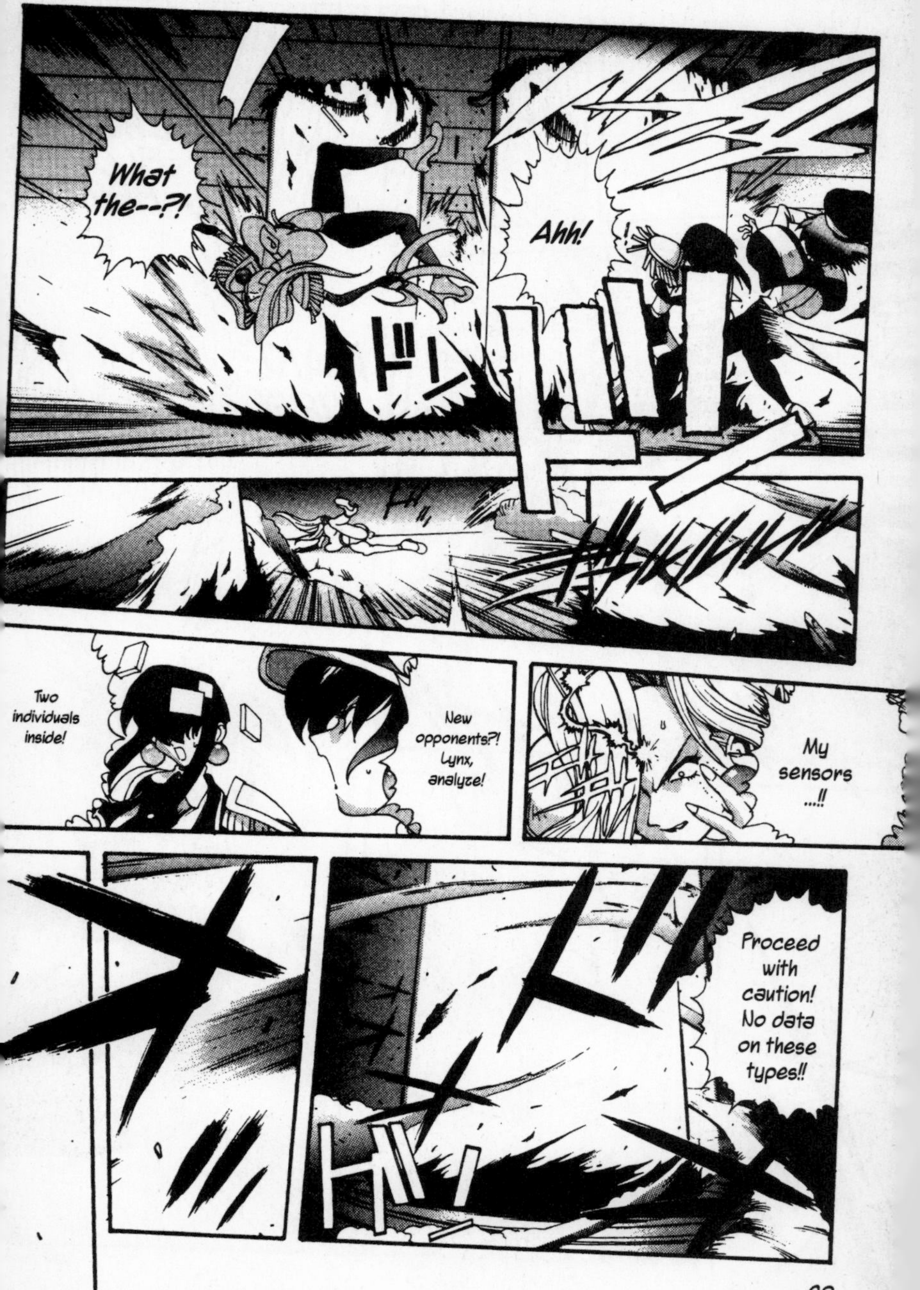
Ahh!
What the--?!
ドン
My sensors ...!!
New opponents?! Lynx, analyze!
Two individuals inside!
Proceed with caution! No data on these types!!

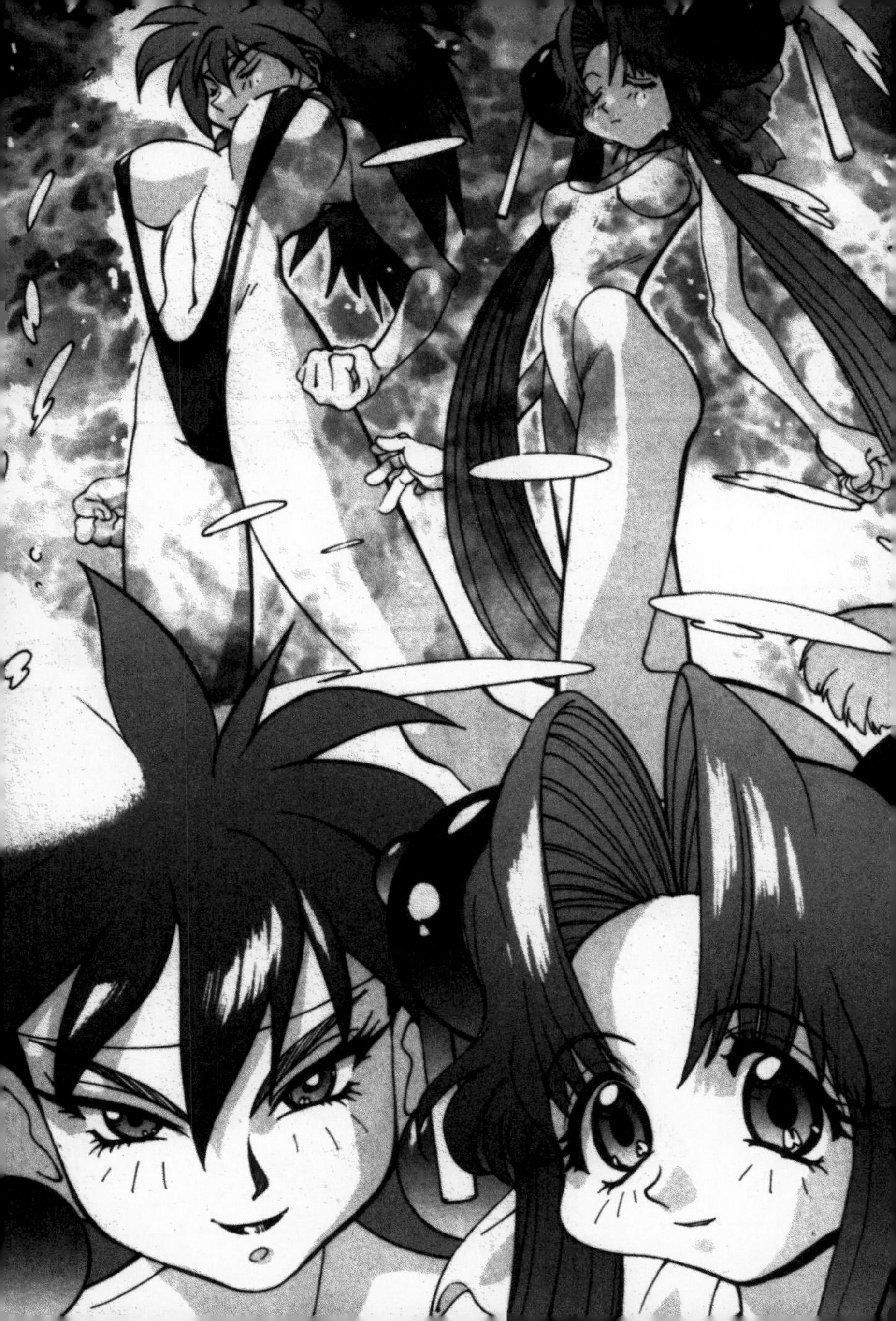

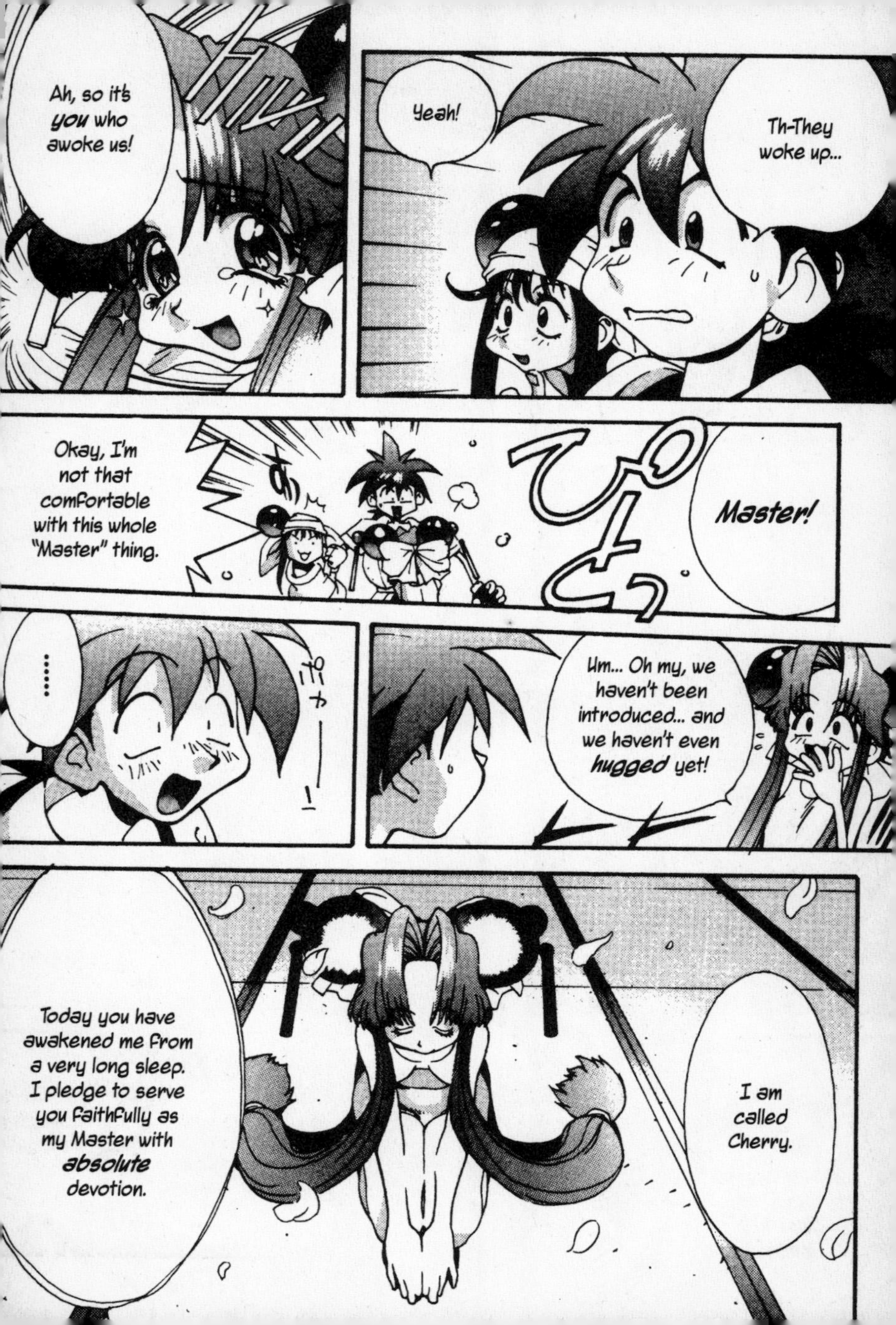
Th-They woke up...
Yeah!
Ah, so it's *you* who awoke us!
Master!
Okay, I'm not that comfortable with this whole "Master" thing.
Um... Oh my, we haven't been introduced... and we haven't even *hugged* yet!
......
I am called Cherry.
Today you have awakened me from a very long sleep. I pledge to serve you faithfully as my Master with *absolute* devotion.

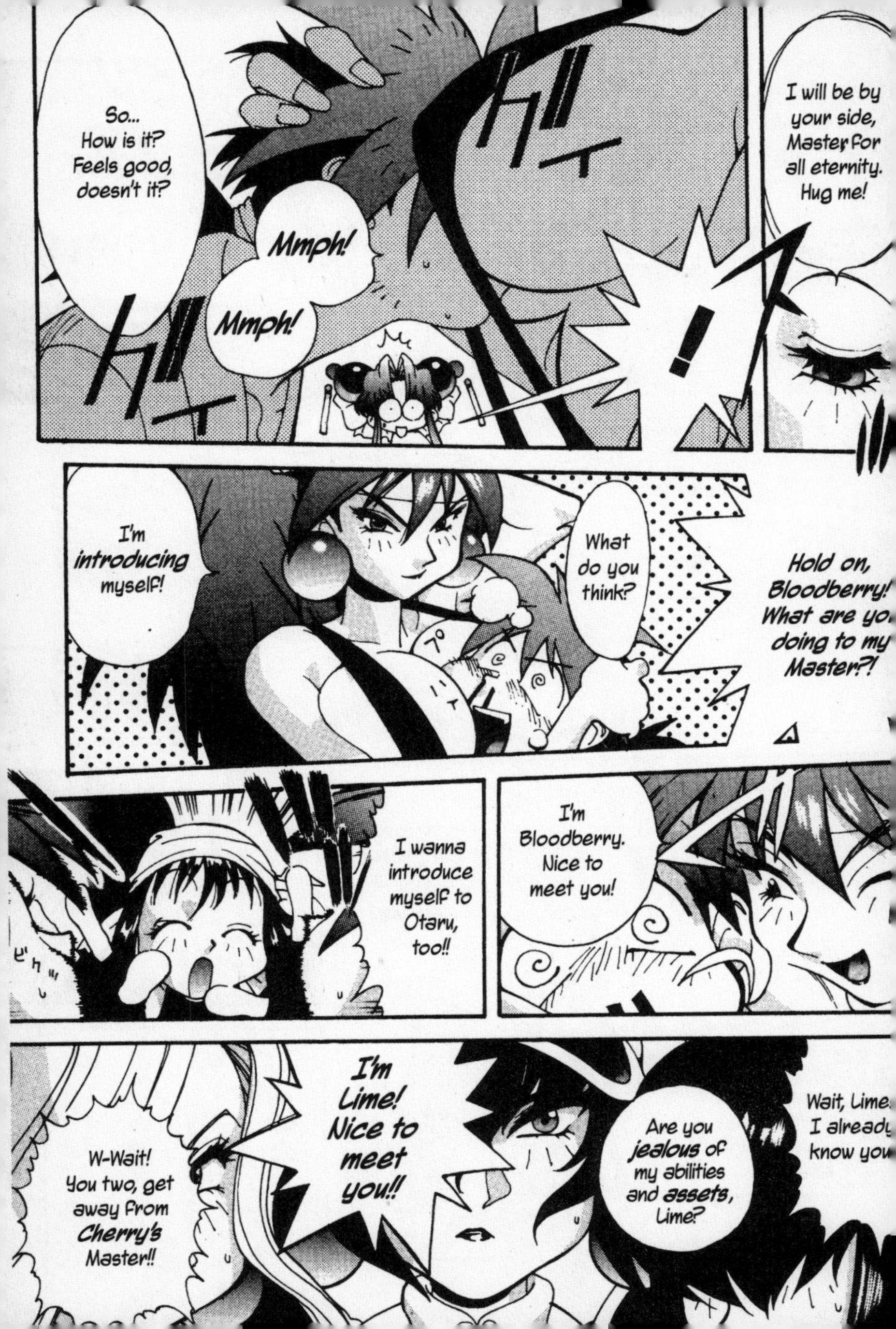
I will be by your side, Master, for all eternity. Hug me!
So... How is it? Feels good, doesn't it?
Mmph!
Mmph!
Hold on, Bloodberry! What are yo doing to my Master?!
What do you think?
I'm *introducing* myself!
I'm Bloodberry. Nice to meet you!
I wanna introduce myself to Otaru, too!!
Wait, Lime. I already know you
Are you *jealous* of my abilities and *assets*, Lime?
I'm Lime! Nice to meet you!!
W-Wait! You two, get away from *Cherry's* Master!!

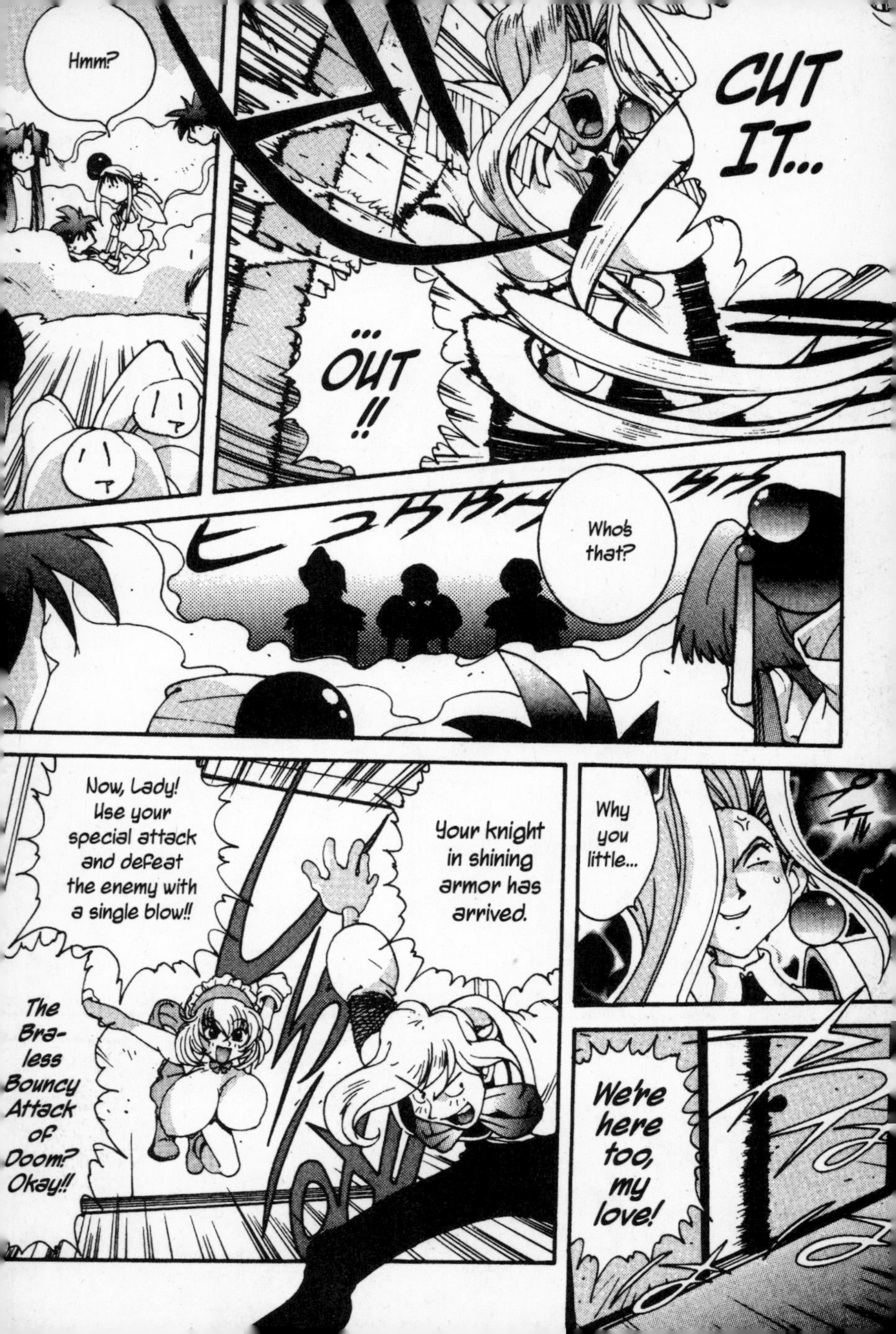
CUT IT...
...ÖUT!!
Hmm?
Who's that?
Why you little...
We're here too, my love!
Your knight in shining armor has arrived.
Now, Lady! Use your special attack and defeat the enemy with a single blow!!
The Bra-less Bouncy Attack of Doom? Okay!!

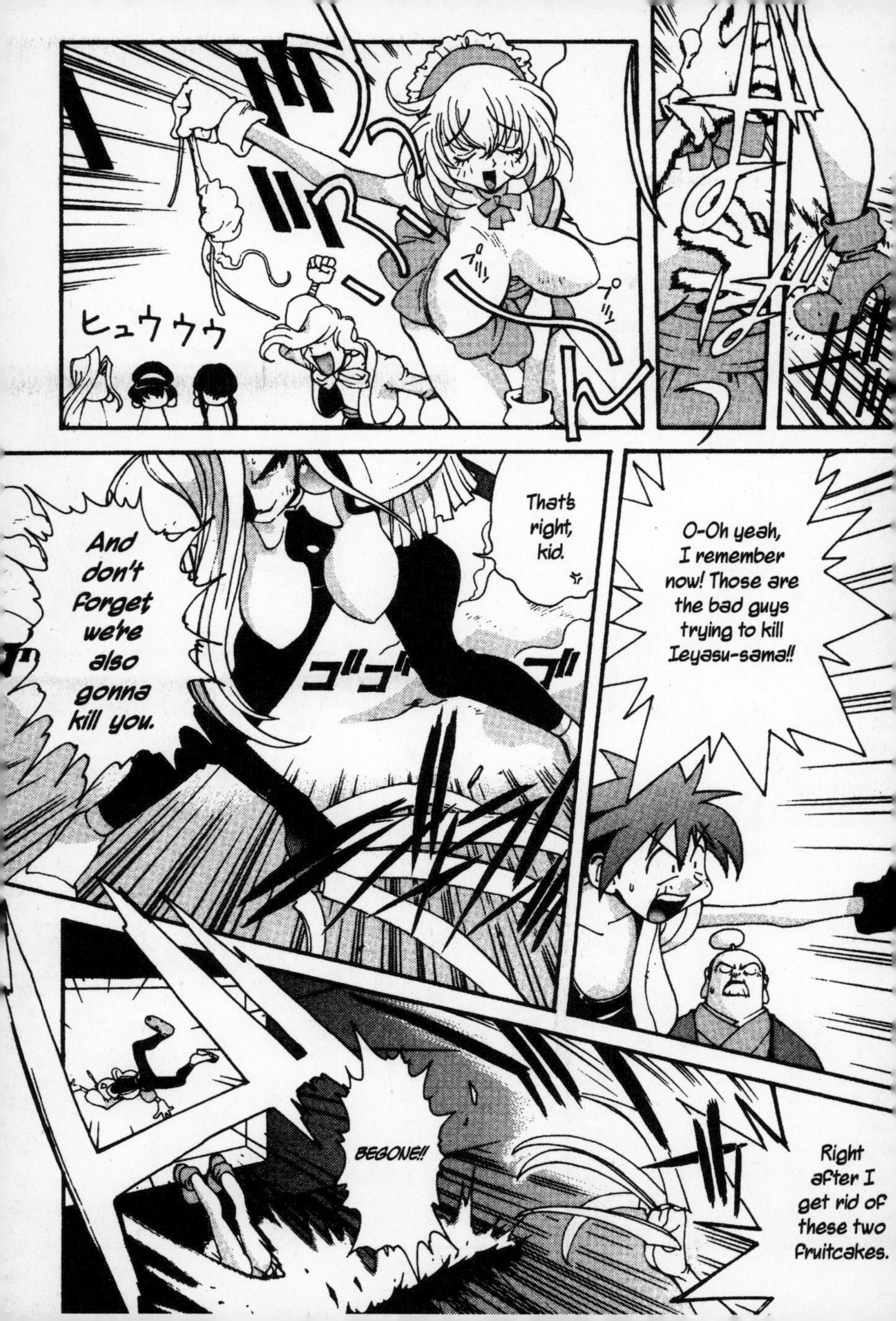
ヒュウウウ
O-Oh yeah, I remember now! Those are the bad guys trying to kill Ieyasu-sama!!
That's right, kid.
And don't forget we're also gonna kill you.
ゴゴゴ
Right after I get rid of these two fruitcakes.
BEGONE!!

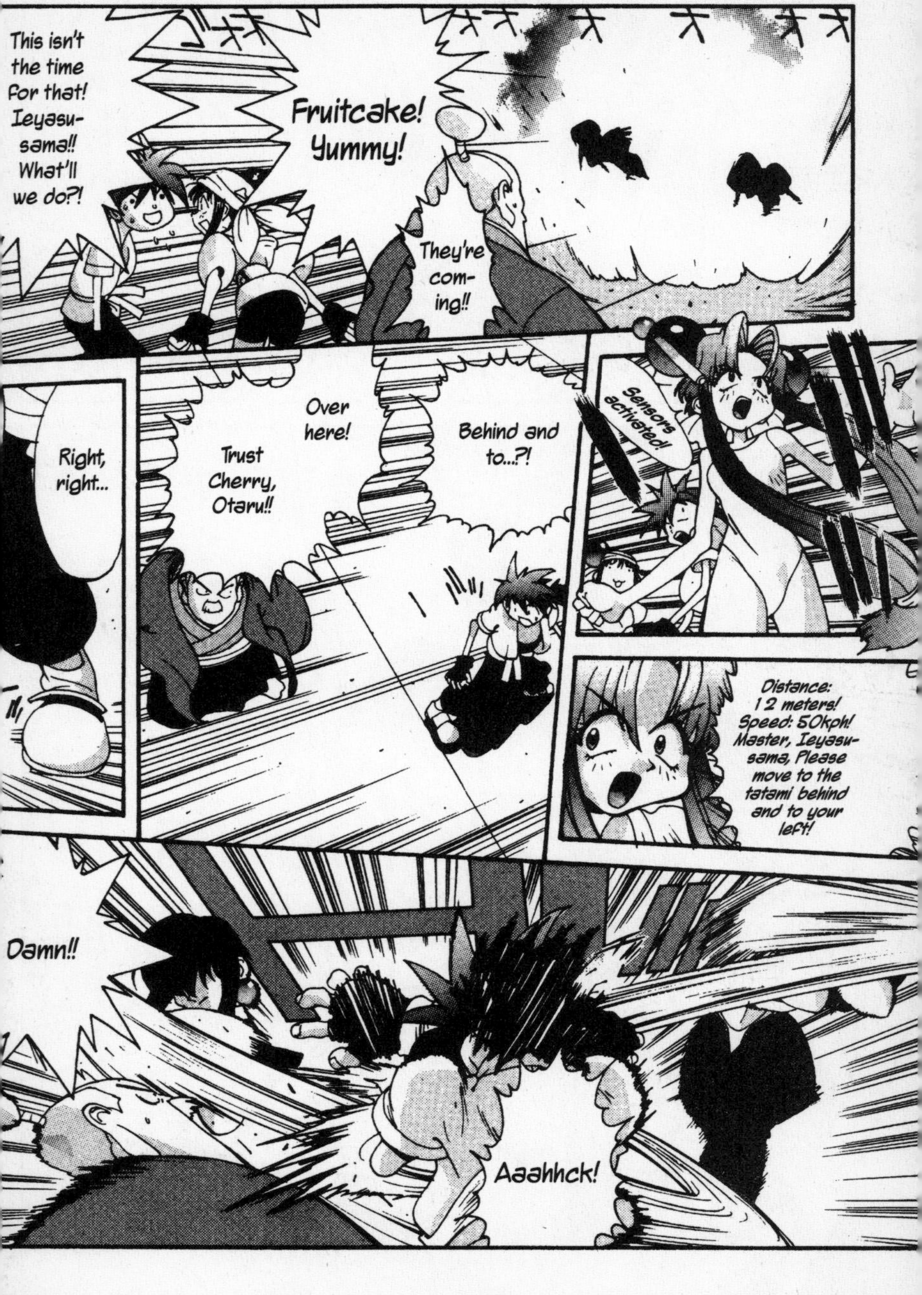
Fruitcake! Yummy!
They're coming!!
This isn't the time for that! Ieyasu-sama!! What'll we do?!
Sensors activated!
Distance: 12 meters! Speed: 50kph! Master, Ieyasu-sama, Please move to the tatami behind and to your left!
Behind and to...?!
Over here!
Trust Cherry, Otaru!!
Right, right...
Aaahhck!
Damn!!

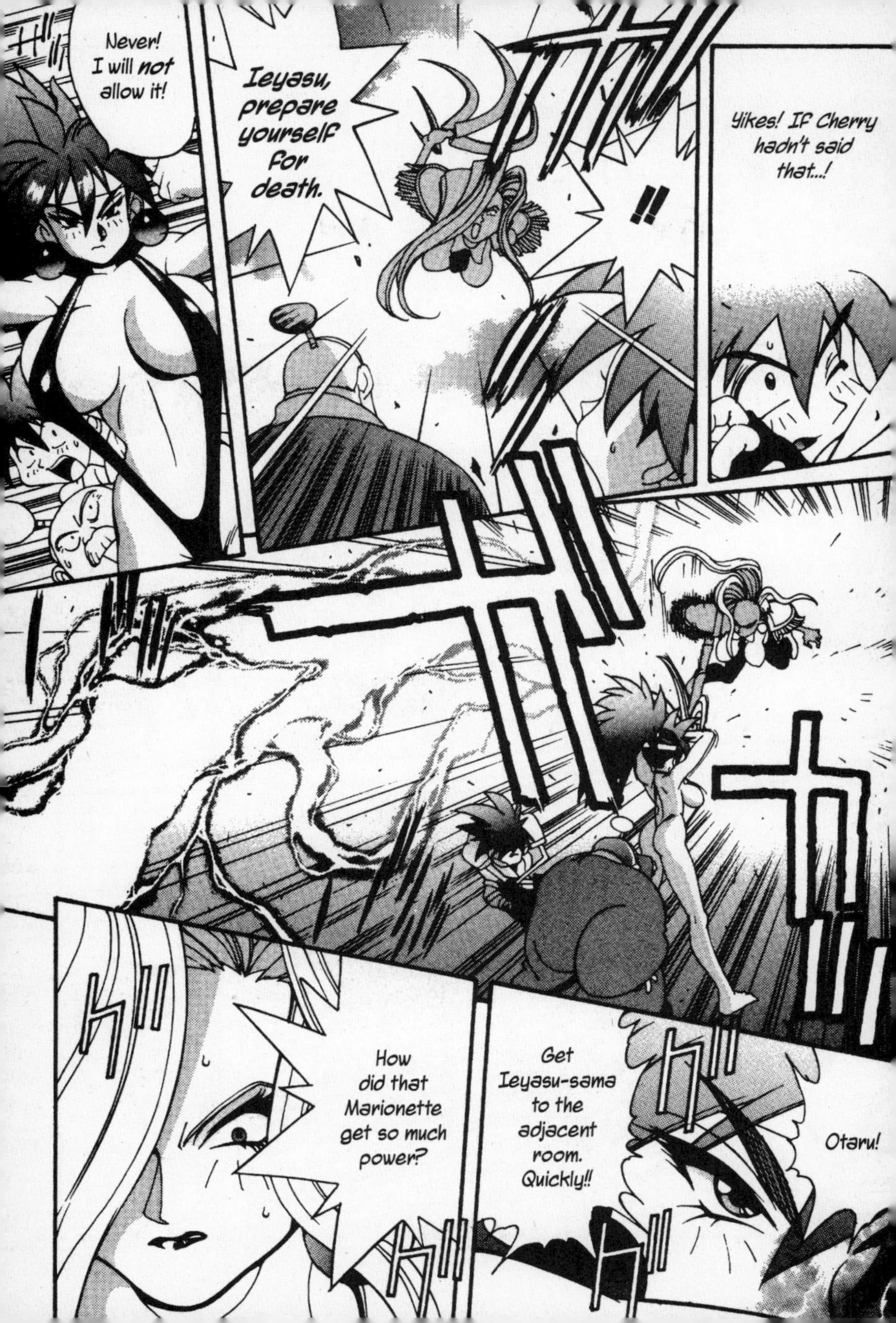
Yikes! If Cherry hadn't said that...!
Ieyasu, prepare yourself for death.
!!
Never! I will *not* allow it!
Otaru!
Get Ieyasu-sama to the adjacent room. Quickly!!
How did that Marionette get so much power?

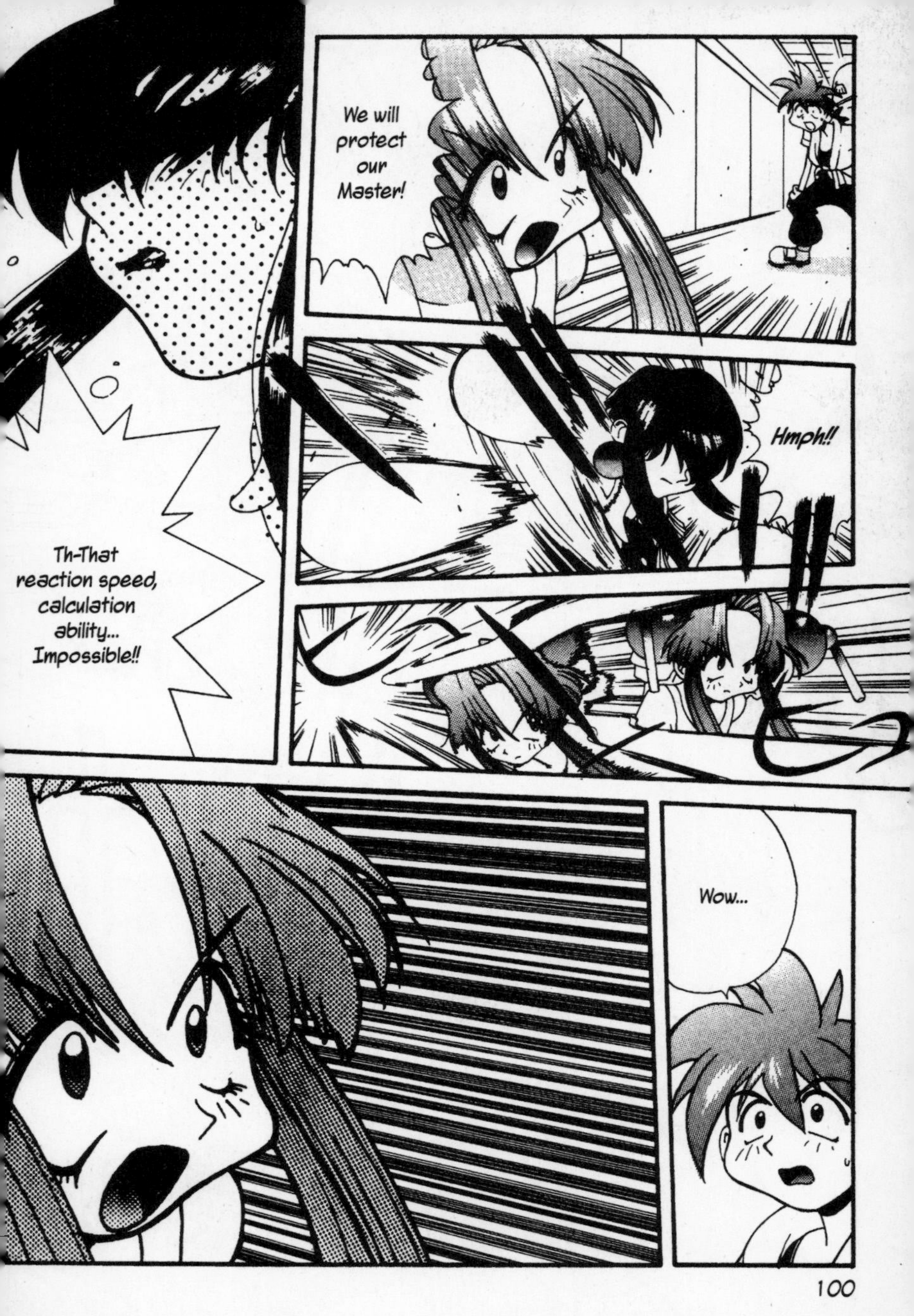
We will protect our Master!
Hmph!!
Th-That reaction speed, calculation ability... Impossible!!
Wow...

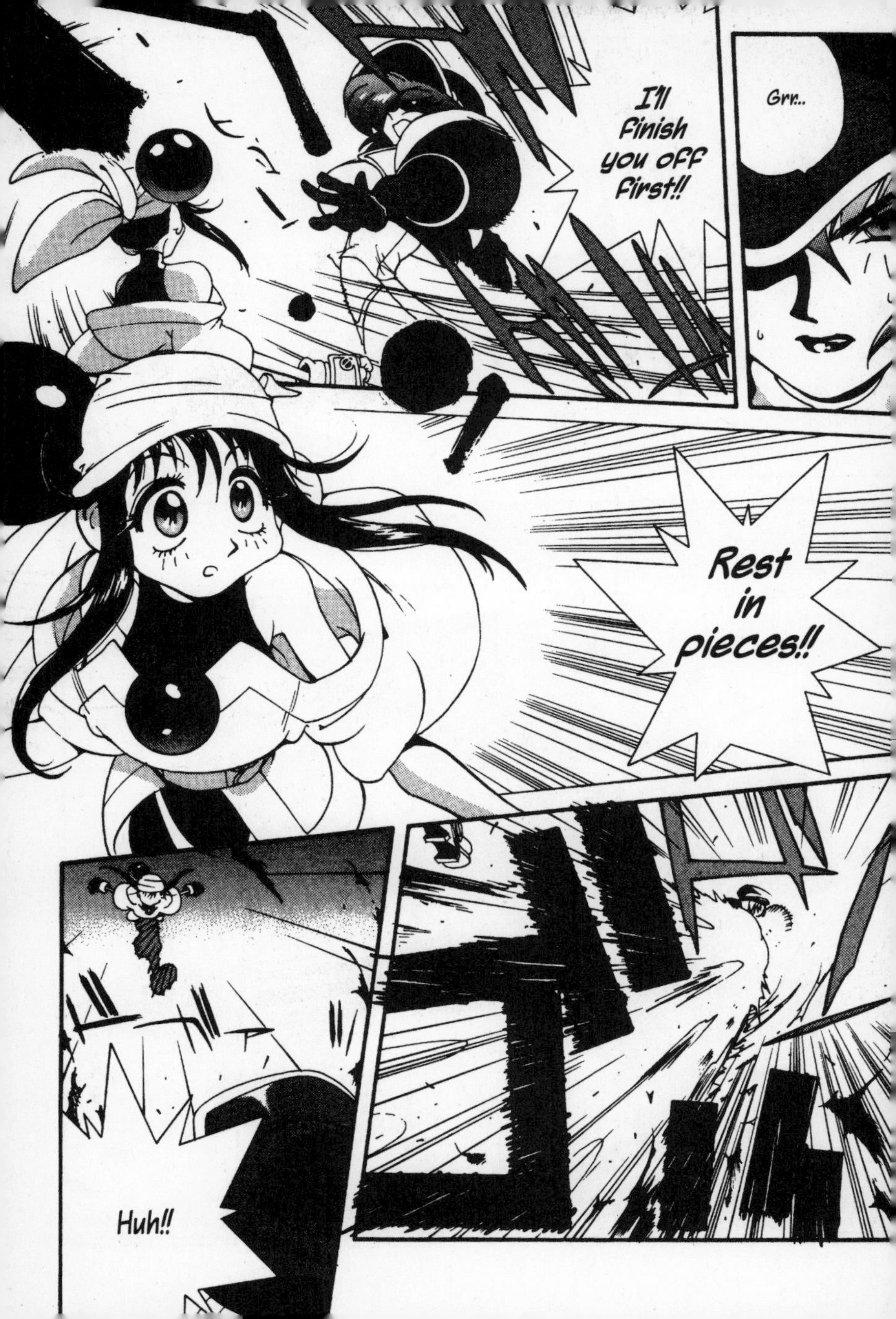
Grr..
I'll finish you off first!!
Rest in pieces!!
Huh!!

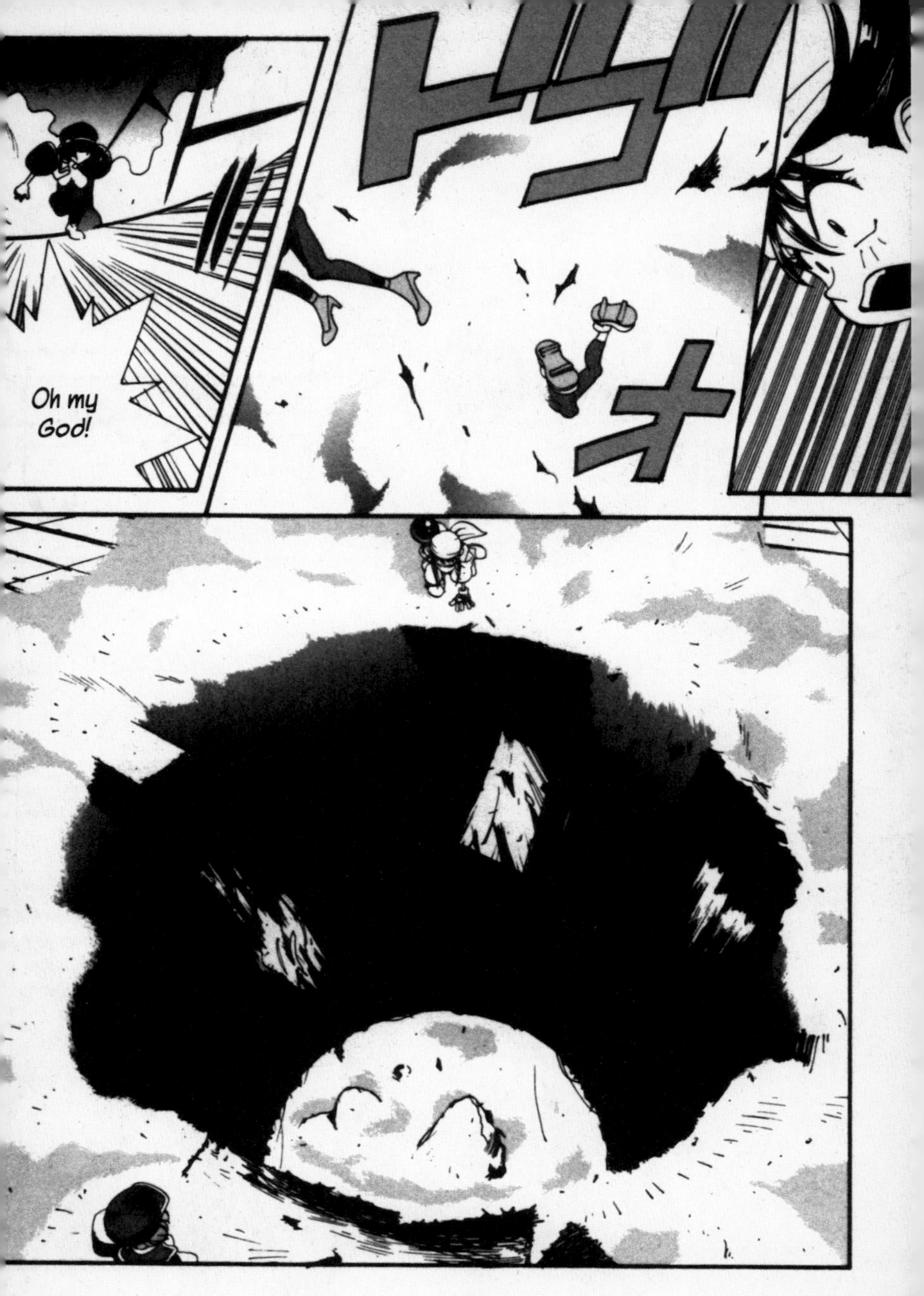
ドッゴ
オ
Oh my God!

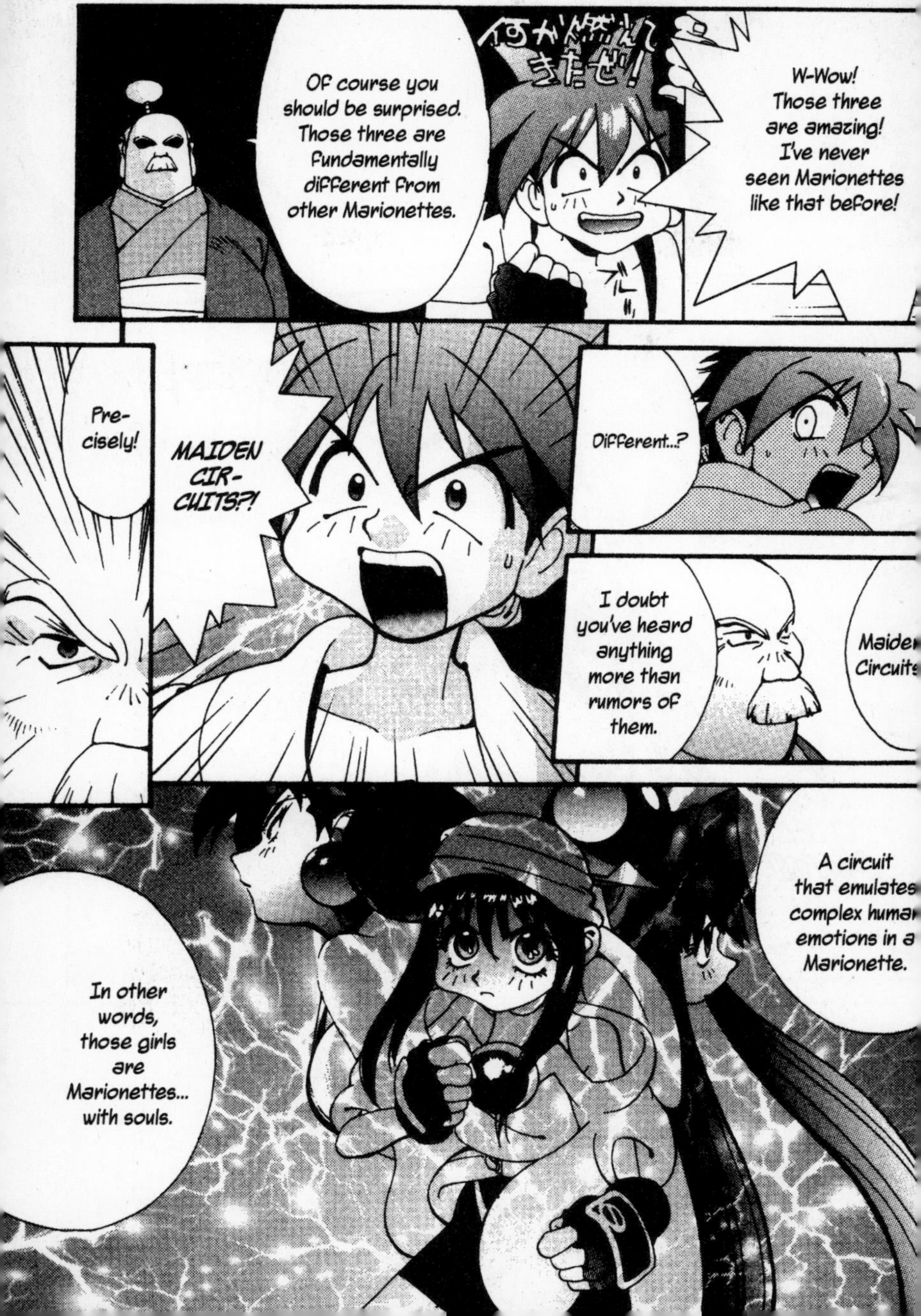

W-Wow! Those three are amazing! I've never seen Marionettes like that before!
Of course you should be surprised. Those three are fundamentally different from other Marionettes.
Different...?
Maide Circuits
I doubt you've heard anything more than rumors of them.
MAIDEN CIR-CUITS?!
Pre-cisely!
A circuit that emulates complex huma emotions in a Marionette.
In other words, those girls are Marionettes... with souls.

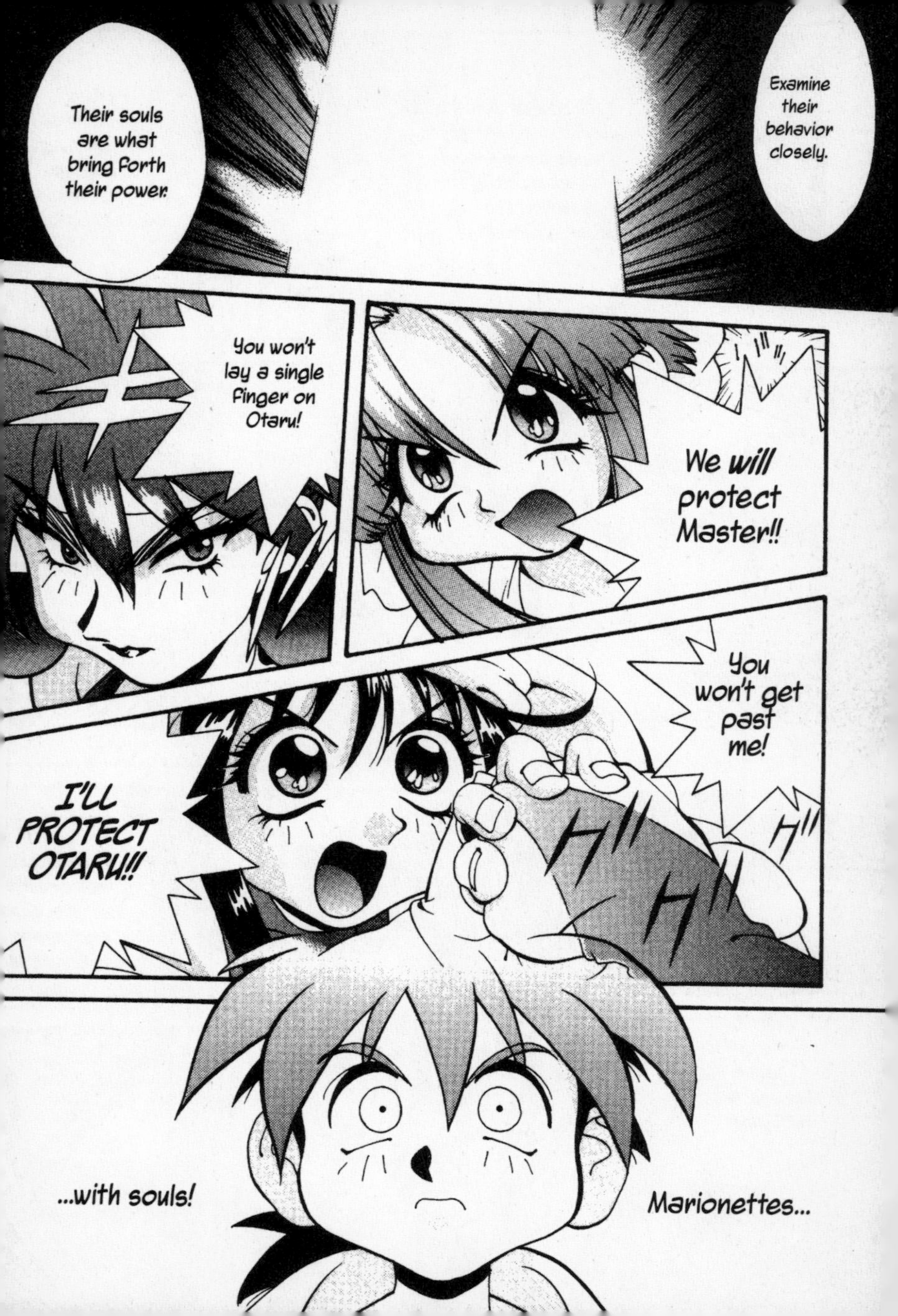

Examine their behavior closely.
Their souls are what bring forth their power.
We will protect Master!!
You won't lay a single finger on Otaru!
You won't get past me!
I'LL PROTECT OTARU!!
Marionettes...
...with souls!

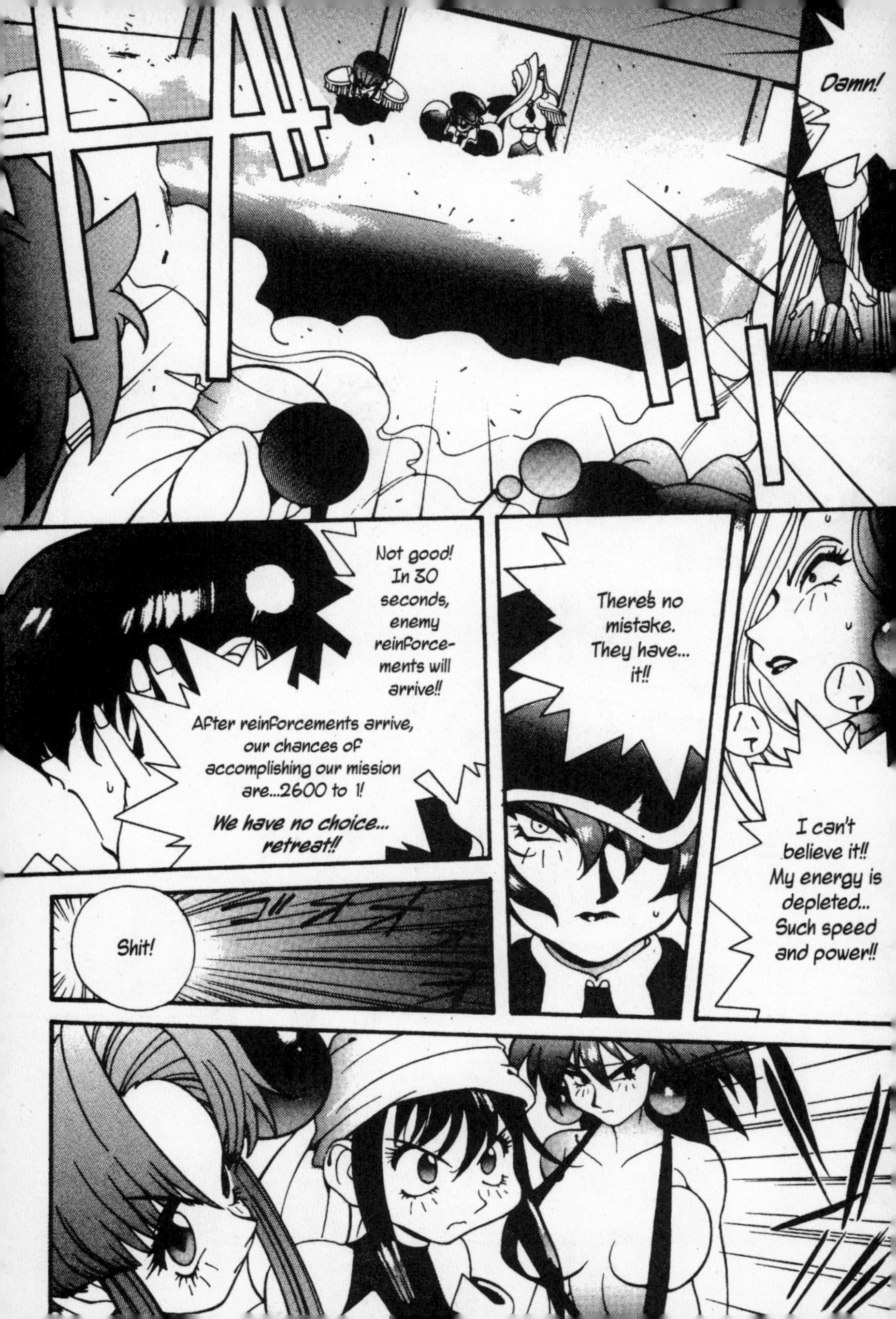
Damn!
I can't believe it!! My energy is depleted... Such speed and power!!
There's no mistake. They have... it!!
Not good! In 30 seconds, enemy reinforcements will arrive!!
After reinforcements arrive, our chances of accomplishing our mission are...2600 to 1!
We have no choice... retreat!!
Shit!

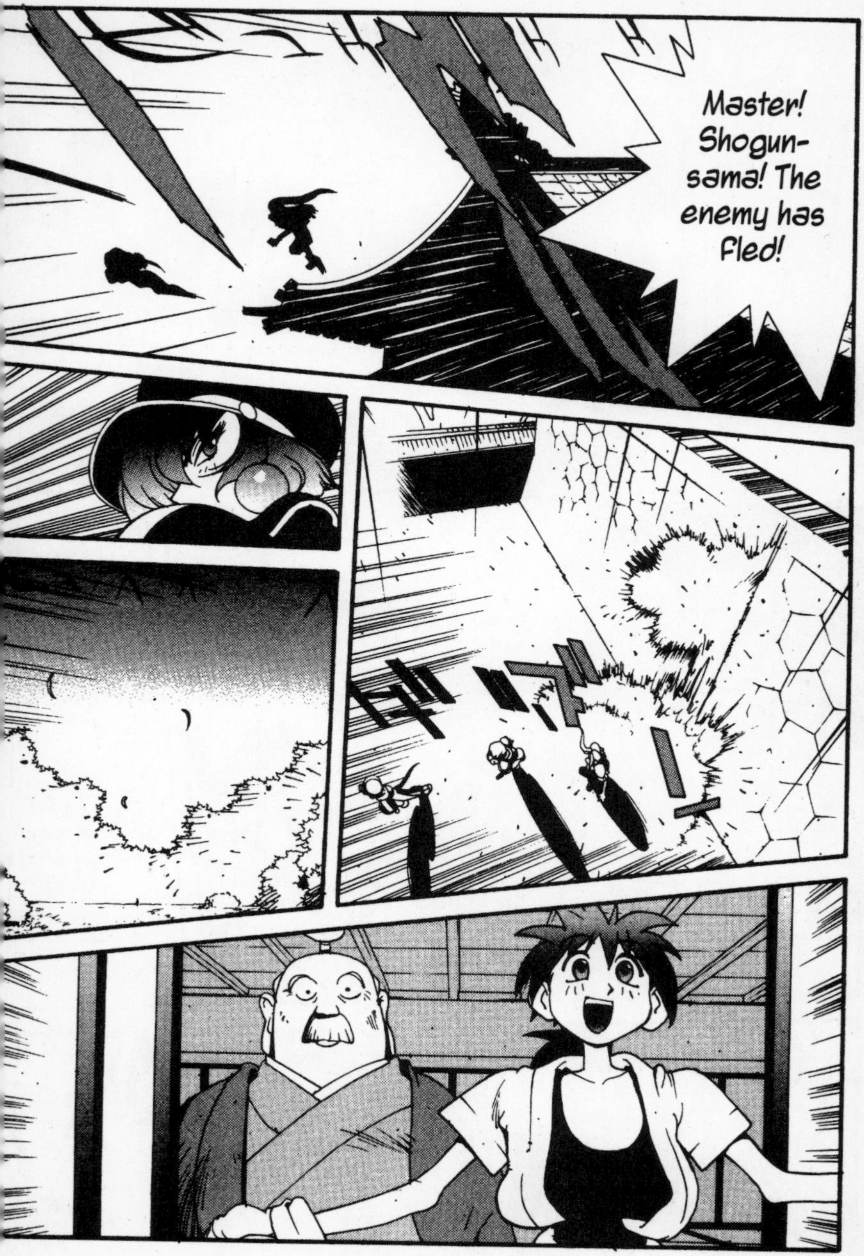
Master! Shogun-sama! The enemy has fled!

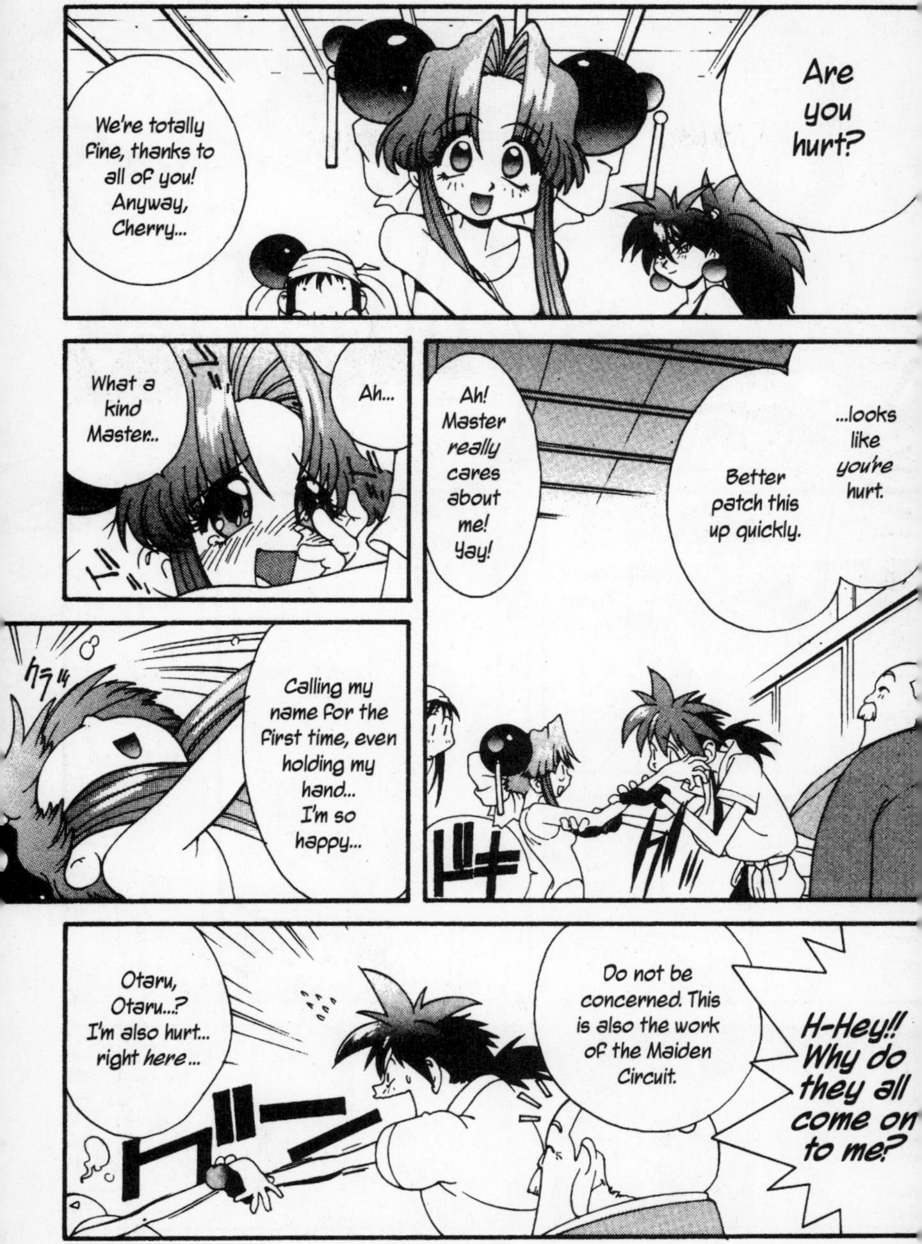

Are you hurt?
We're totally fine, thanks to all of you! Anyway, Cherry...
...looks like you're hurt.
Better patch this up quickly.
Ah! Master really cares about me! Yay!
Ah...
What a kind Master..
Calling my name for the first time, even holding my hand... I'm so happy...
H-Hey!! Why do they all come on to me?
Do not be concerned. This is also the work of the Maiden Circuit.
Otaru, Otaru...? I'm also hurt... right here...

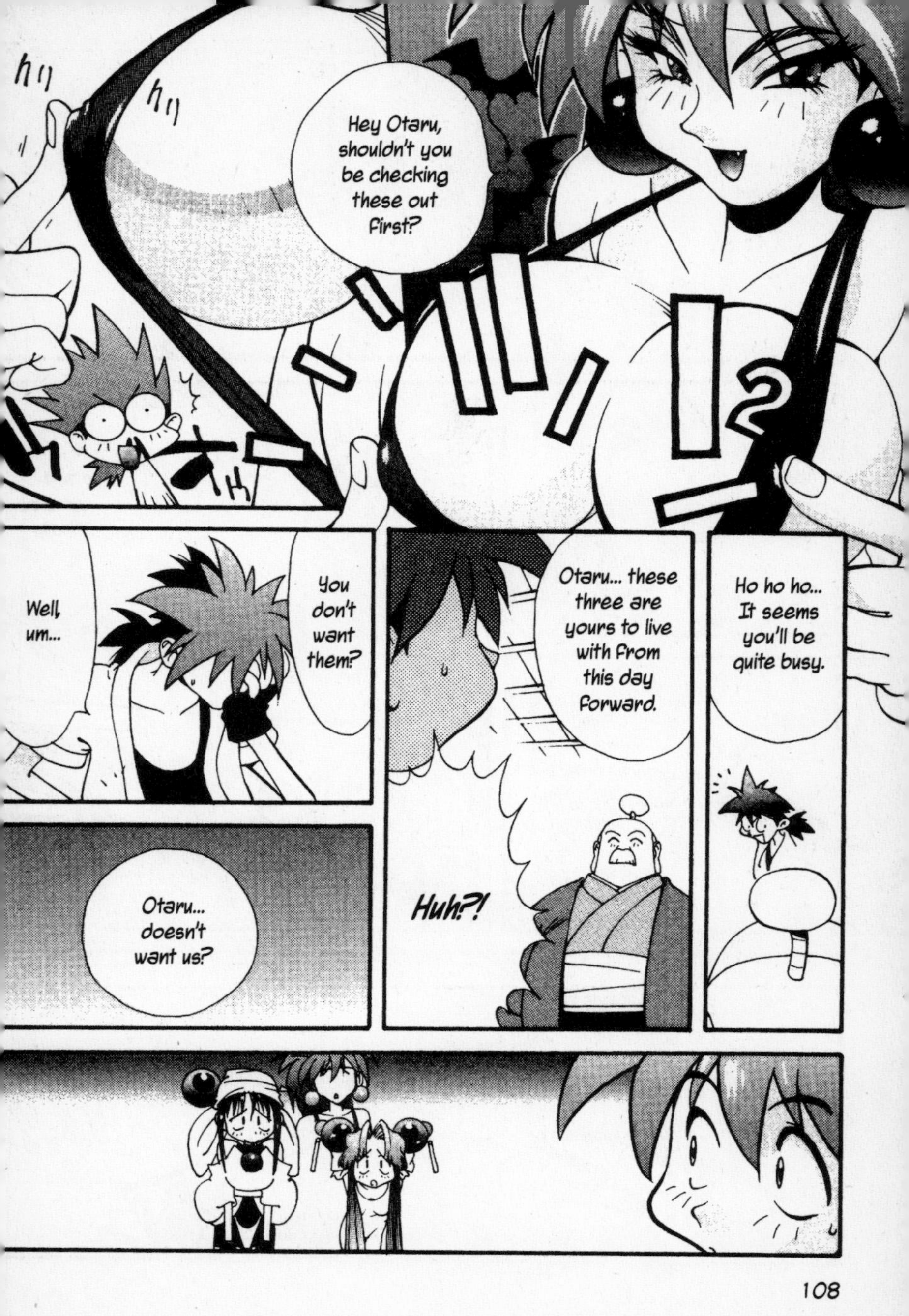
Hey Otaru, shouldn't you be checking these out first?
Ho ho ho... It seems you'll be quite busy.
Otaru... these three are yours to live with from this day forward.
Huh?!
You don't want them?
Well, um...
Otaru... doesn't want us?

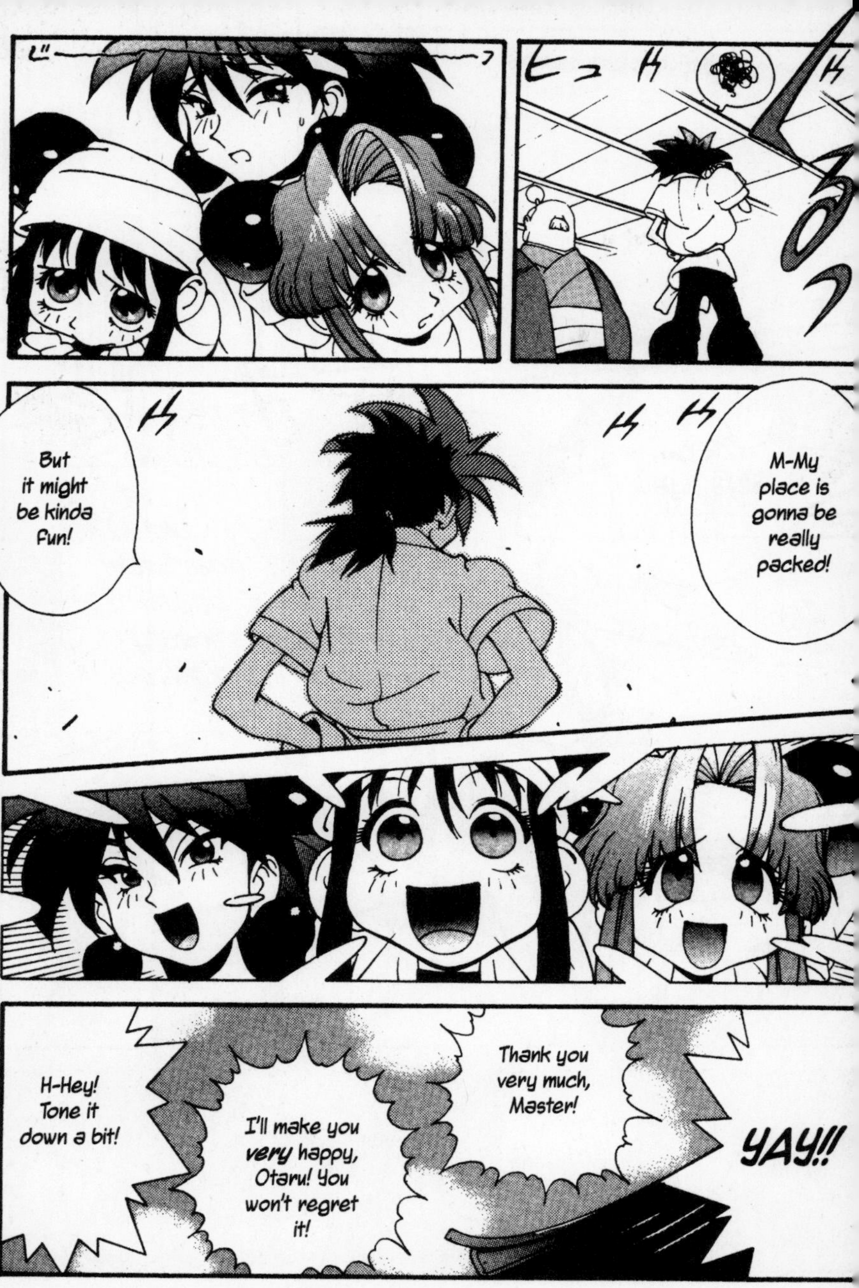
M-My place is gonna be really packed!
But it might be kinda fun!
YAY!!
Thank you very much, Master!
I'll make you *very* happy, Otaru! You won't regret it!
H-Hey! Tone it down a bit!

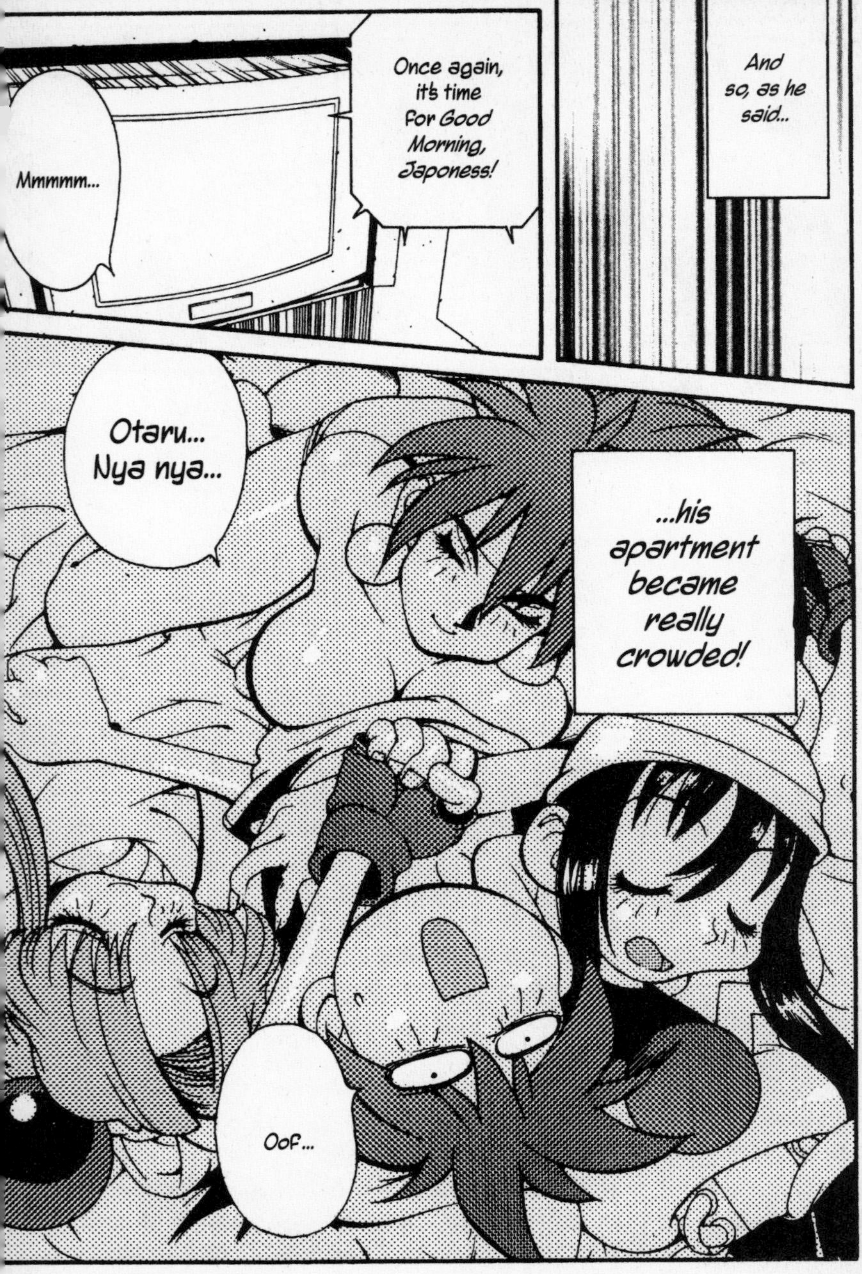
And so, as he said...
Once again, it's time for Good Morning, Japoness!
Mmmmm...
...his apartment became really crowded!
Otaru... Nya nya...
Oof...

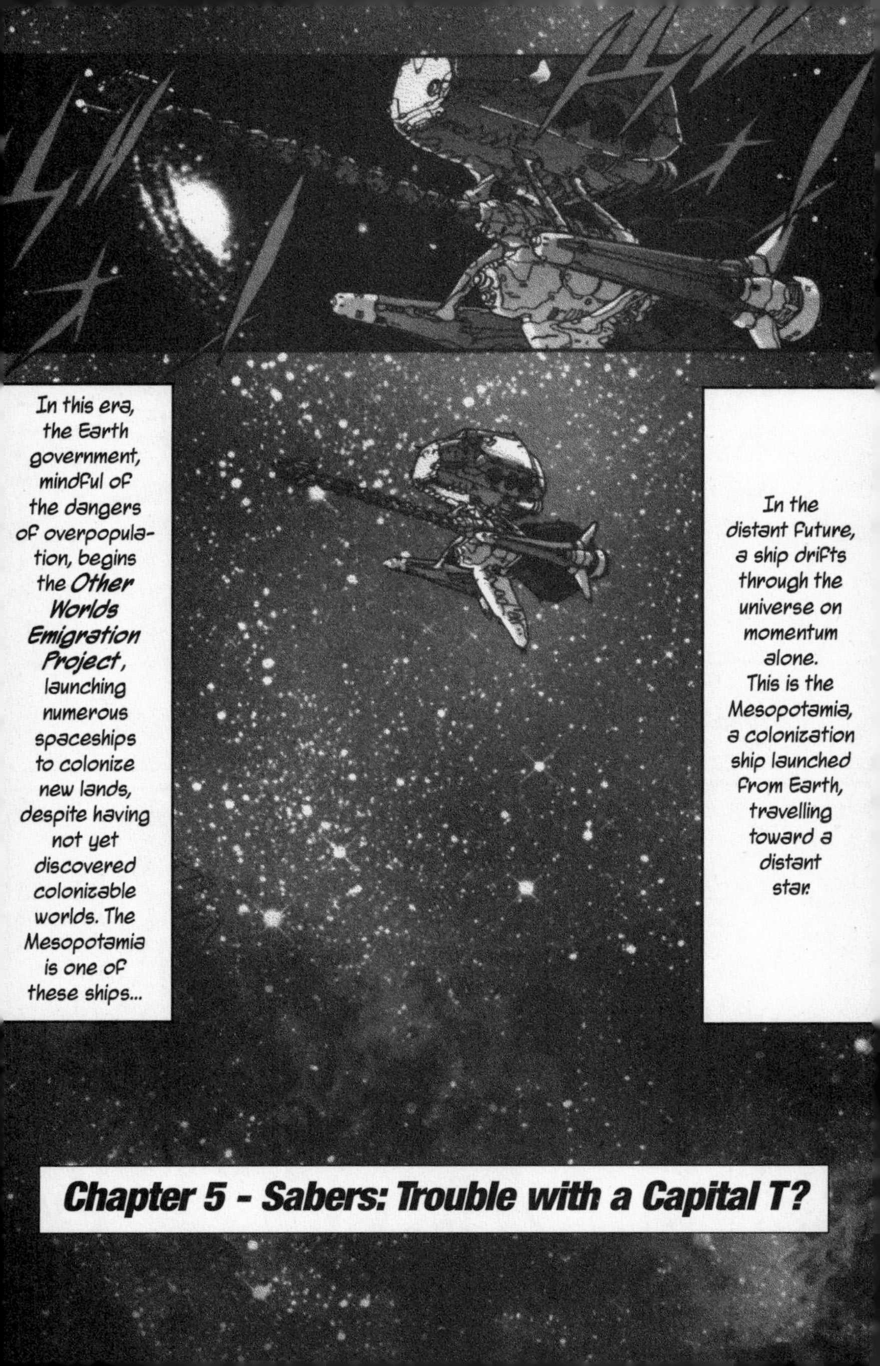
In the distant future, a ship drifts through the universe on momentum alone. This is the Mesopotamia, a colonization ship launched from Earth, travelling toward a distant star.
In this era, the Earth government, mindful of the dangers of overpopulation, begins the *Other Worlds Emigration Project*, launching numerous spaceships to colonize new lands, despite having not yet discovered colonizable worlds. The Mesopotamia is one of these ships...
Chapter 5 - Sabers: Trouble with a Capital T?

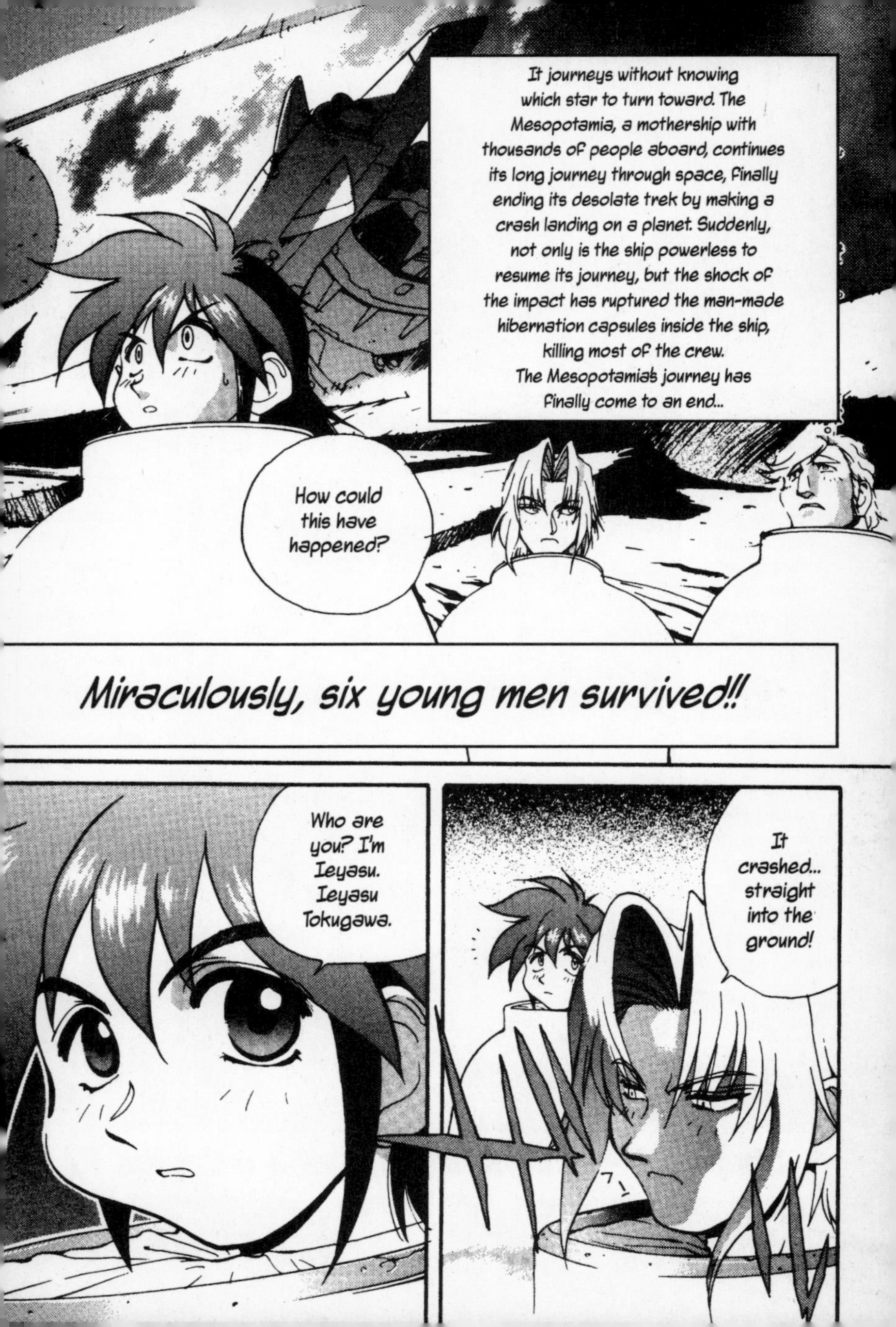
It journeys without knowing which star to turn toward. The Mesopotamia, a mothership with thousands of people aboard, continues its long journey through space, finally ending its desolate trek by making a crash landing on a planet. Suddenly, not only is the ship powerless to resume its journey, but the shock of the impact has ruptured the man-made hibernation capsules inside the ship, killing most of the crew. The Mesopotamia's journey has finally come to an end...
How could this have happened?
Miraculously, six young men survived!!
It crashed... straight into the ground!
Who are you? I'm Ieyasu. Ieyasu Tokugawa.

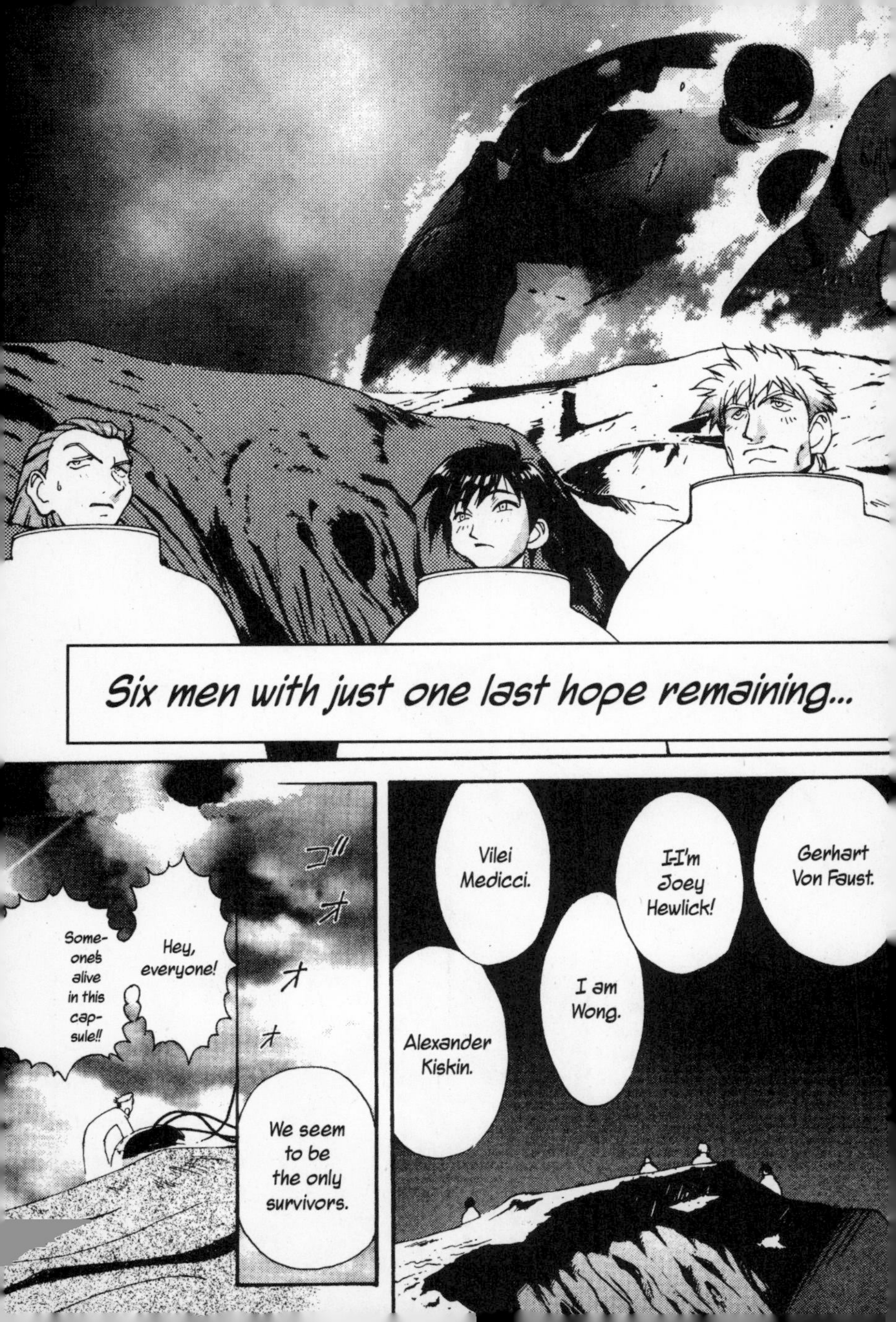
Six men with just one last hope remaining...
Gerhart Von Faust.
I-I'm Joey Hewlick!
Vilei Medicci.
I am Wong.
Alexander Kiskin.
ゴオオオ
We seem to be the only survivors.
Hey, everyone!
Some-one's alive in this cap-sule!!

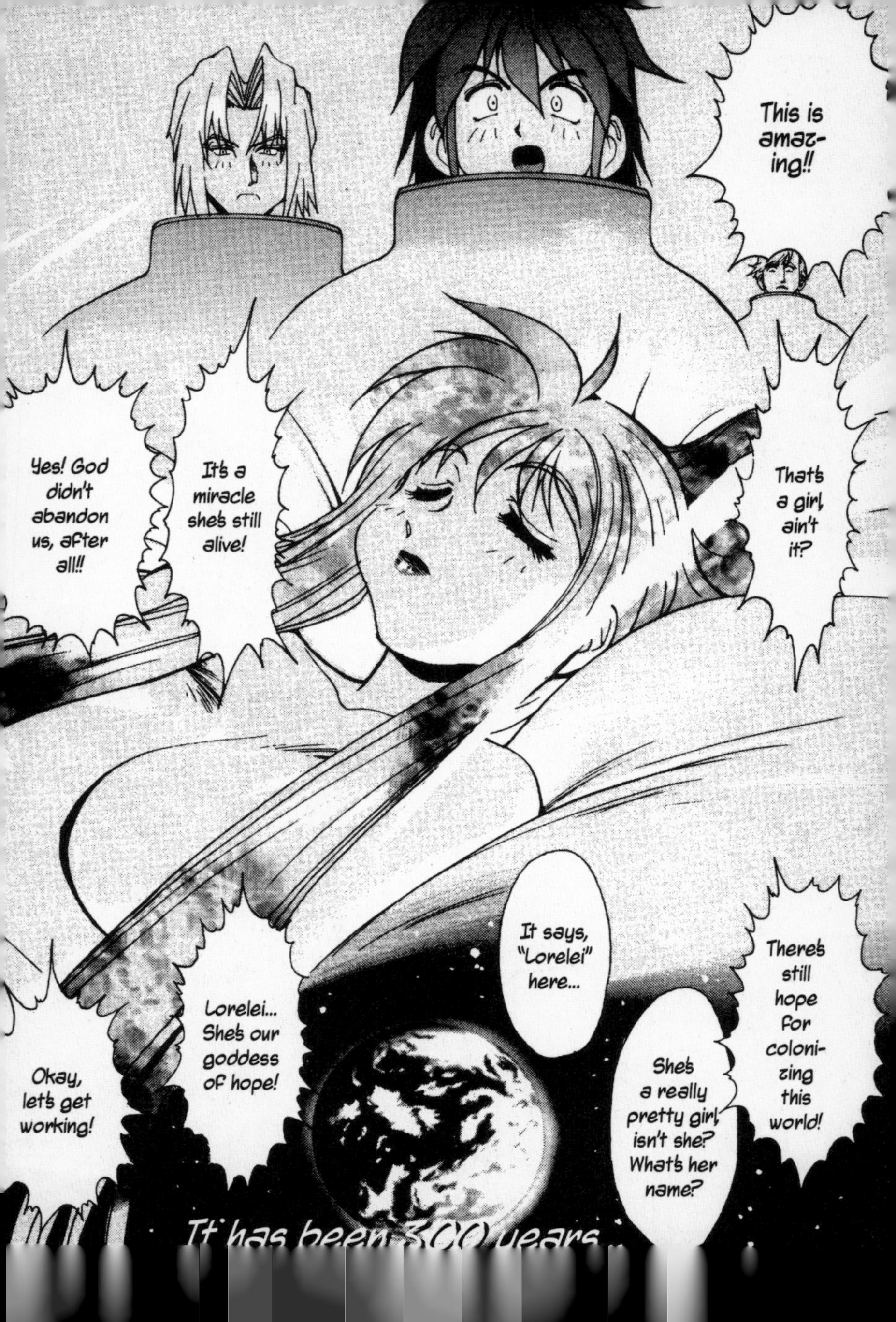
This is amaz-ing!!
That's a girl, ain't it?
It's a miracle she's still alive!
Yes! God didn't abandon us, after all!!
There's still hope for coloni-zing this world!
She's a really pretty girl, isn't she? What's her name?
It says, "Lorelei" here...
Lorelei... She's our goddess of hope!
Okay, let's get working!
It has been 300 years...

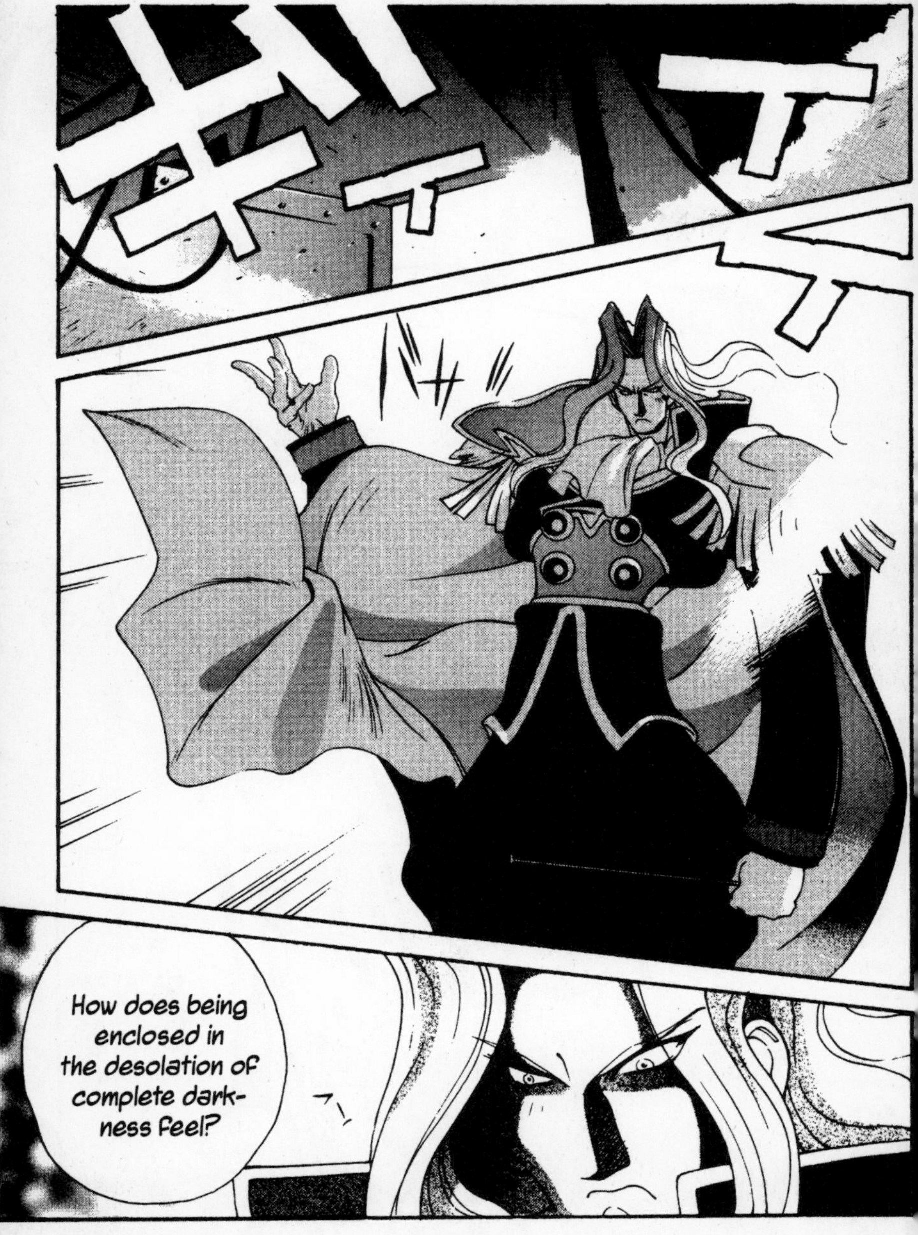
How does being enclosed in the desolation of complete dark-ness feel?

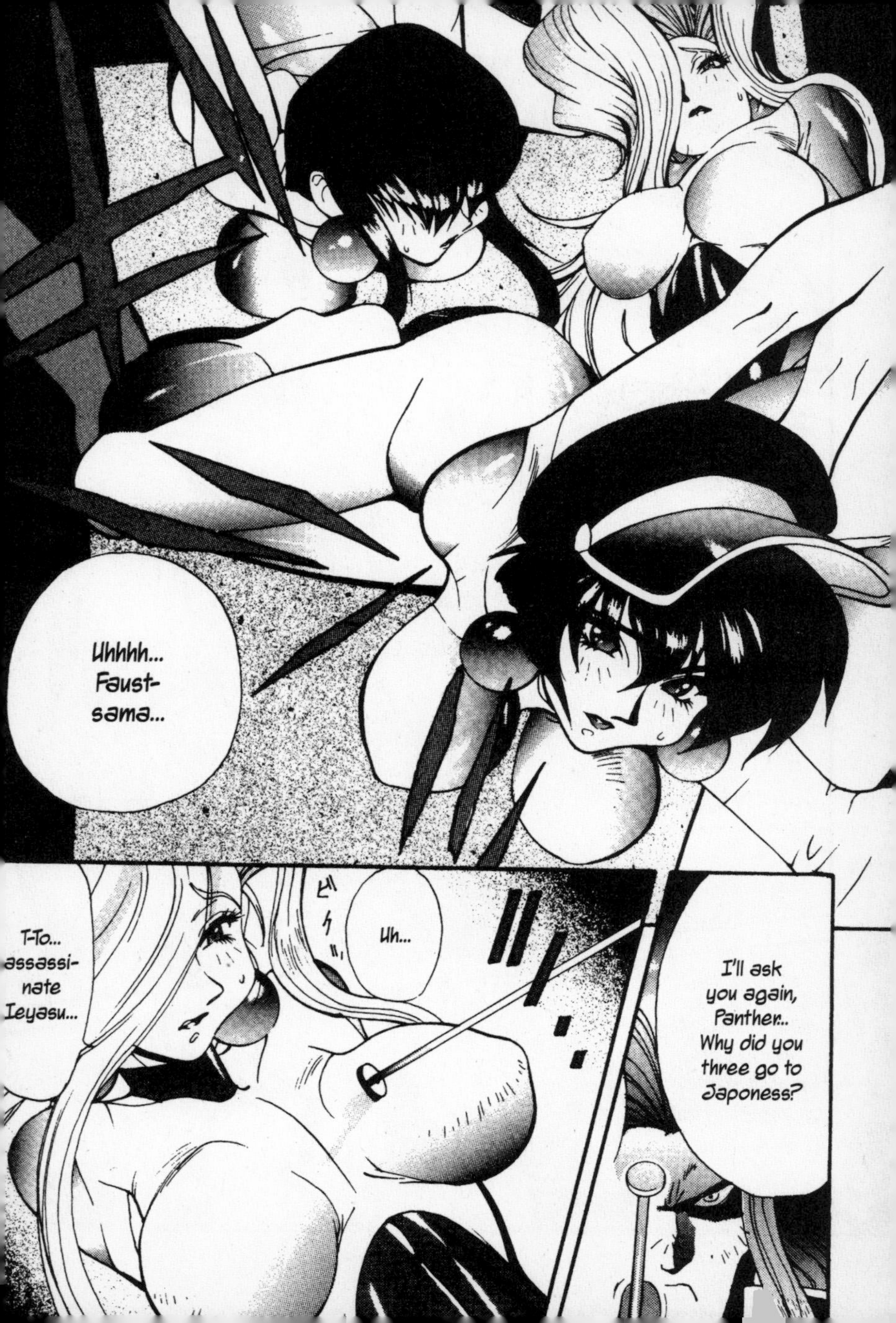
Uhhhh... Faust-sama...
I'll ask you again, Panther... Why did you three go to Japoness?
Uh...
ビク
T-To... assassi-nate Ieyasu...

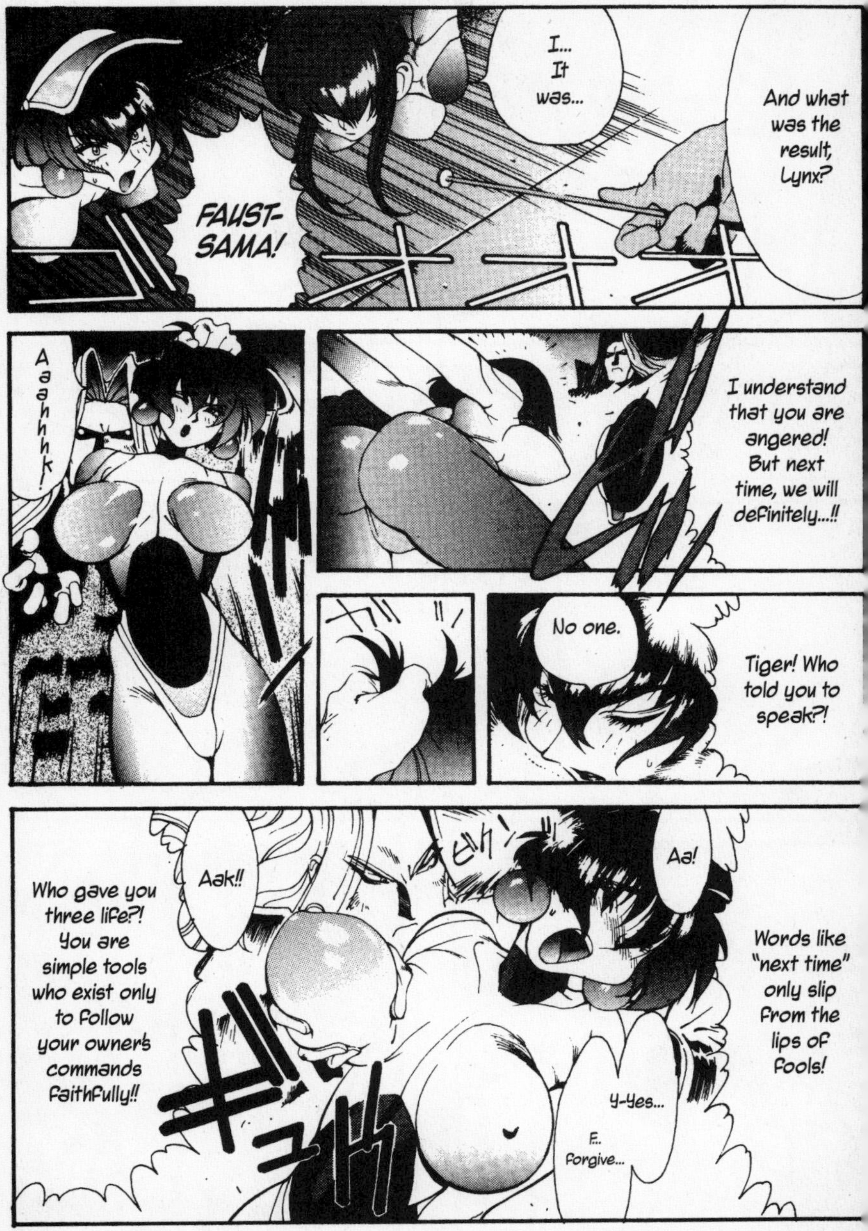
And what was the result, Lynx?
I... It was...
FAUST-SAMA!
I understand that you are angered! But next time, we will definitely...!!
Tiger! Who told you to speak?!
No one.
Aaahhhk!
Aa!
Words like "next time" only slip from the lips of fools!
Aak!!
Who gave you three life?! You are simple tools who exist only to follow your owner's commands faithfully!!
Y-Yes...
F.. Forgive...

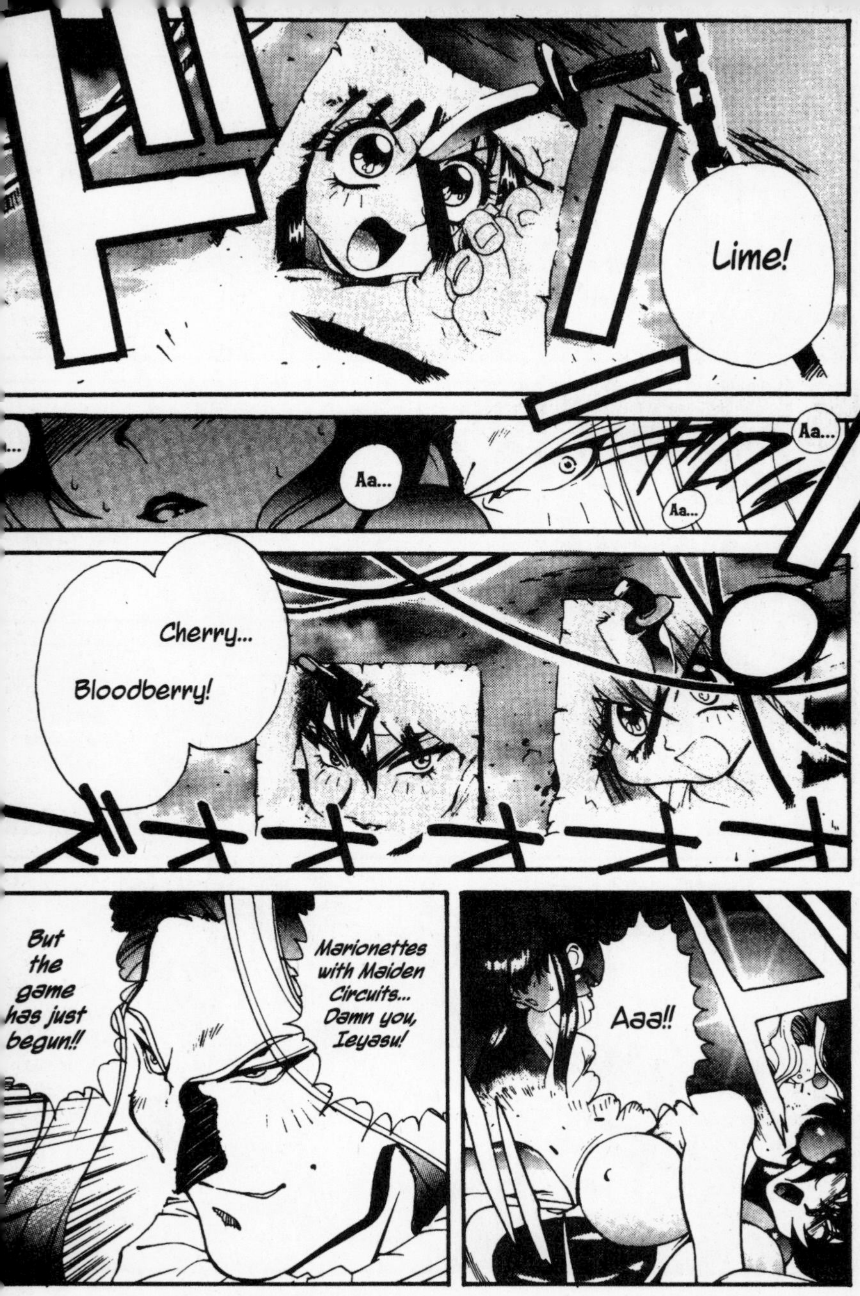
Lime!
Aa...
Aa...
Aa...
...
Cherry... Bloodberry!
Aaa!!
Marionettes with Maiden Circuits... Damn you, Ieyasu!
But the game has just begun!!

Japoness... Petersburg... New Texas... Romania... Shiyan... and Gartland!
We will soon see which one of us is the Chosen Land.

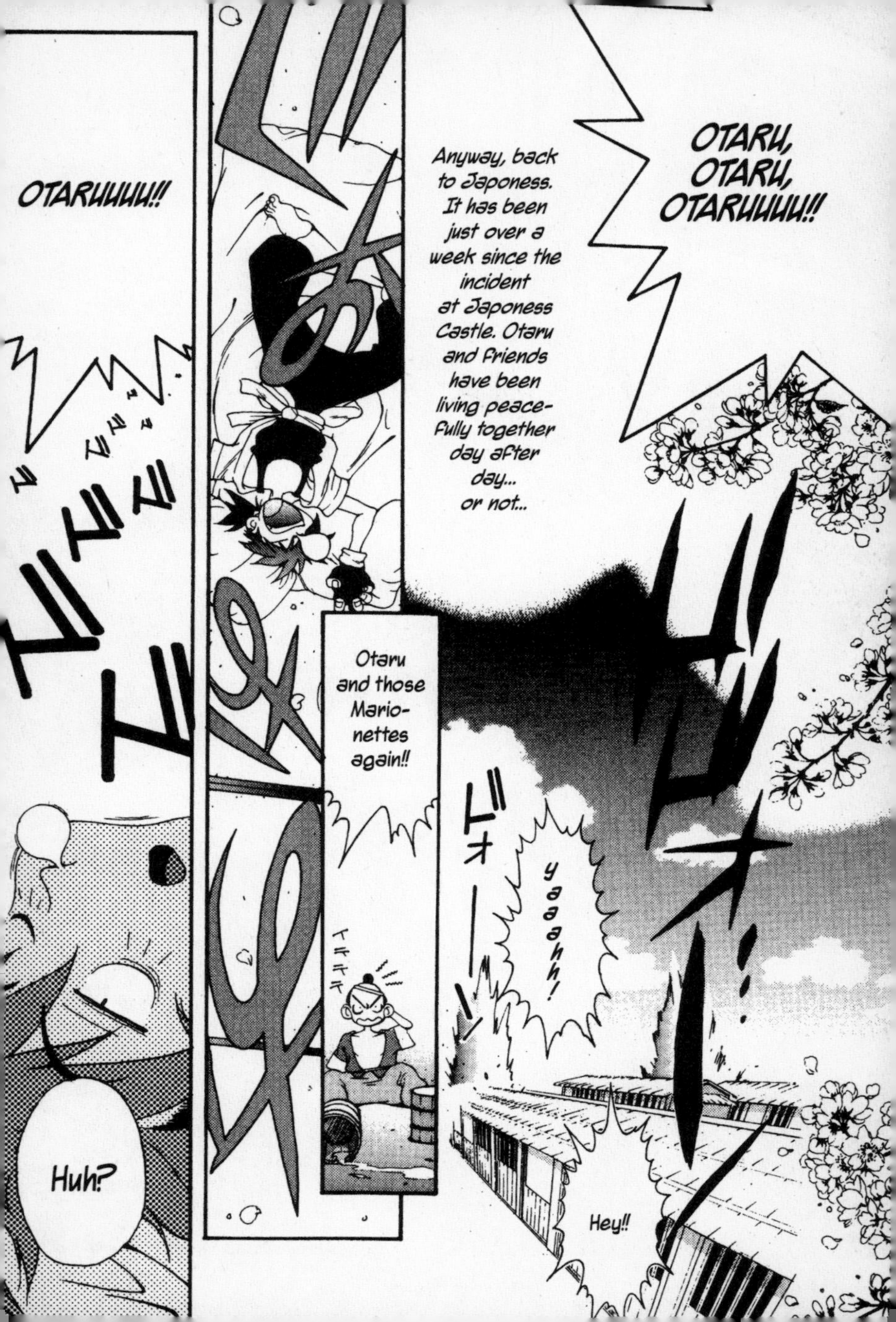
OTARU, OTARU, OTARUUUU!!
Anyway, back to Japoness. It has been just over a week since the incident at Japoness Castle. Otaru and friends have been living peacefully together day after day... or not...
yaaahh!
Hey!!
Otaru and those Marionettes again!!
OTARUUUU!!
Huh?

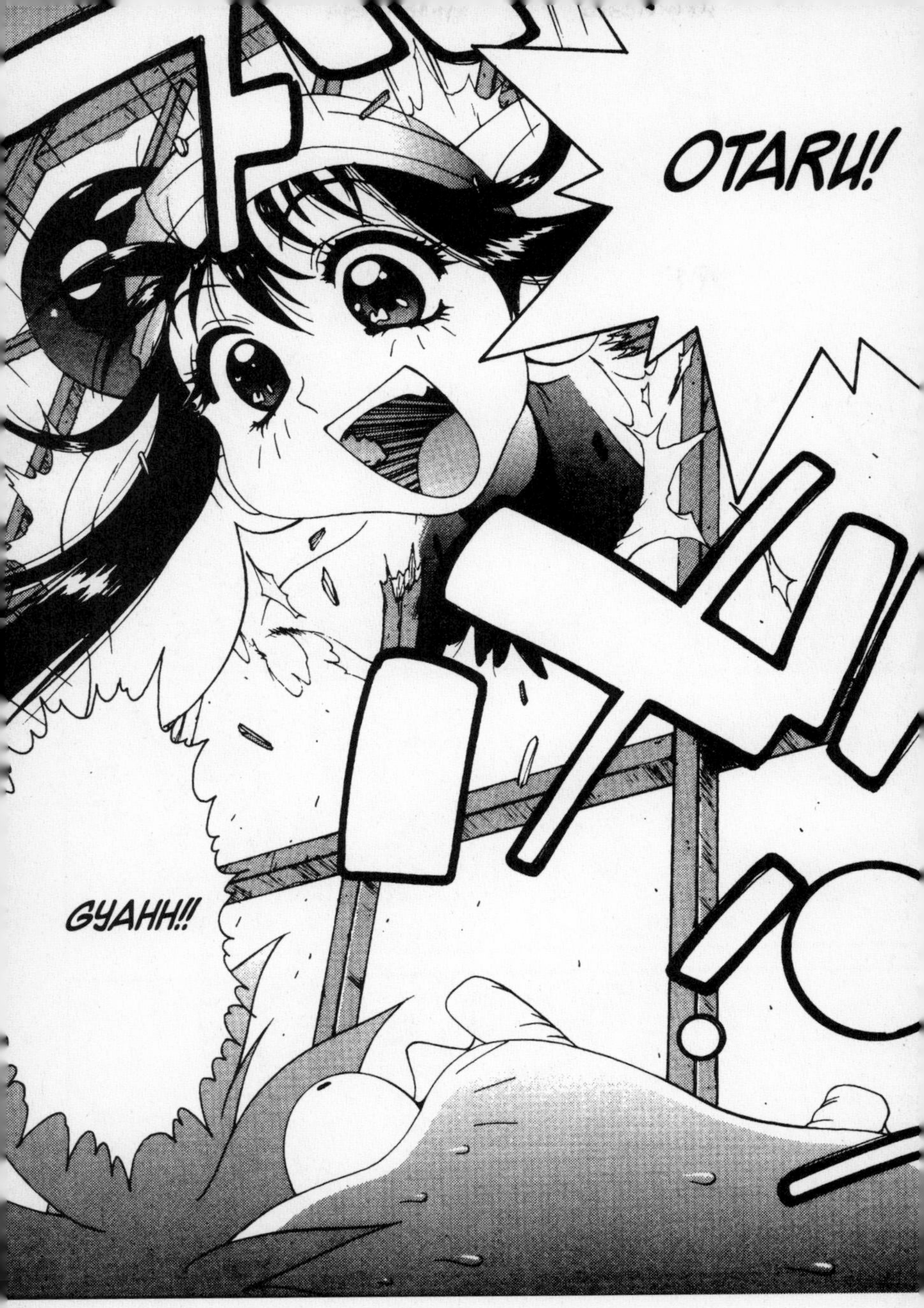
OTARU!
GYAHH!!

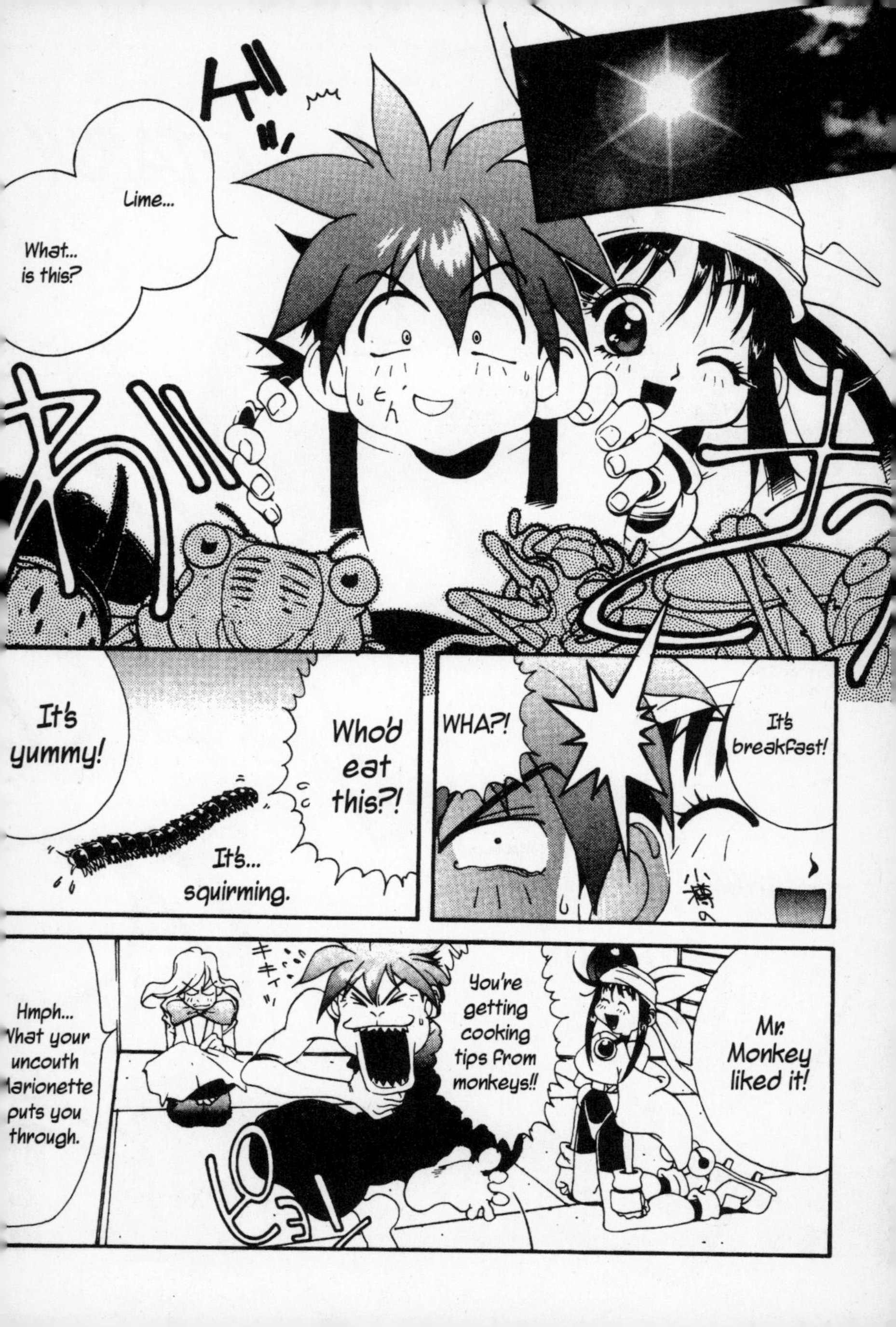
Lime...
What... is this?
It's breakfast!
WHA?!
Who'd eat this?!
It's yummy!
It's... squirming.
Mr. Monkey liked it!
You're getting cooking tips from monkeys!!
Hmph... What your uncouth Marionette puts you through.

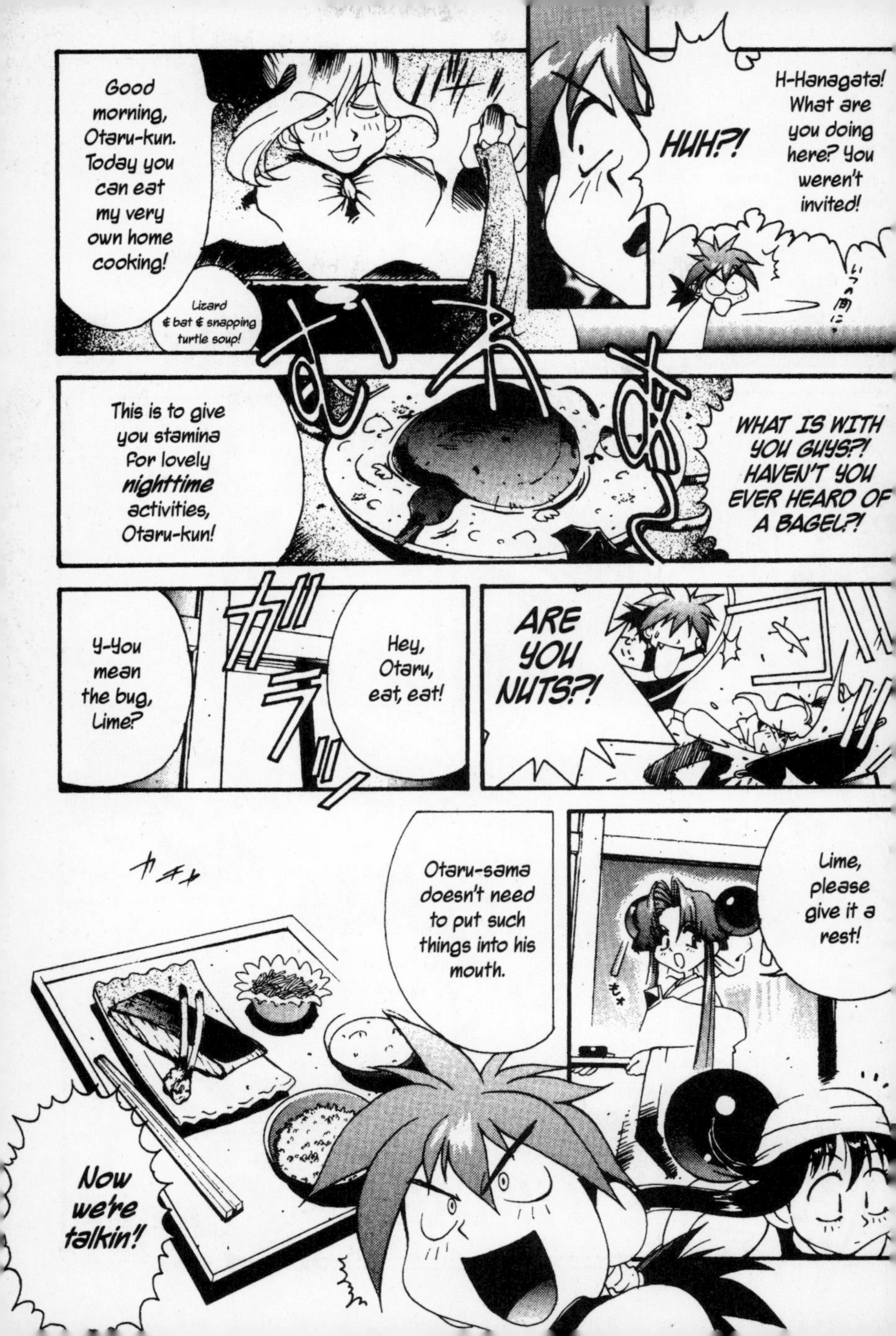
HUH?!
H-Hanagata! What are you doing here? You weren't invited!
Good morning, Otaru-kun. Today you can eat my very own home cooking!
Lizard & bat & snapping turtle soup!
WHAT IS WITH YOU GUYS?! HAVEN'T YOU EVER HEARD OF A BAGEL?!
This is to give you stamina for lovely nighttime activities, Otaru-kun!
ARE YOU NUTS?!
Hey, Otaru, eat, eat!
Y-You mean the bug, Lime?
Lime, please give it a rest!
Otaru-sama doesn't need to put such things into his mouth.
Now we're talkin'!

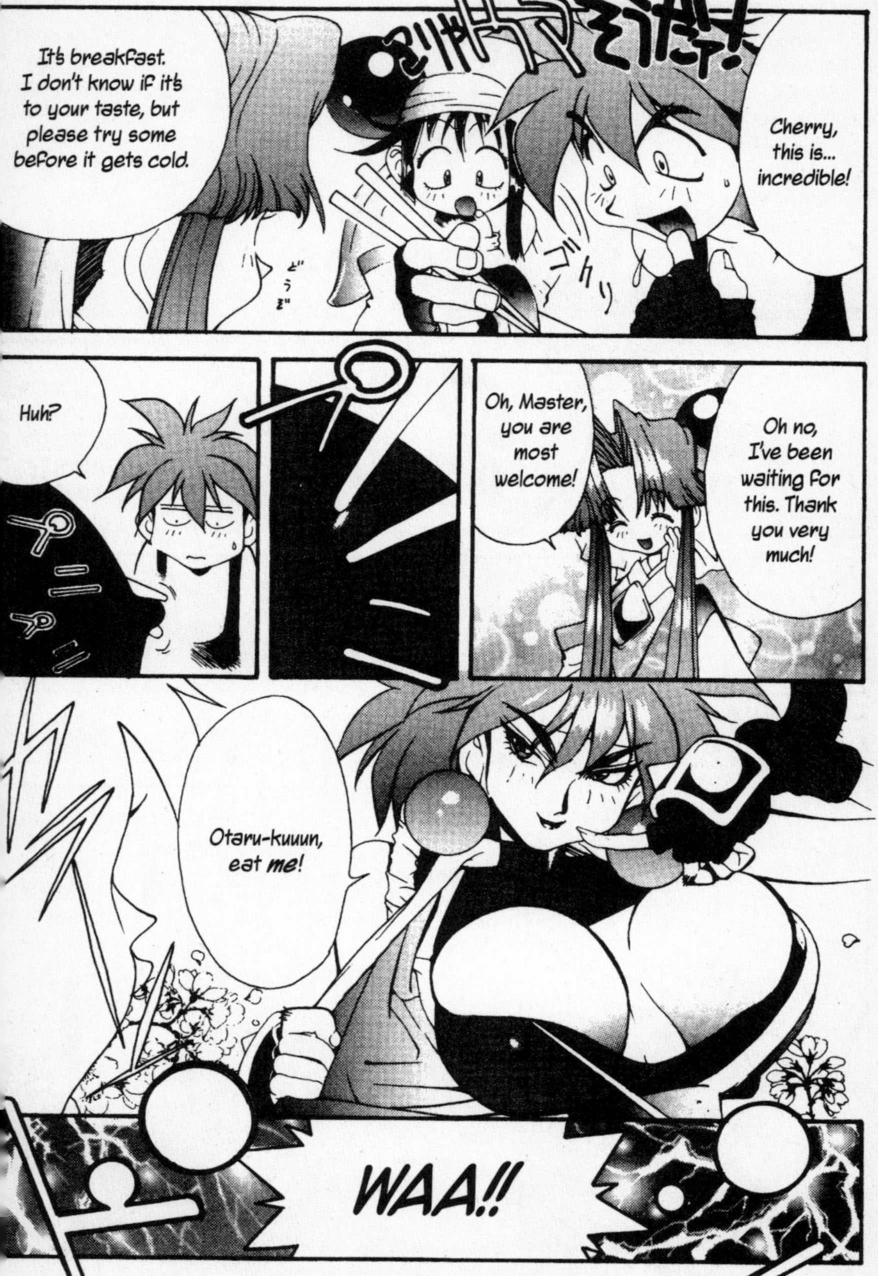
Cherry, this is... incredible!
It's breakfast. I don't know if it's to your taste, but please try some before it gets cold.
Oh no, I've been waiting for this. Thank you very much!
Oh, Master, you are most welcome!
Huh?
Otaru-kuuun, eat *me*!
WAA!!

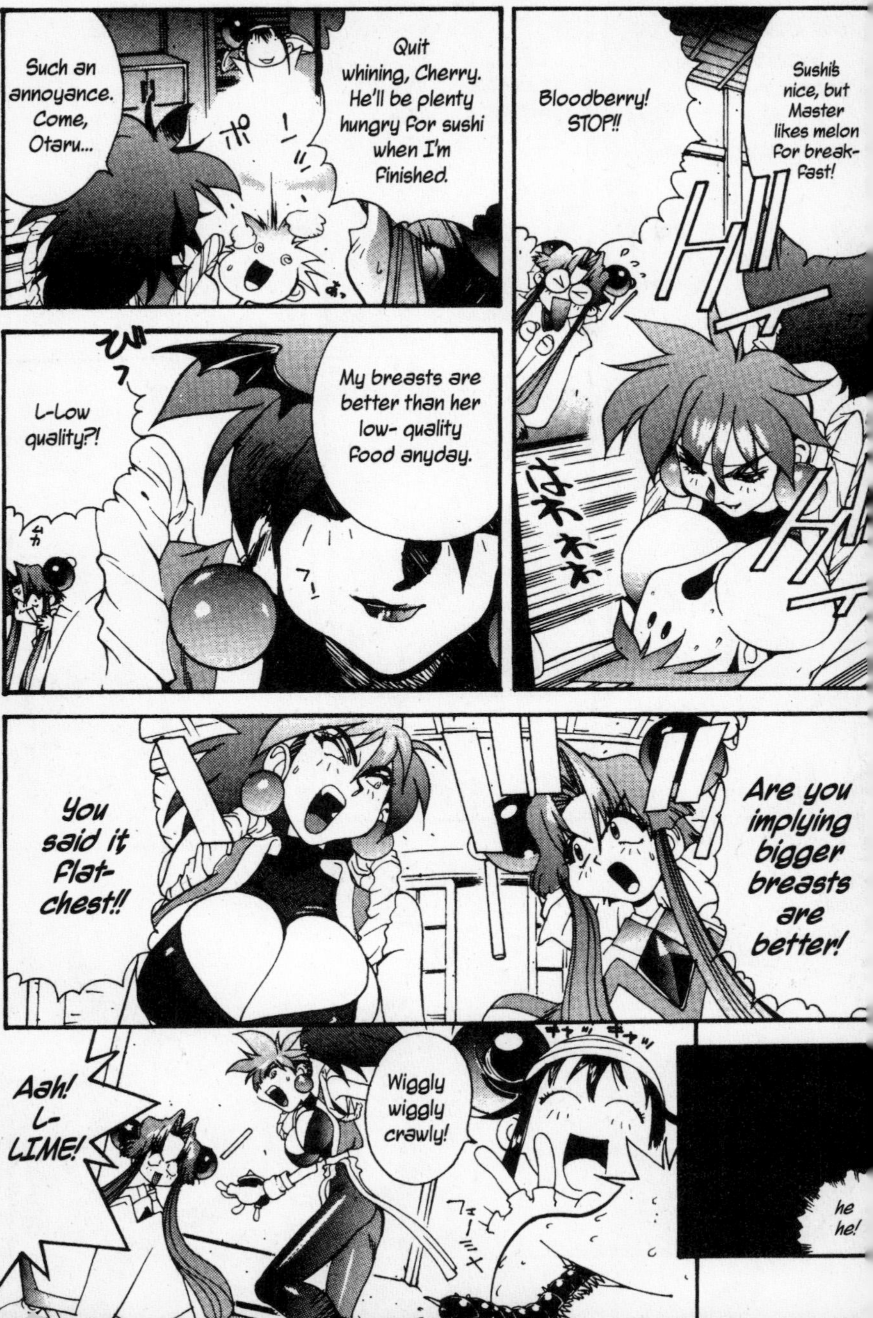

Sushi's nice, but Master likes melon for break-fast!
Bloodberry! STOP!!
Quit whining, Cherry. He'll be plenty hungry for sushi when I'm finished.
Such an annoyance. Come, Otaru...
My breasts are better than her low- quality food anyday.
L-Low quality?!
Are you implying bigger breasts are better!
You said it flat-chest!!
he he!
Wiggly wiggly crawly!
Aah! L-LIME!

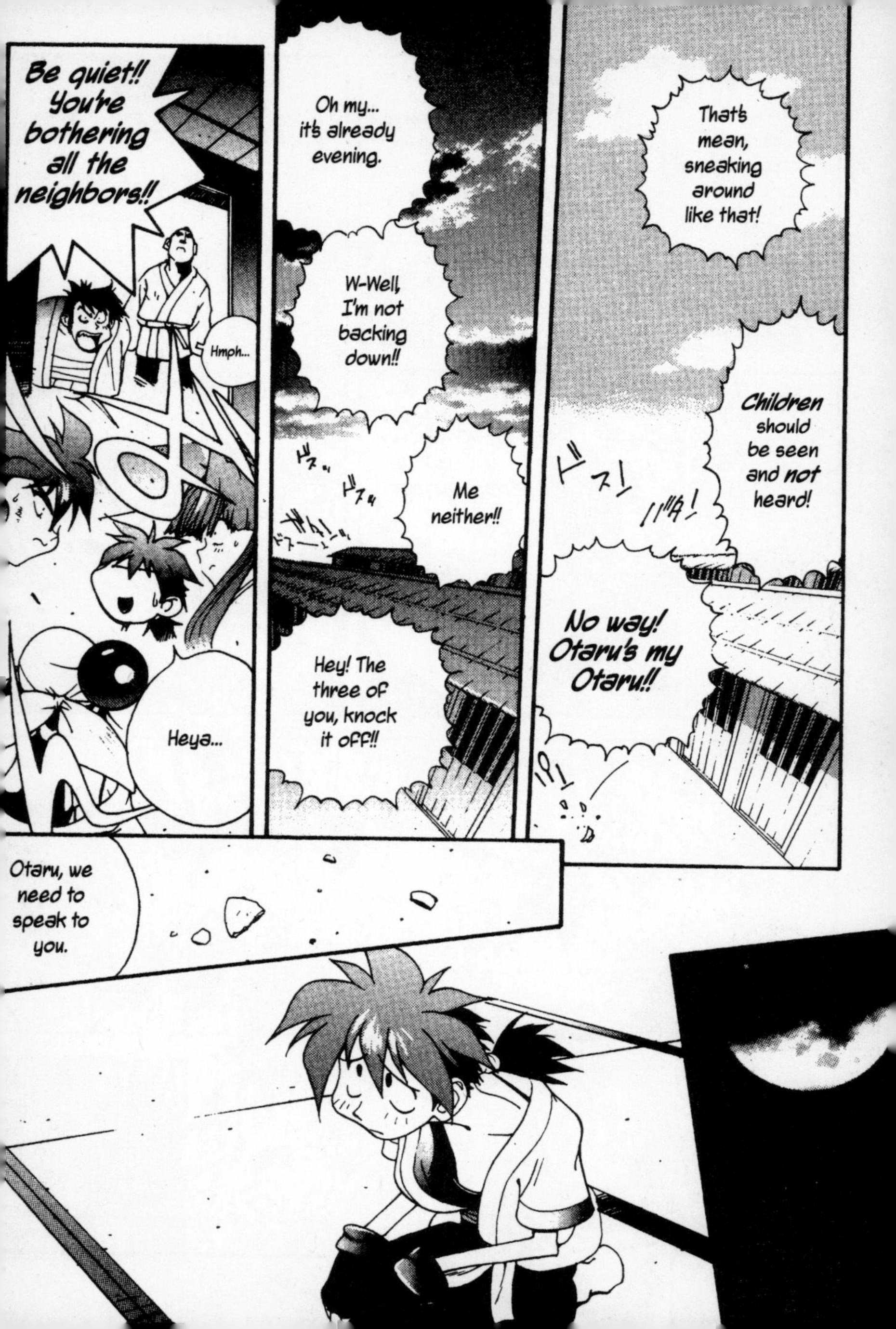
That's mean, sneaking around like that!
Children should be seen and not heard!
No way! Otaru's my Otaru!!
Oh my... it's already evening.
W-Well, I'm not backing down!!
Me neither!!
Hey! The three of you, knock it off!!
Be quiet!! You're bothering all the neighbors!!
Hmph...
Heya...
Otaru, we need to speak to you.

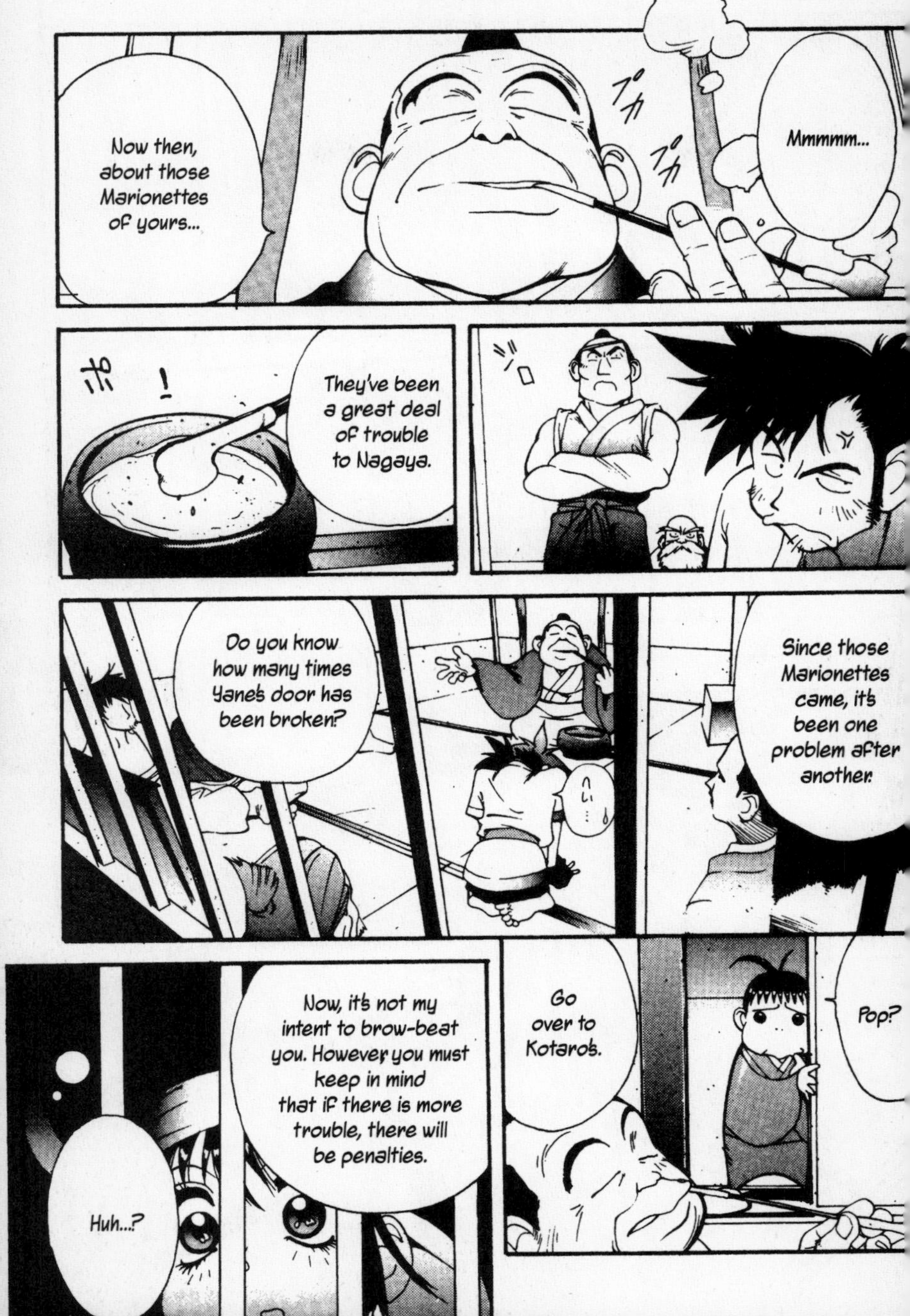
Mmmmm...
ぷか ぷか
Now then, about those Marionettes of yours...
!
They've been a great deal of trouble to Nagaya.
Since those Marionettes came, it's been one problem after another.
Do you know how many times Yane's door has been broken?
Pop?
Go over to Kotaro's.
Now, it's not my intent to brow-beat you. However, you must keep in mind that if there is more trouble, there will be penalties.
Huh...?

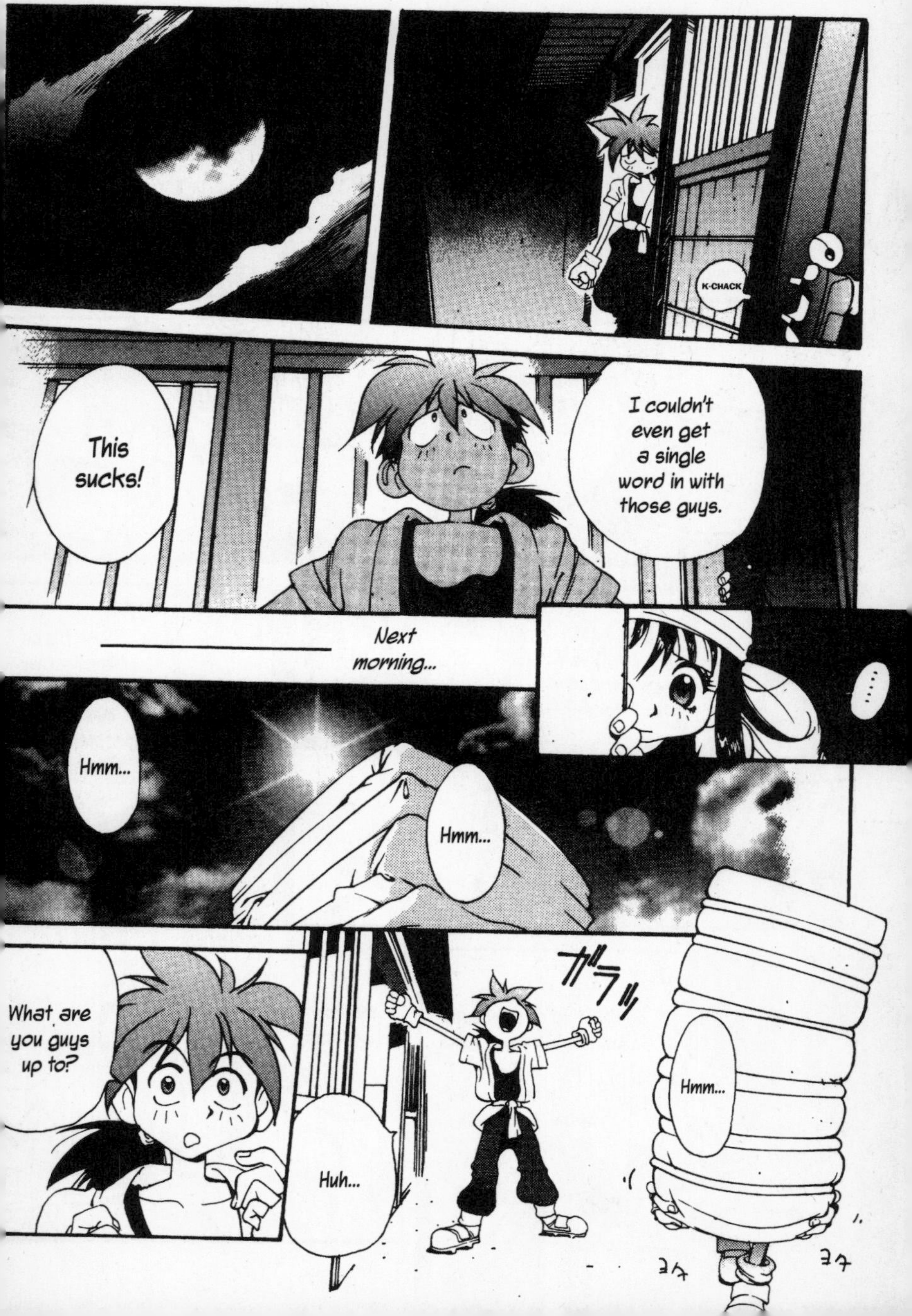
K-CHACK
I couldn't even get a single word in with those guys.
This sucks!
.....
Next morning...
Hmm...
Hmm...
Hmm...
ガラッ
Huh...
What are you guys up to?

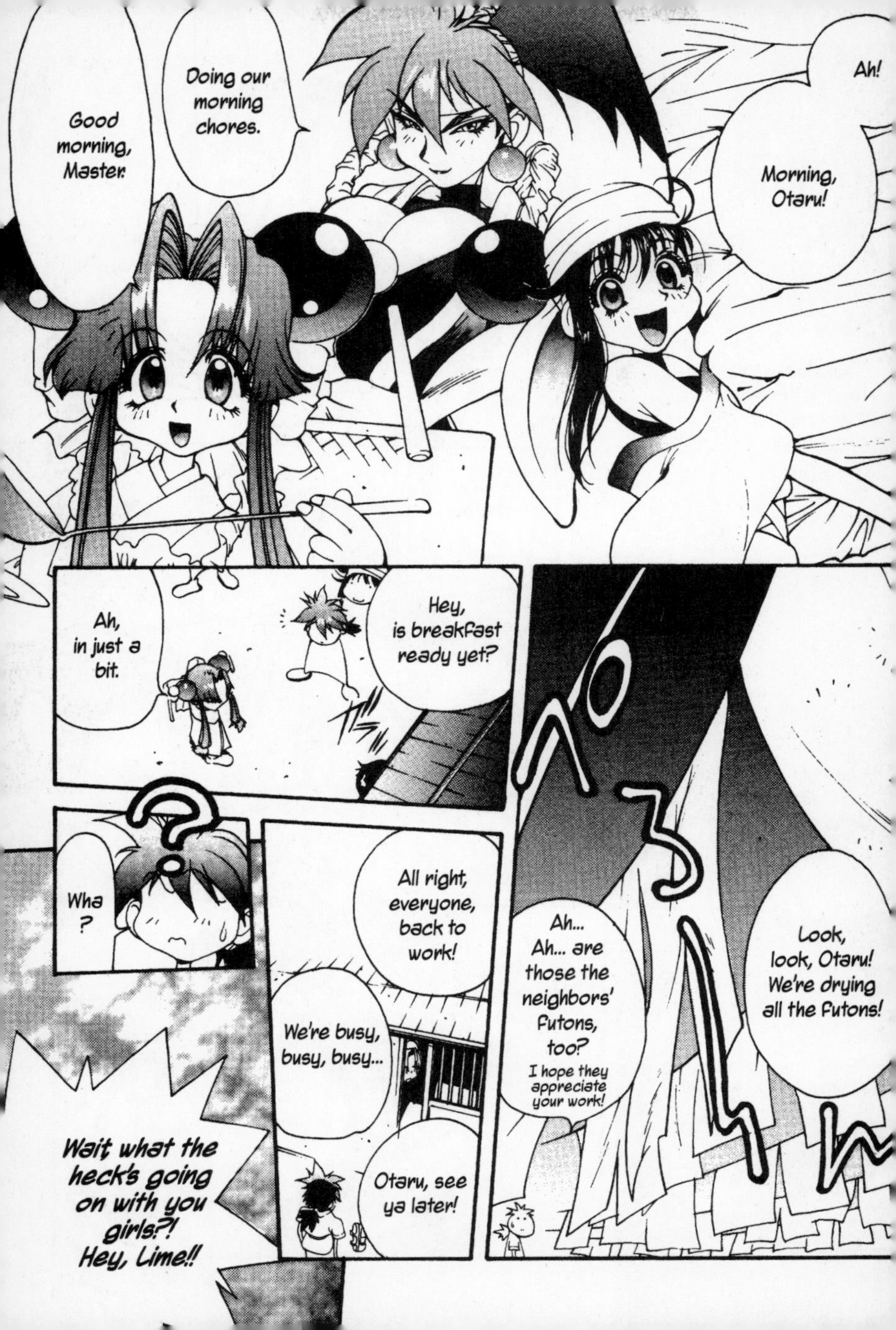
Ah!
Morning, Otaru!
Doing our morning chores.
Good morning, Master.
Look, look, Otaru! We're drying all the futons!
Ah... Ah... are those the neighbors' futons, too?
I hope they appreciate your work!
Hey, is breakfast ready yet?
Ah, in just a bit.
All right, everyone, back to work!
We're busy, busy, busy...
Otaru, see ya later!
Wha ?
Wait, what the heck's going on with you girls?! Hey, Lime!!

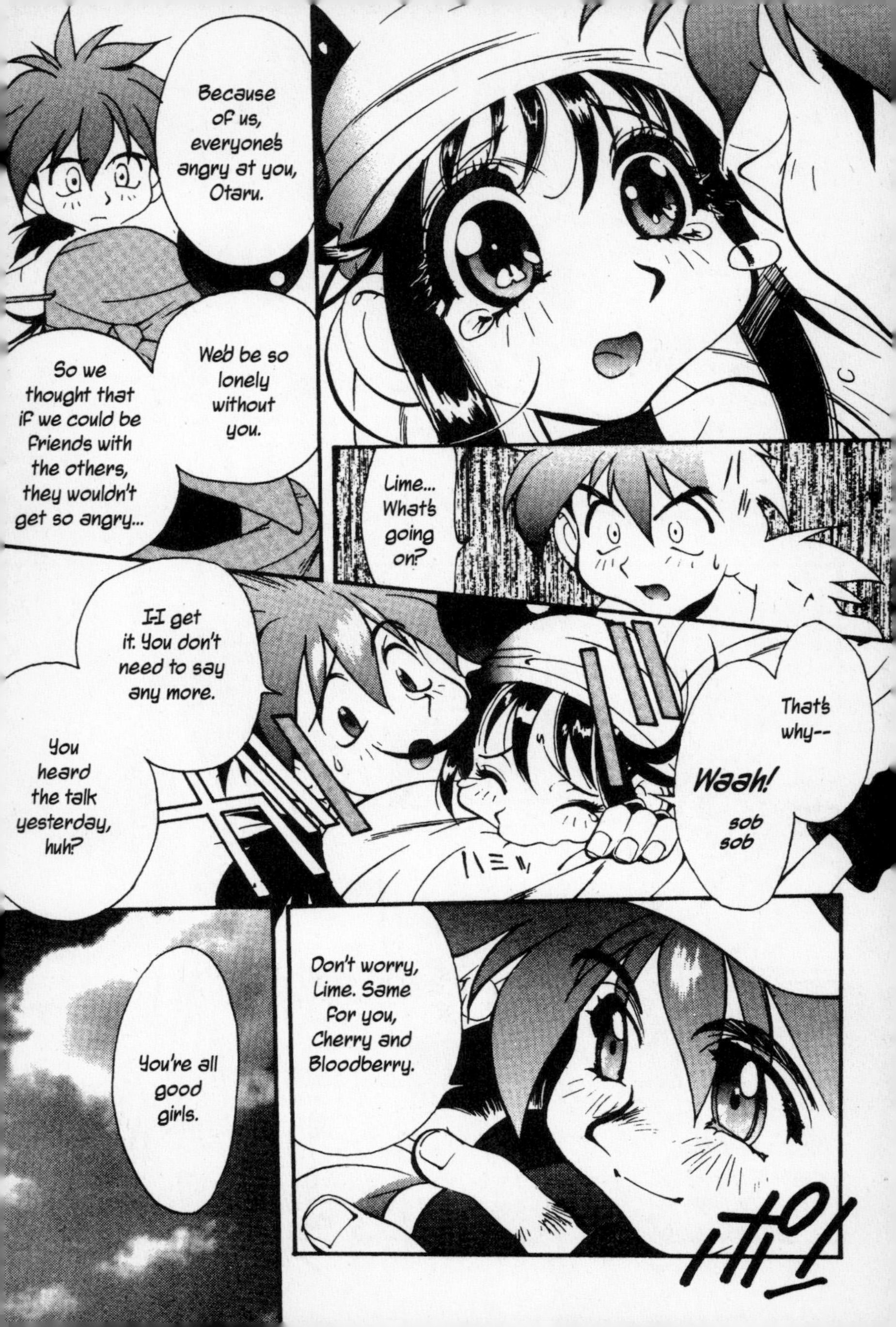
Lime... What's going on?
Because of us, everyone's angry at you, Otaru.
We'd be so lonely without you.
So we thought that if we could be friends with the others, they wouldn't get so angry...
That's why--
Waah!
sob sob
I-I get it. You don't need to say any more.
You heard the talk yesterday, huh?
Don't worry, Lime. Same for you, Cherry and Bloodberry.
You're all good girls.

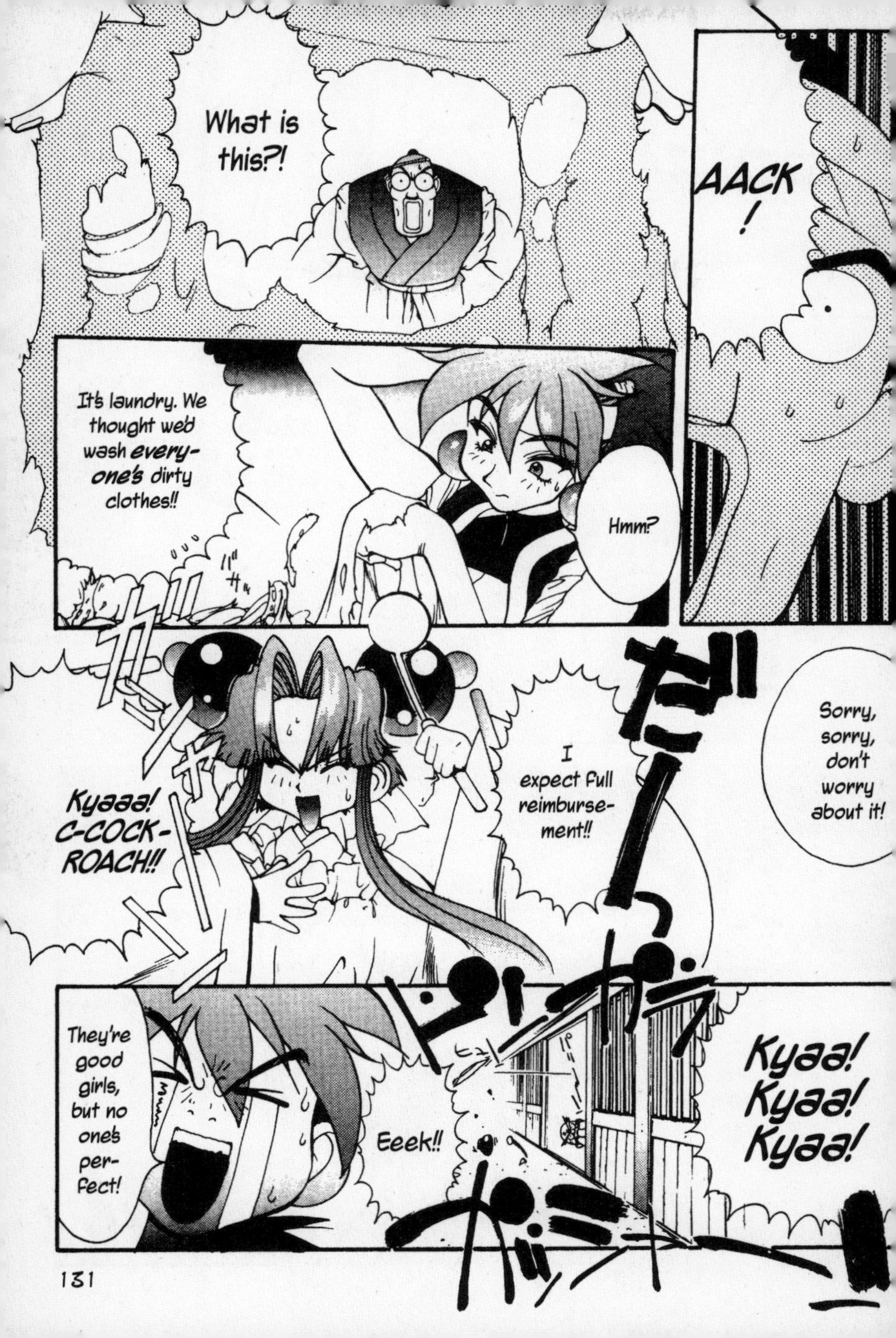
AACK!
What is this?!
Hmm?
It's laundry. We thought we'd wash *everyone's* dirty clothes!!
Sorry, sorry, don't worry about it!
I expect full reimbursement!!
Kyaaa! C-COCKROACH!!
Kyaa! Kyaa! Kyaa!
Eeek!!
They're good girls, but no one's perfect!

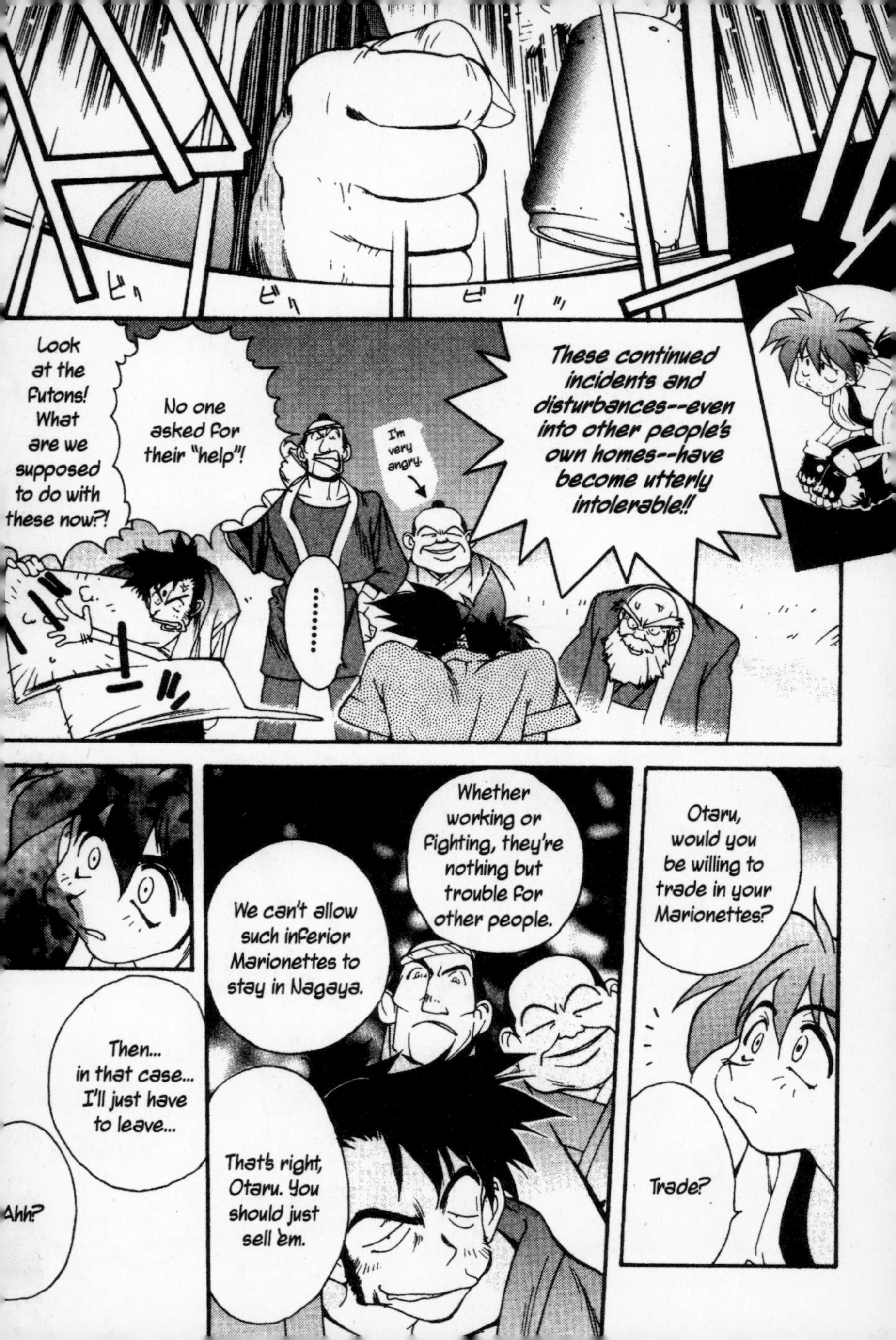
ビリッ
ビッ
ビッ
These continued incidents and disturbances--even into other people's own homes--have become utterly intolerable!!
I'm very angry.
No one asked for their "help"!
Look at the futons! What are we supposed to do with these now?!
....
Otaru, would you be willing to trade in your Marionettes?
Trade?
Whether working or fighting, they're nothing but trouble for other people.
We can't allow such inferior Marionettes to stay in Nagaya.
That's right, Otaru. You should just sell 'em.
Then... in that case... I'll just have to leave...
Ahh?

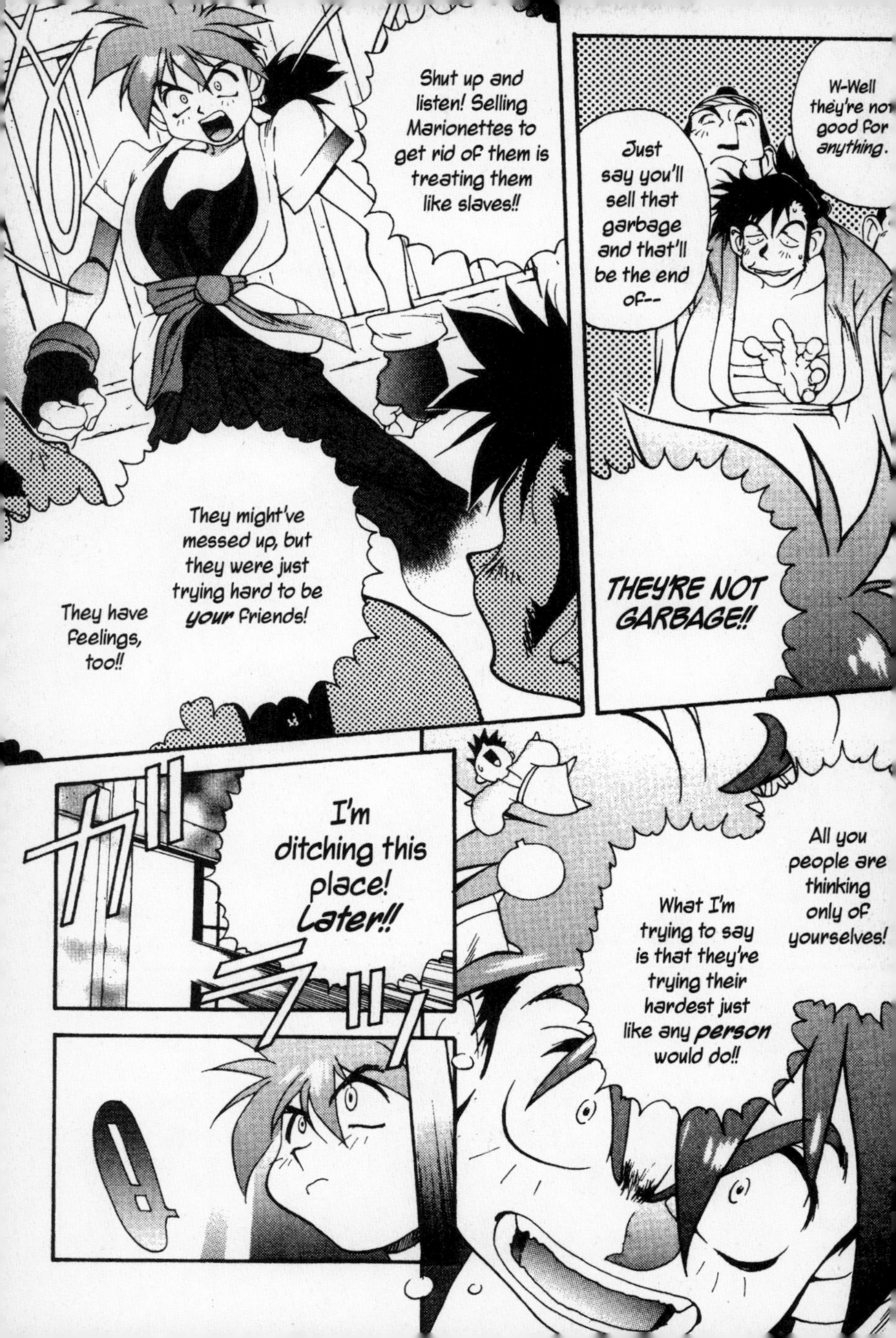
W-Well they're not good for anything.
Just say you'll sell that garbage and that'll be the end of--
THEY'RE NOT GARBAGE!!
Shut up and listen! Selling Marionettes to get rid of them is treating them like slaves!!
They might've messed up, but they were just trying hard to be *your* friends!
They have feelings, too!!
All you people are thinking only of yourselves!
What I'm trying to say is that they're trying their hardest just like any *person* would do!!
I'm ditching this place! *Later!!*
!?

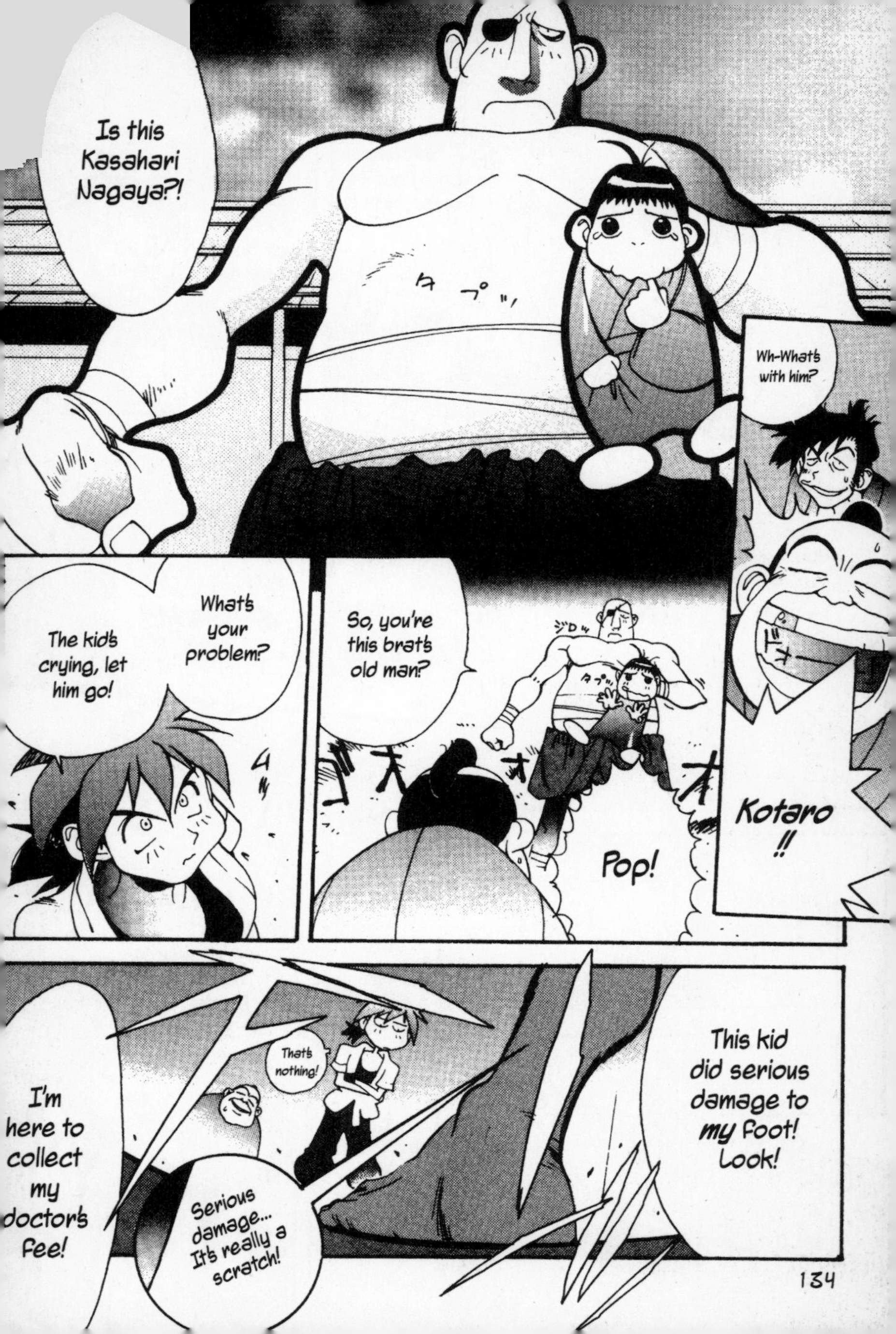
Is this Kasahari Nagaya?!
タプッ
Wh-What's with him?
Kotaro!!
So, you're this brat's old man?
Pop!
What's your problem?
The kid's crying, let him go!
This kid did serious damage to my foot! Look!
That's nothing!
Serious damage... It's really a scratch!
I'm here to collect my doctor's fee!

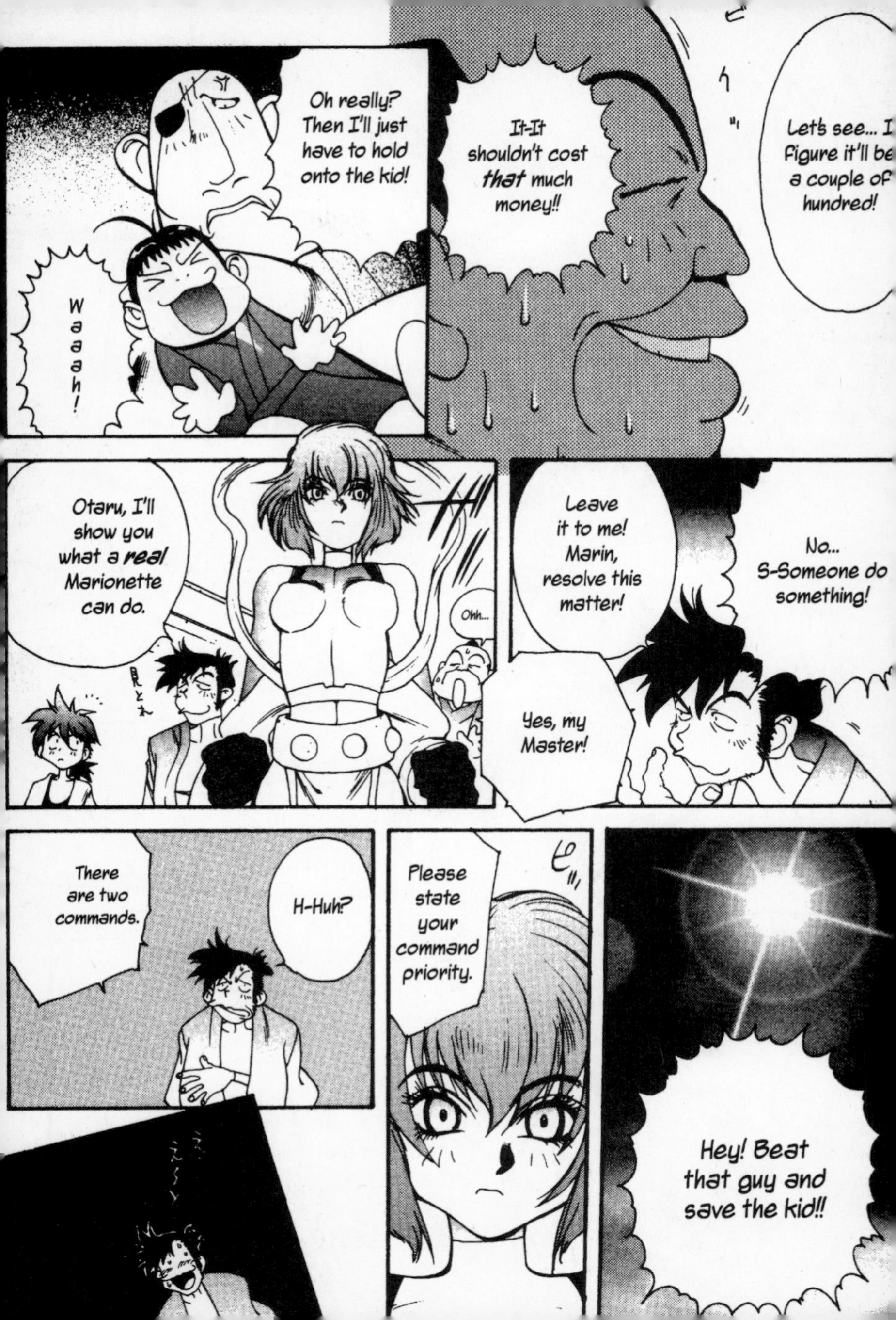
Let's see... I figure it'll be a couple of hundred!
It-It shouldn't cost *that* much money!!
Oh really? Then I'll just have to hold onto the kid!
Waaaah!
No... S-Someone do something!
Leave it to me! Marin, resolve this matter!
Yes, my Master!
Otaru, I'll show you what a *real* Marionette can do.
Ohh...
Hey! Beat that guy and save the kid!!
Please state your command priority.
H-Huh?
There are two commands.

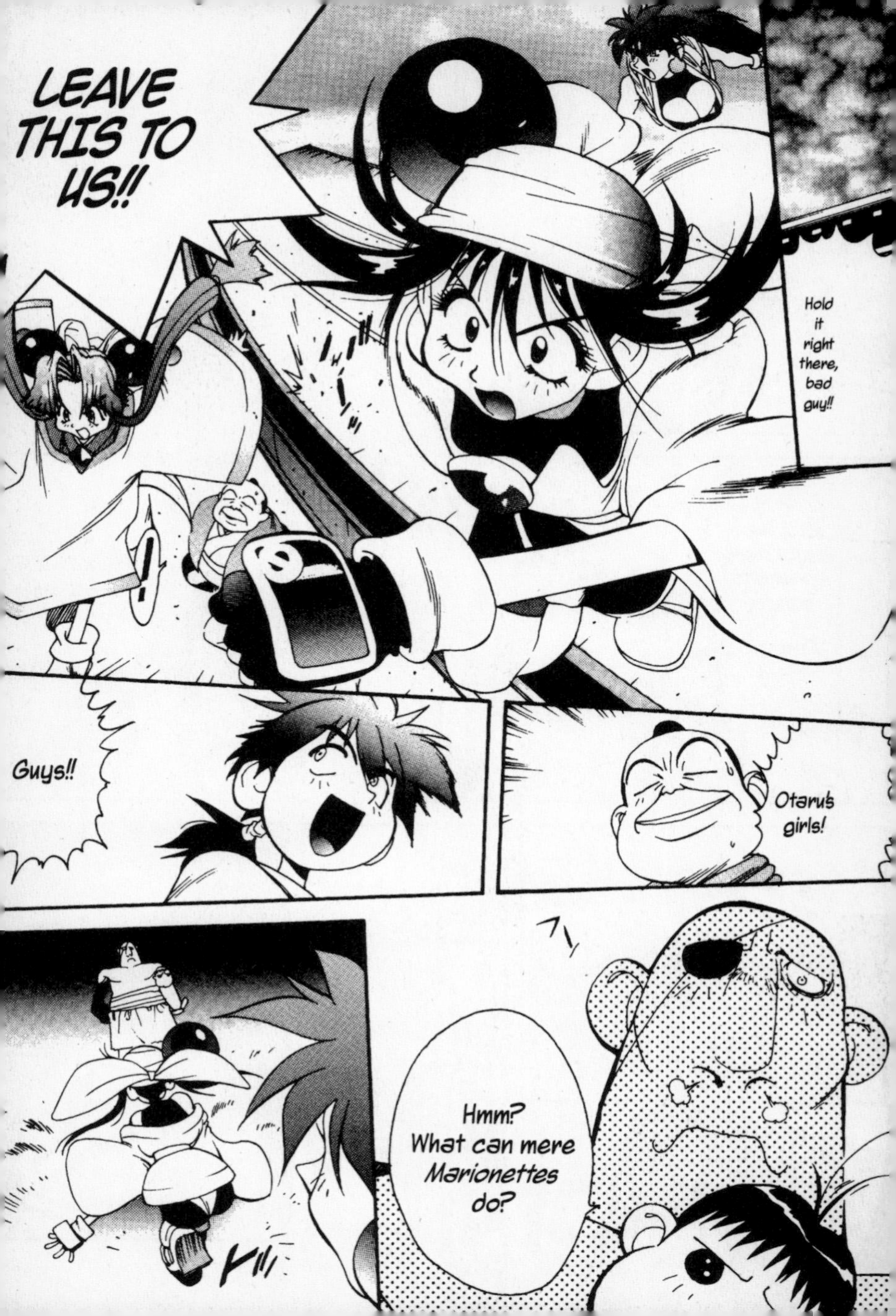
Hold it right there, bad guy!!
LEAVE THIS TO US!!
Otaru's girls!
Guys!!
Hmm? What can mere Marionettes do?

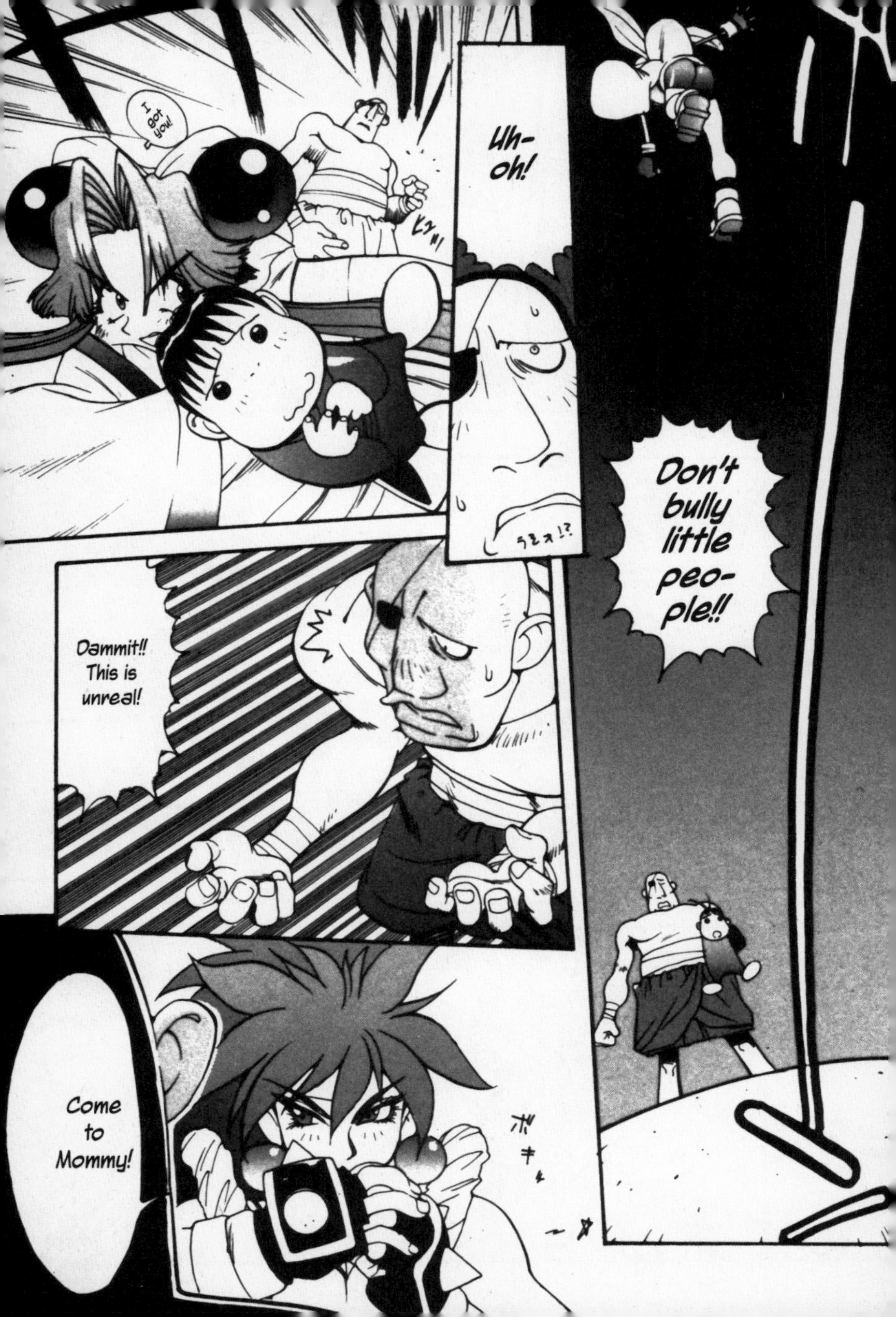

Don't bully little peo-ple!!
Uh-oh!
I got you!
Dammit!! This is unreal!
Come to Mommy!

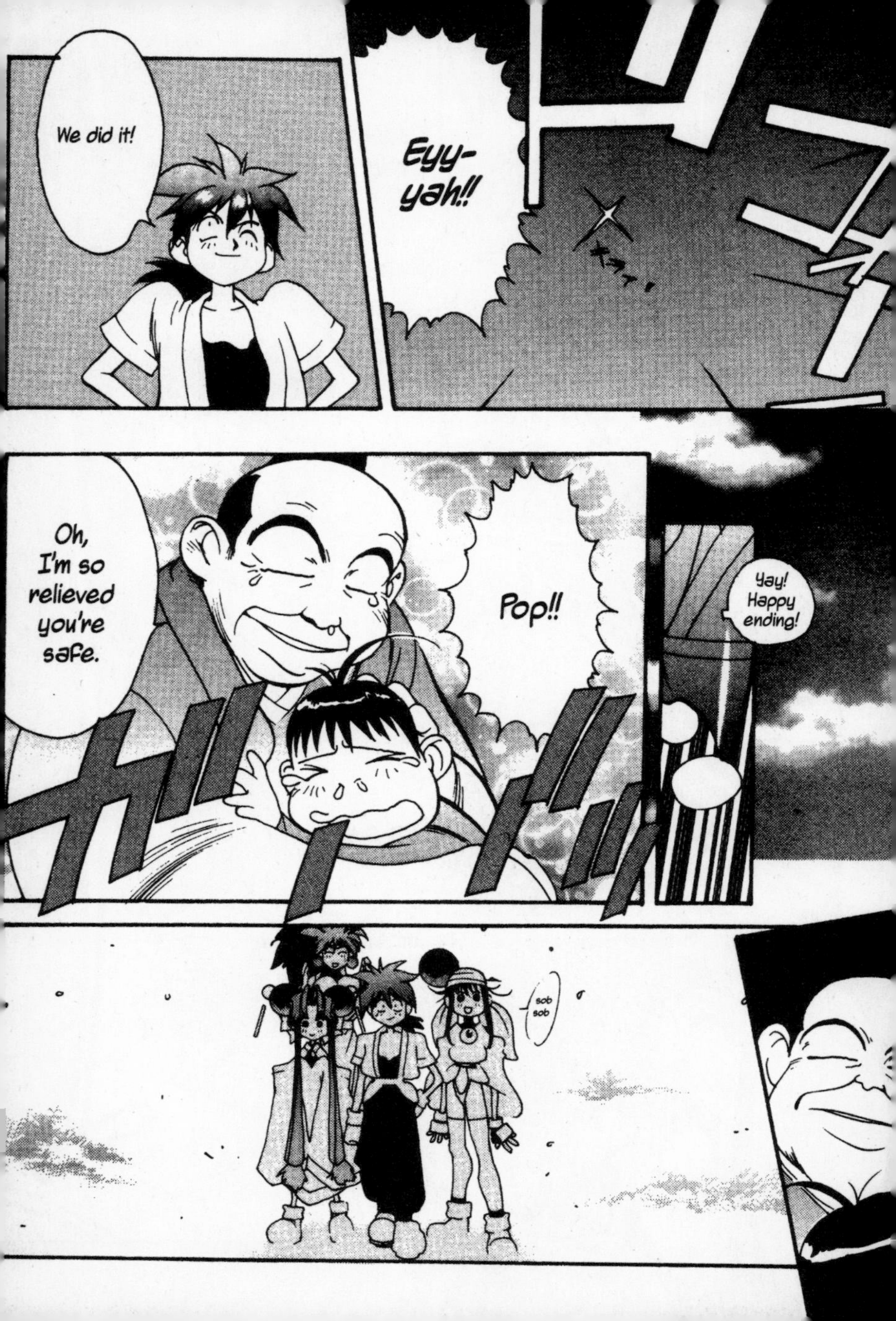
Eyy-yah!!
We did it!
Yay! Happy ending!
Pop!!
Oh, I'm so relieved you're safe.
sob sob

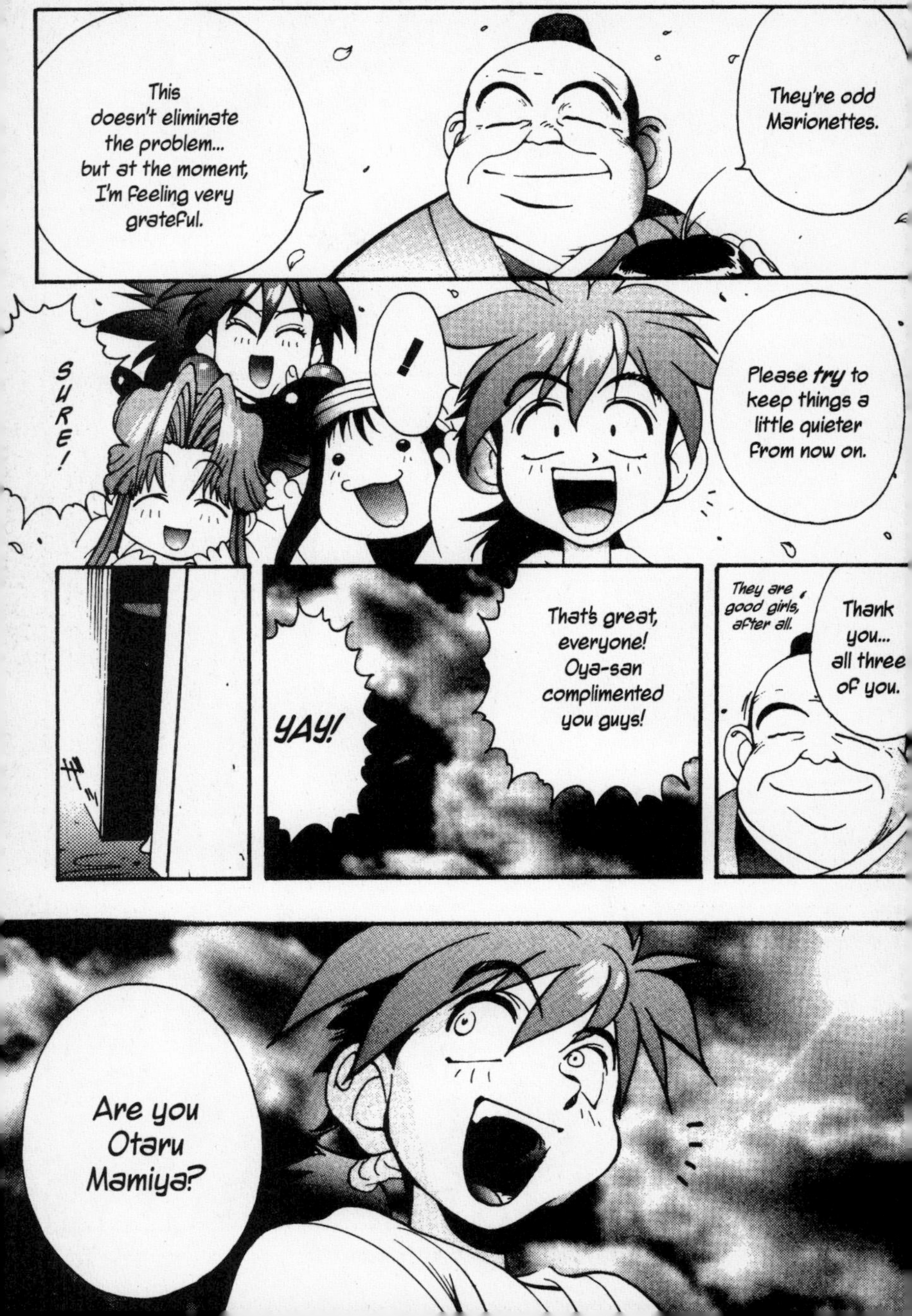
They're odd Marionettes.
This doesn't eliminate the problem... but at the moment, I'm feeling very grateful.
Please *try* to keep things a little quieter from now on.
!
SURE!
Thank you... all three of you.
They are good girls, after all.
That's great, everyone! Oya-san complimented you guys!
YAY!
Are you Otaru Mamiya?

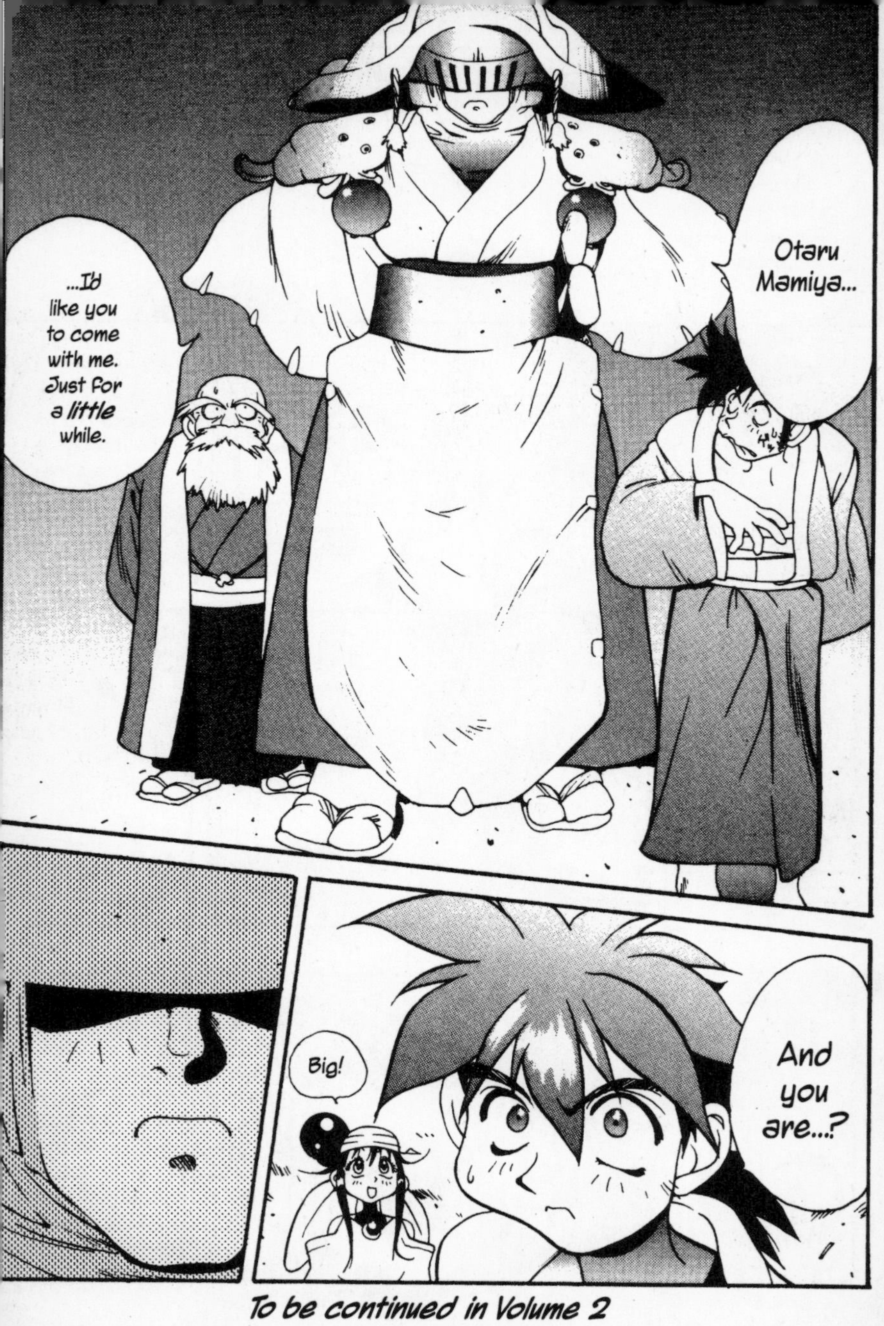
Otaru Mamiya...
...I'd like you to come with me. Just for a *little* while.
And you are...?
Big!

To be continued in Volume 2

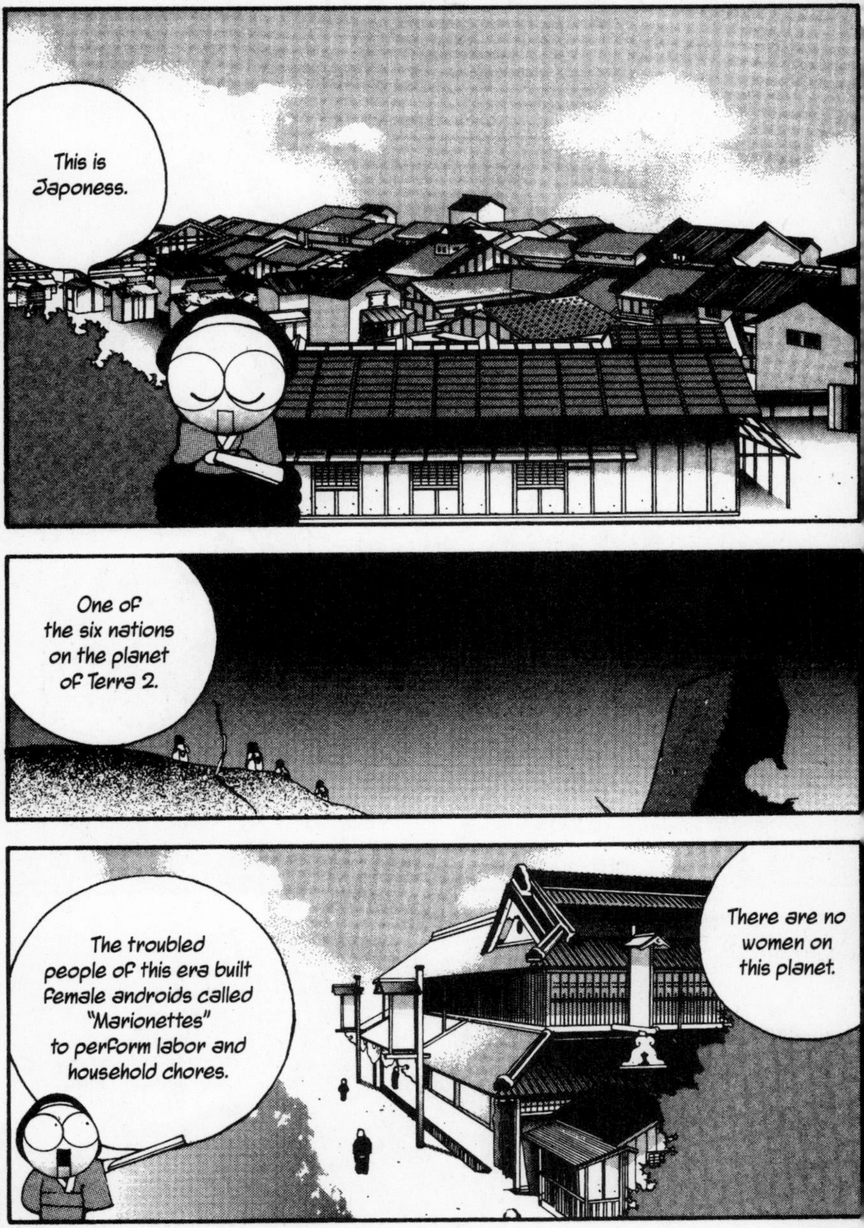
This is Japoness.
One of the six nations on the planet of Terra 2.
There are no women on this planet.
The troubled people of this era built female androids called "Marionettes" to perform labor and household chores.

The main character of this story is Otaru Mamiya.
These are the mysterious Marionettes who love Otaru... despite being machines.
From the left: Lime, Cherry and Bloodberry.
The focus of this tale is the deep, forbidden love and romance between these Saber Marionettes and our protagonist, Otaru Mamiya!
Ahem... Ahem...

Bonus Story - It's Summer! It's a Ghost! Is it a Love Comic?!

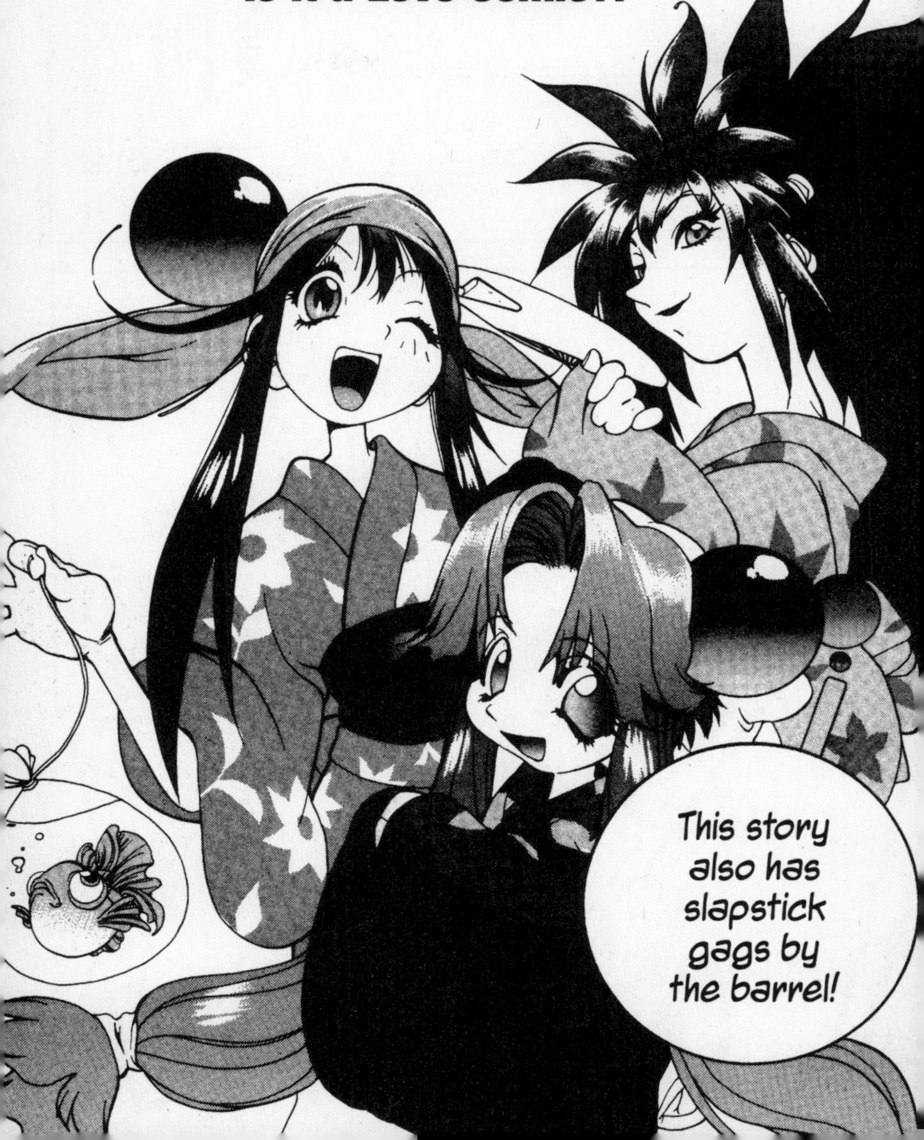
This story also has slapstick gags by the barrel!

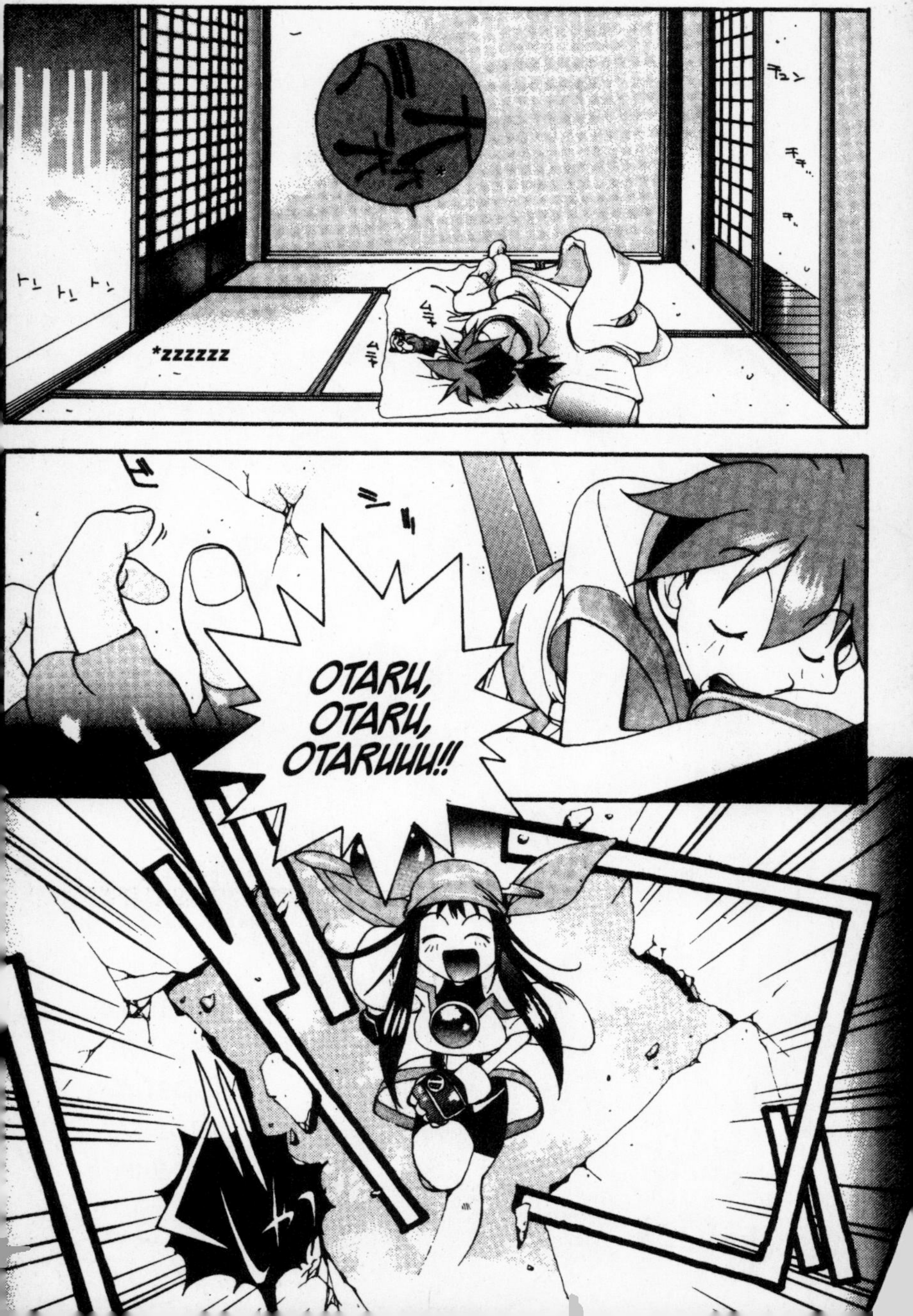
*ZZZZZZ
OTARU, OTARU, OTARUUU!!

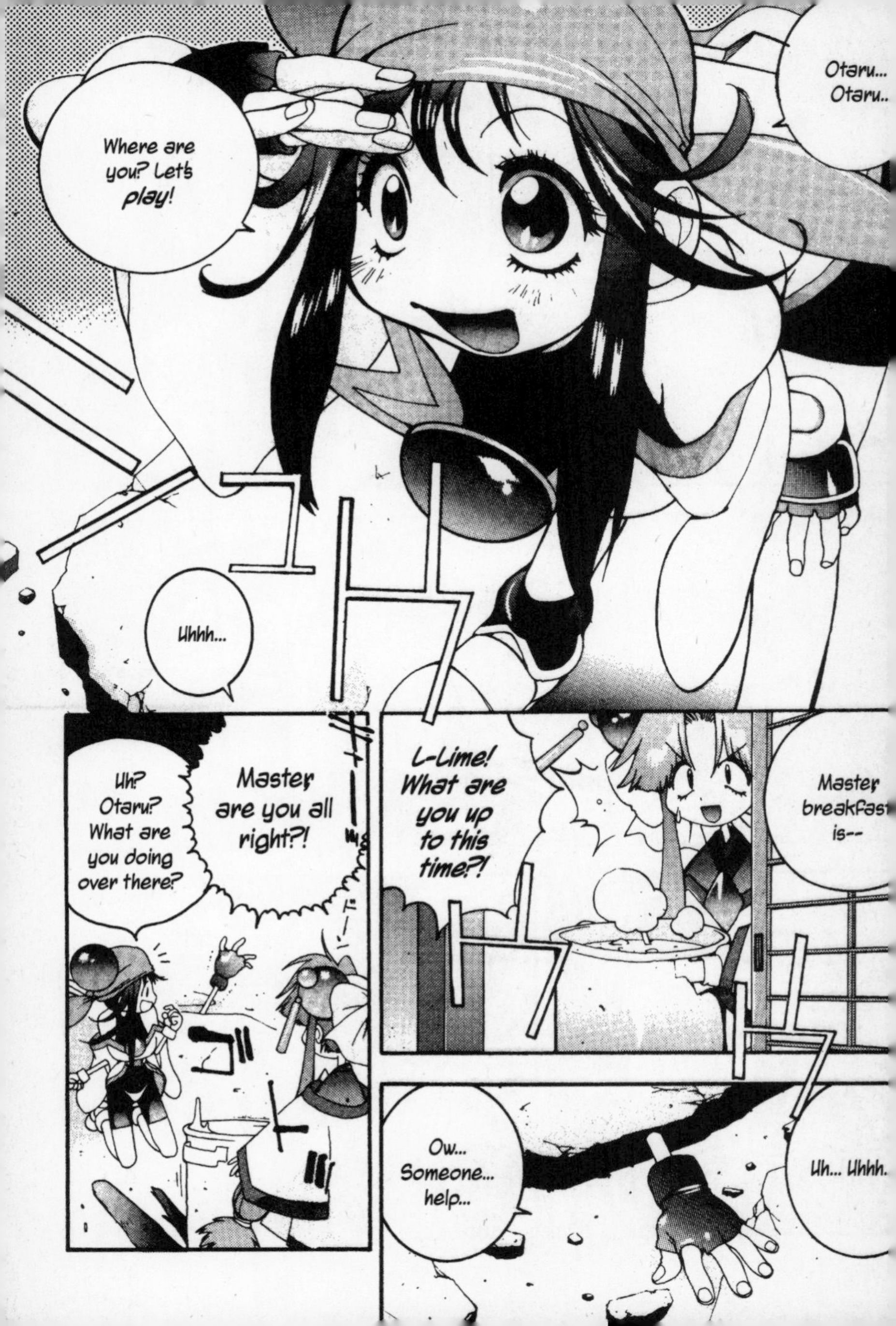
Otaru... Otaru...
Where are you? Let's play!
Uhhh...
Master, breakfast is--
L-Lime! What are you up to this time?!
Uh... Uhhh.
Ow... Someone... help...
Master, are you all right?!
Uh? Otaru? What are you doing over there?

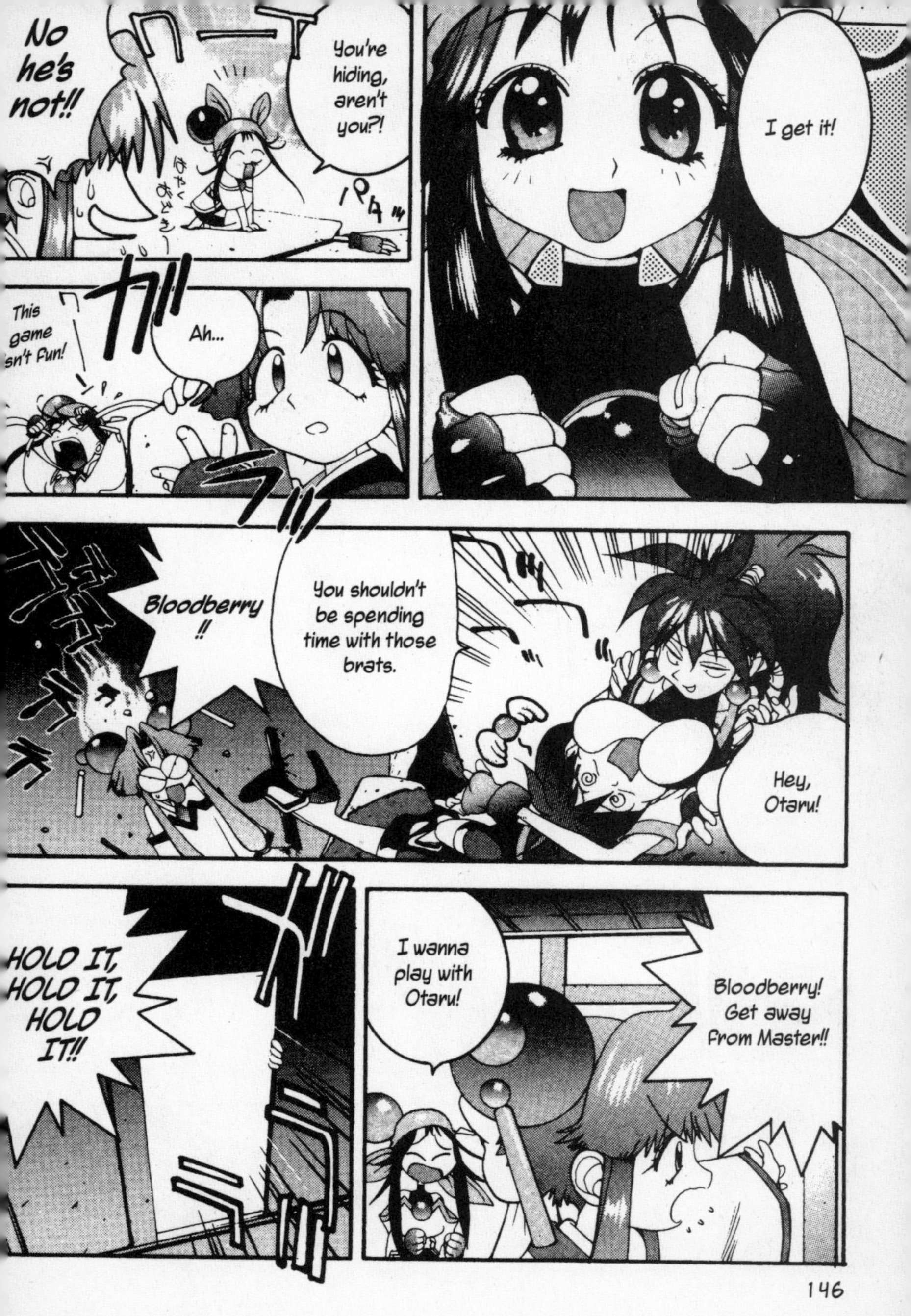
I get it!
You're hiding, aren't you?!
No he's not!!
Ah...
This game sn't fun!
Hey, Otaru!
You shouldn't be spending time with those brats.
Bloodberry!!
Bloodberry! Get away from Master!!
I wanna play with Otaru!
HOLD IT, HOLD IT, HOLD IT!!

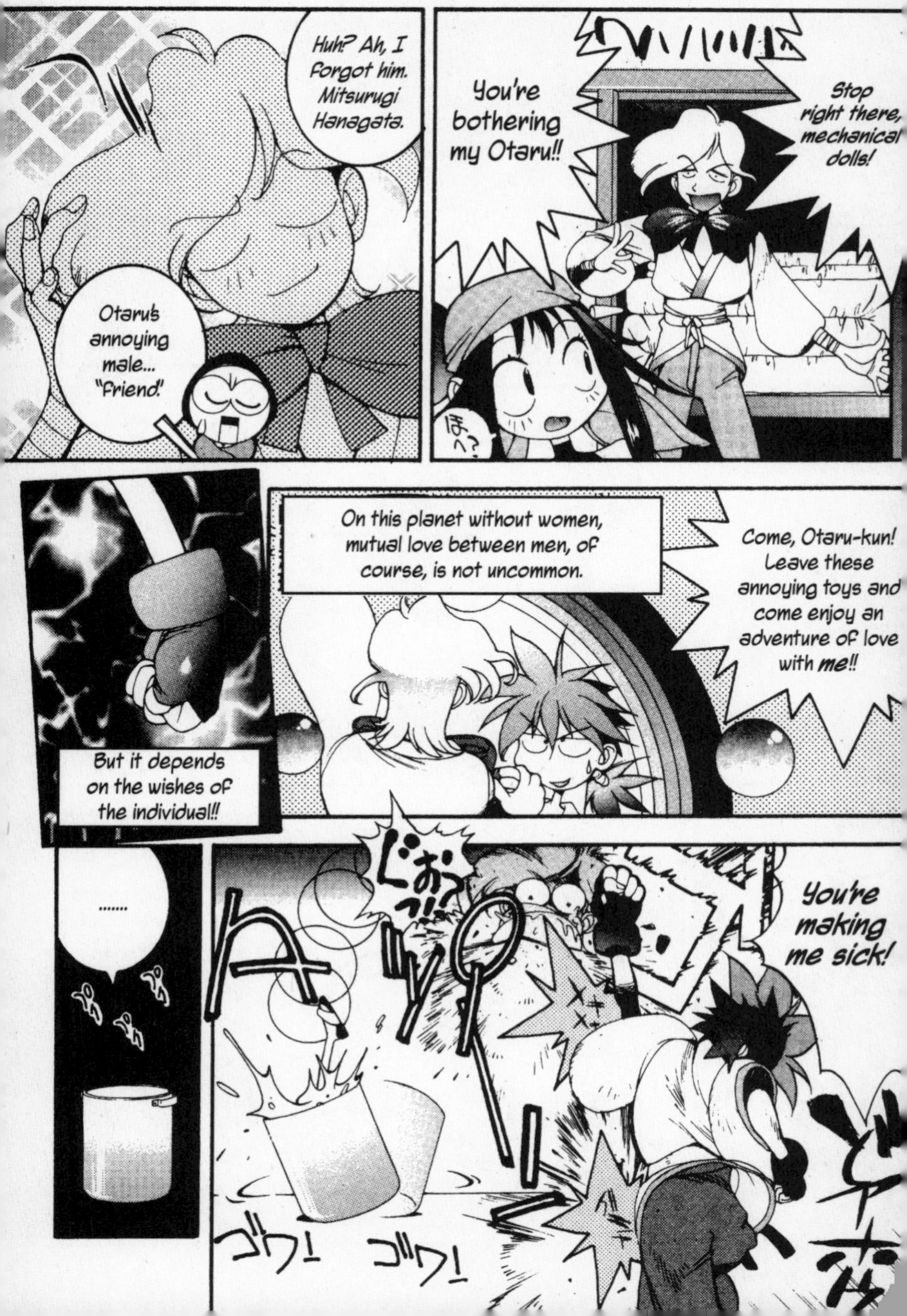
Stop right there, mechanical dolls!
You're bothering my Otaru!!
ほへ?
Huh? Ah, I forgot him. Mitsurugi Hanagata.
Otaru's annoying male... "friend."
On this planet without women, mutual love between men, of course, is not uncommon.
Come, Otaru-kun! Leave these annoying toys and come enjoy an adventure of love with *me*!!
But it depends on the wishes of the individual!!
You're making me sick!
......

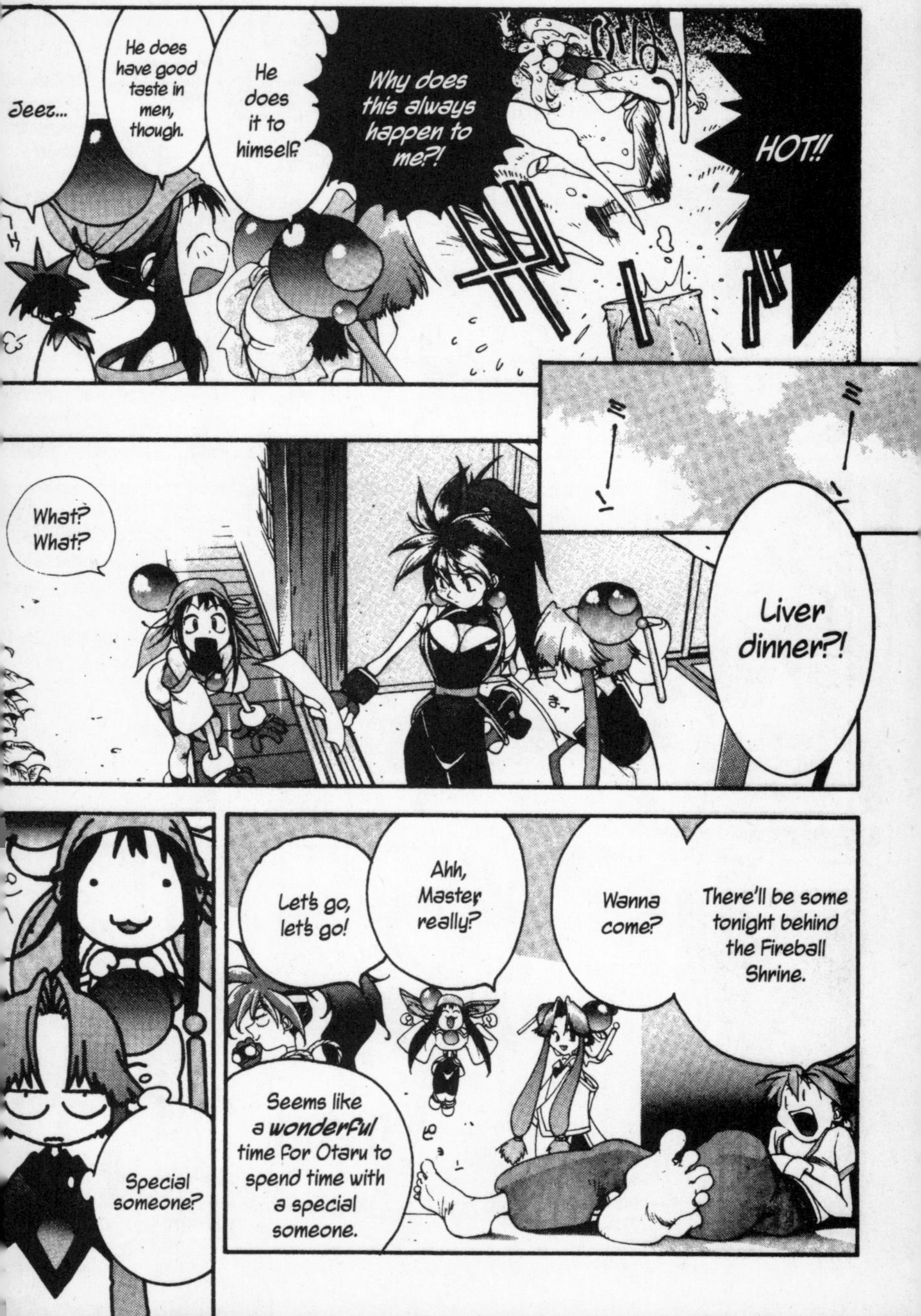
HOT!!
Why does this always happen to me?!
He does it to himself.
He does have good taste in men, though.
Jeez...
Liver dinner?!
What? What?
There'll be some tonight behind the Fireball Shrine.
Wanna come?
Ahh, Master, really?
Let's go, let's go!
Seems like a *wonderful* time for Otaru to spend time with a special someone.
Special someone?

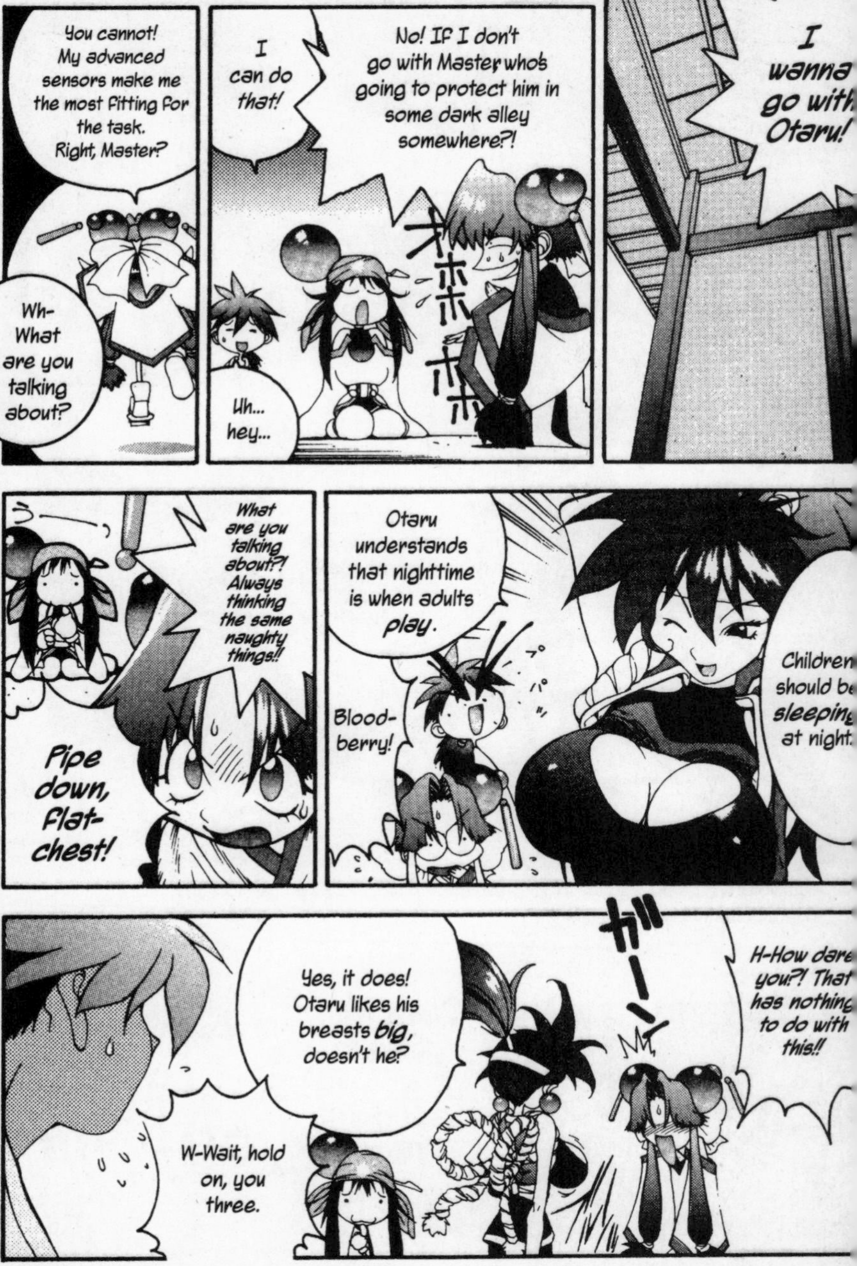
I wanna go with Otaru!
No! If I don't go with Master, who's going to protect him in some dark alley somewhere?!
I can do that!
Uh... hey...
You cannot! My advanced sensors make me the most fitting for the task. Right, Master?
Wh- What are you talking about?
Children should b sleeping at night.
Otaru understands that nighttime is when adults play.
Blood-berry!
What are you talking about?! Always thinking the same naughty things!!
Pipe down, Flat-chest!
H-How dare you?! Tha has nothing to do with this!!
Yes, it does! Otaru likes his breasts big, doesn't he?
W-Wait, hold on, you three.

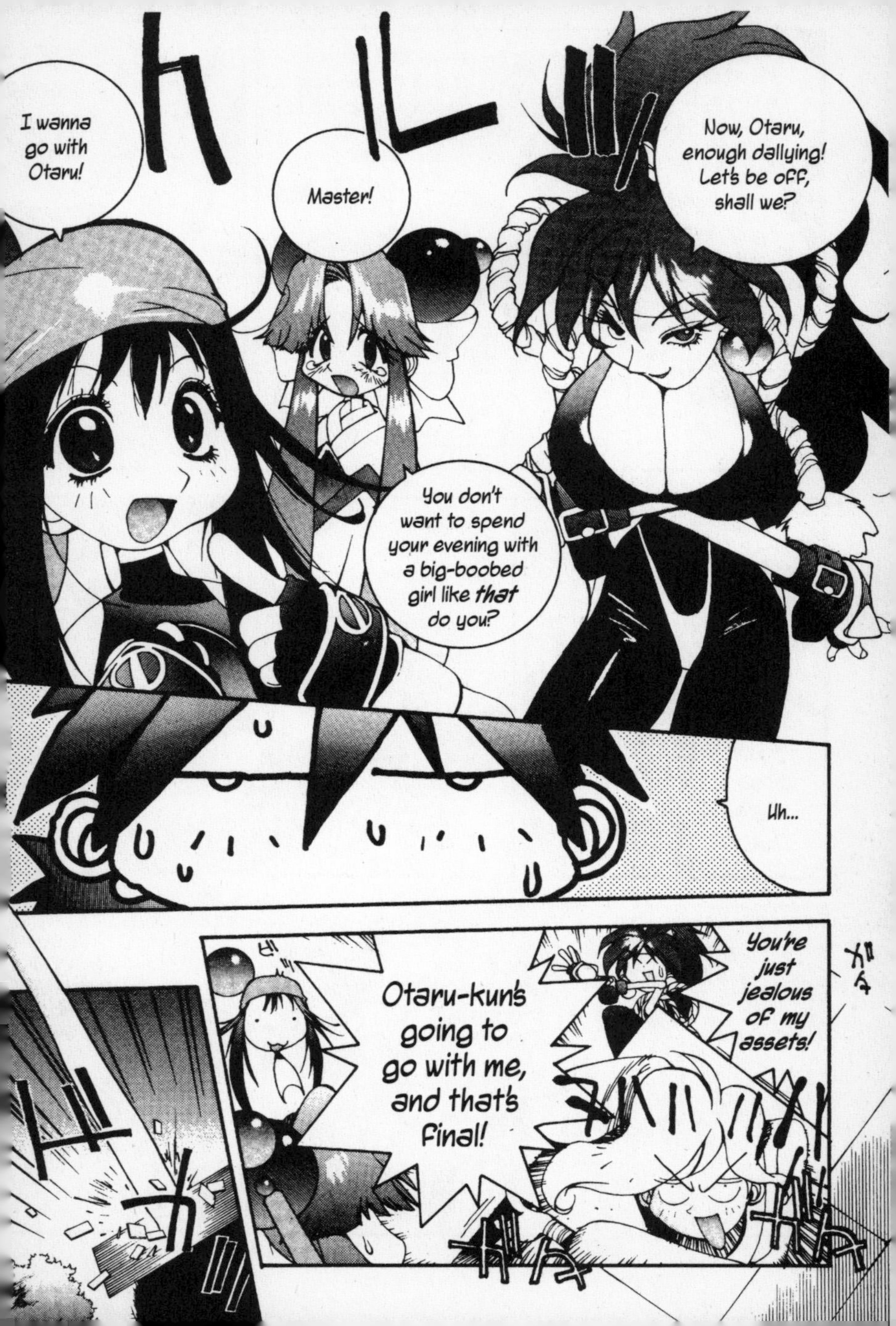
Now, Otaru, enough dallying! Let's be off, shall we?
Master!
I wanna go with Otaru!
You don't want to spend your evening with a big-boobed girl like *that* do you?
Uh...
You're just jealous of my assets!
Otaru-kun's going to go with me, and that's final!

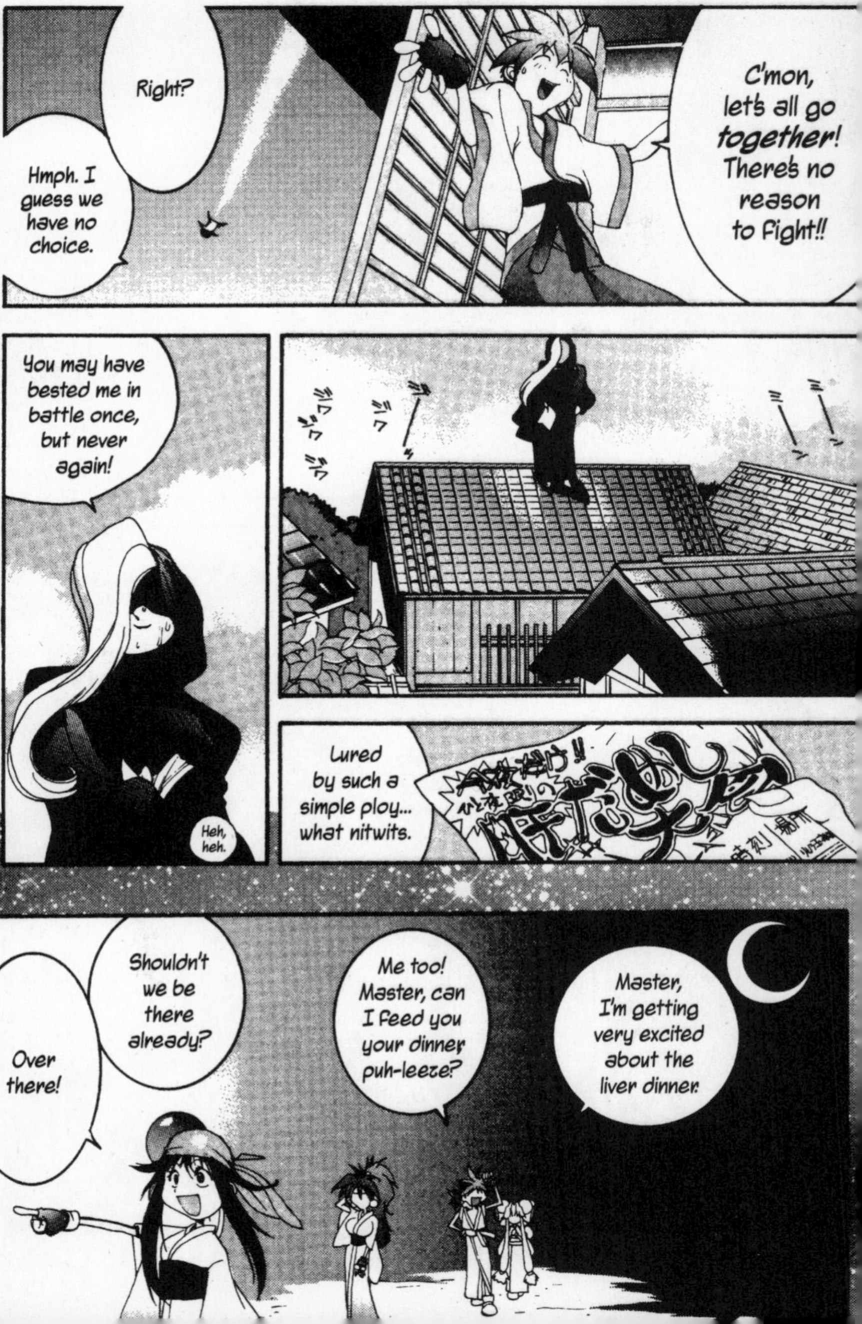
C'mon, let's all go *together*! There's no reason to fight!!
Right?
Hmph. I guess we have no choice.
Lured by such a simple ploy... what nitwits.
You may have bested me in battle once, but never again!
Heh, heh.
Master, I'm getting very excited about the liver dinner.
Me too! Master, can I feed you your dinner, puh-leeze?
Shouldn't we be there already?
Over there!

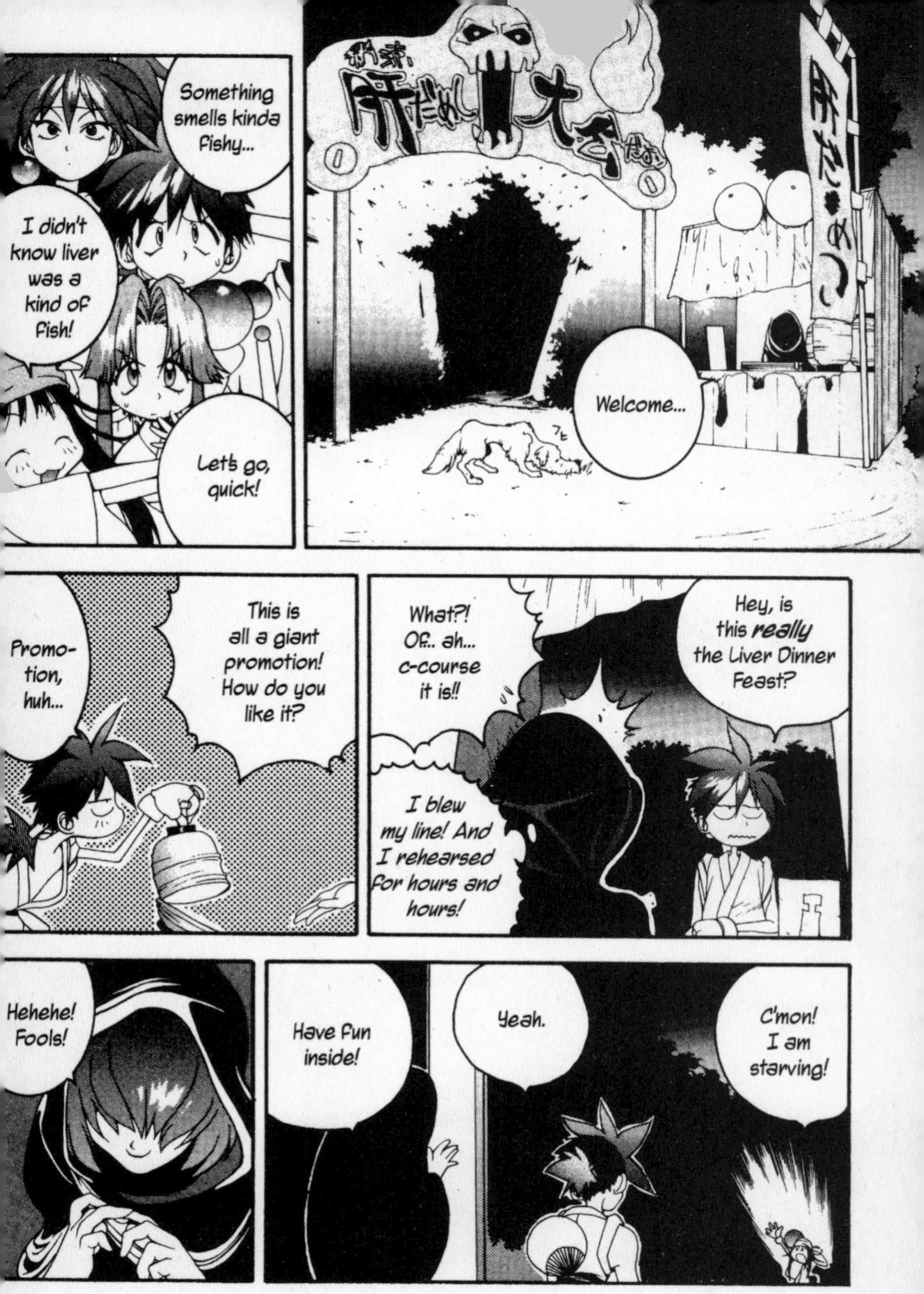
Welcome...
Something smells kinda fishy...
I didn't know liver was a kind of fish!
Let's go, quick!
Hey, is this really the Liver Dinner Feast?
What?! Of.. ah... c-course it is!!
I blew my line! And I rehearsed for hours and hours!
This is all a giant promotion! How do you like it?
Promo-tion, huh...
C'mon! I am starving!
Yeah.
Have fun inside!
Hehehe! Fools!

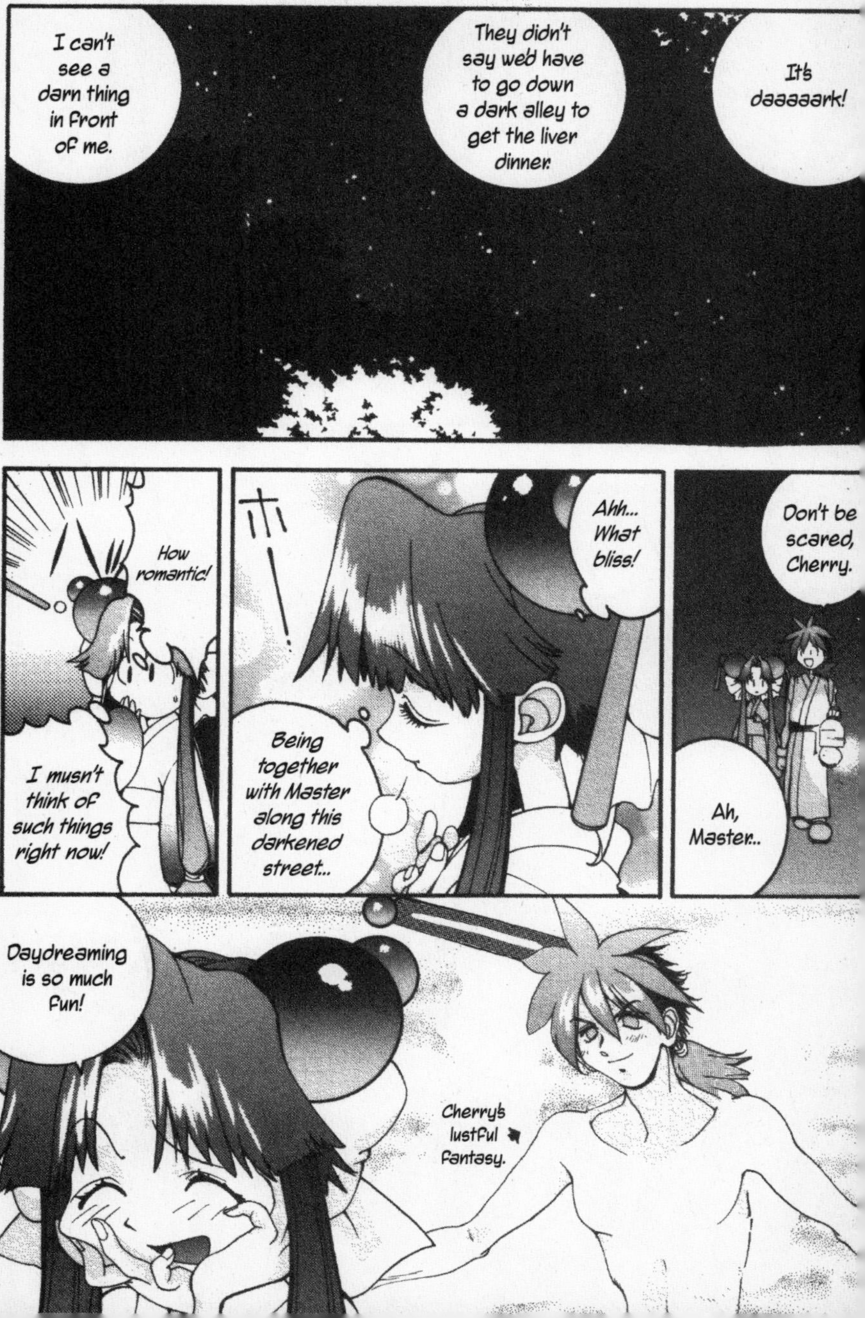
It's daaaaaark!
They didn't say we'd have to go down a dark alley to get the liver dinner.
I can't see a darn thing in front of me.
Don't be scared, Cherry.
Ah, Master...
Ahh... What bliss!
Being together with Master along this darkened street...
How romantic!
I musn't think of such things right now!
Daydreaming is so much fun!
Cherry's lustful fantasy.

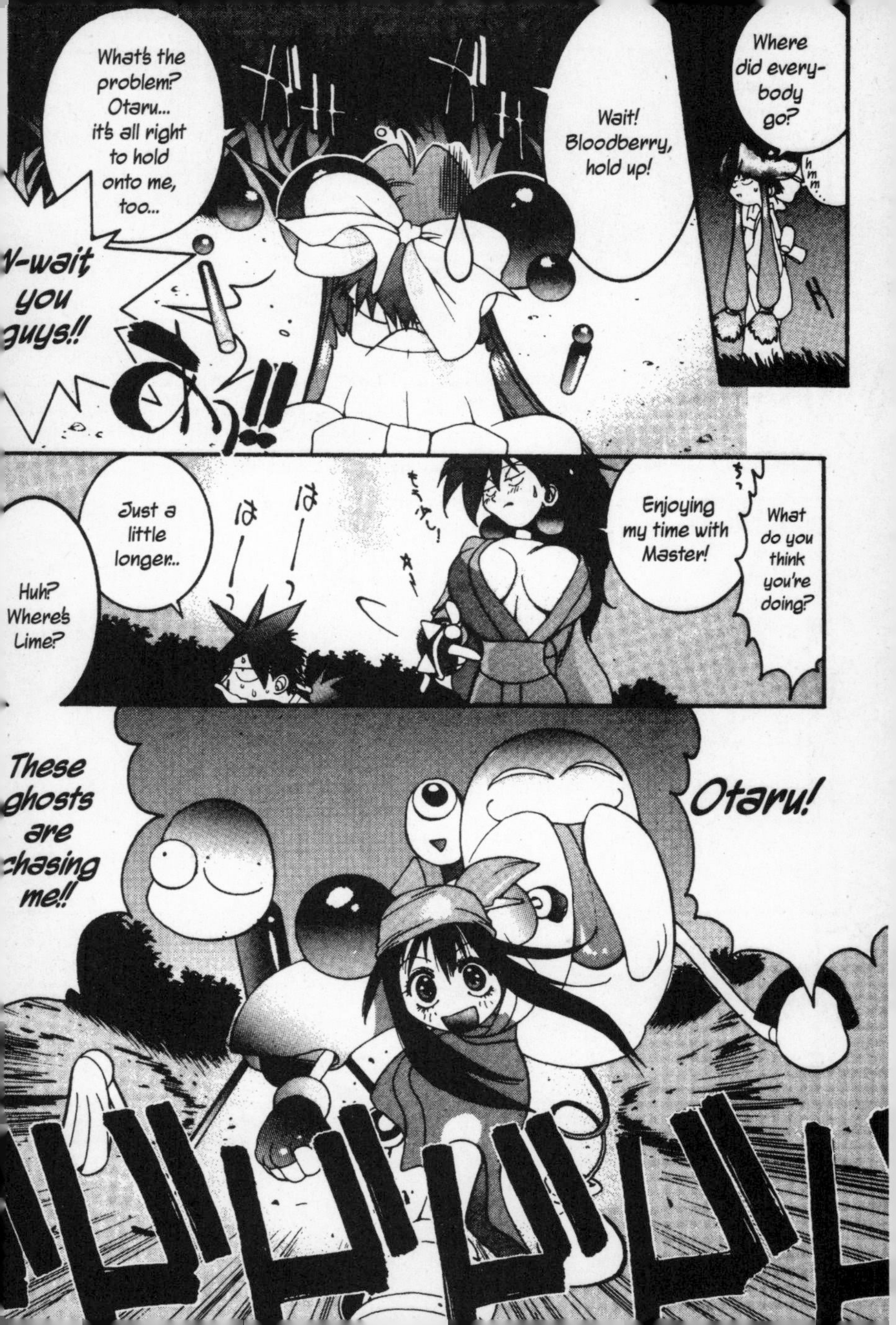

Where did every-body go?
hmm...
Wait! Bloodberry, hold up!
What's the problem? Otaru... it's all right to hold onto me, too...
-wait you guys!!
What do you think you're doing?
Enjoying my time with Master!
は―っ
は―っ
Just a little longer...
Huh? Where's Lime?
Otaru!
These ghosts are chasing me!!

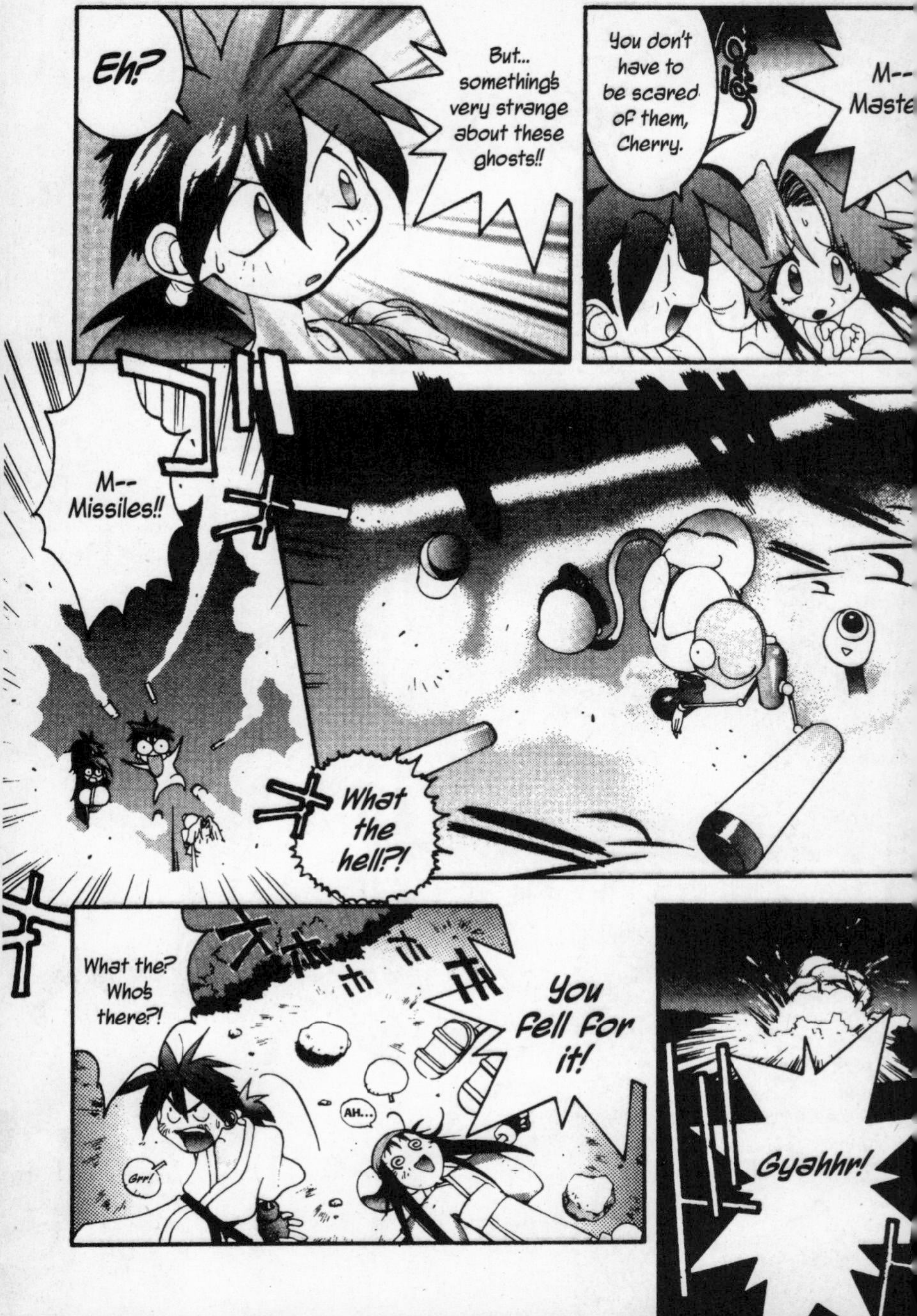
M-- Maste
You don't have to be scared of them, Cherry.
But... something's very strange about these ghosts!!
Eh?
What the hell?!
M-- Missiles!!
Gyahhr!
You fell for it!
AH...
What the? Who's there?!
Grr!

SABER DOLLS!!
The Saber Dolls! Considered the strongest Marionettes from Gartland, an enemy of the Japoness nation!!
They're as bad as hey look, and the als of Lime, herry and oodberry!

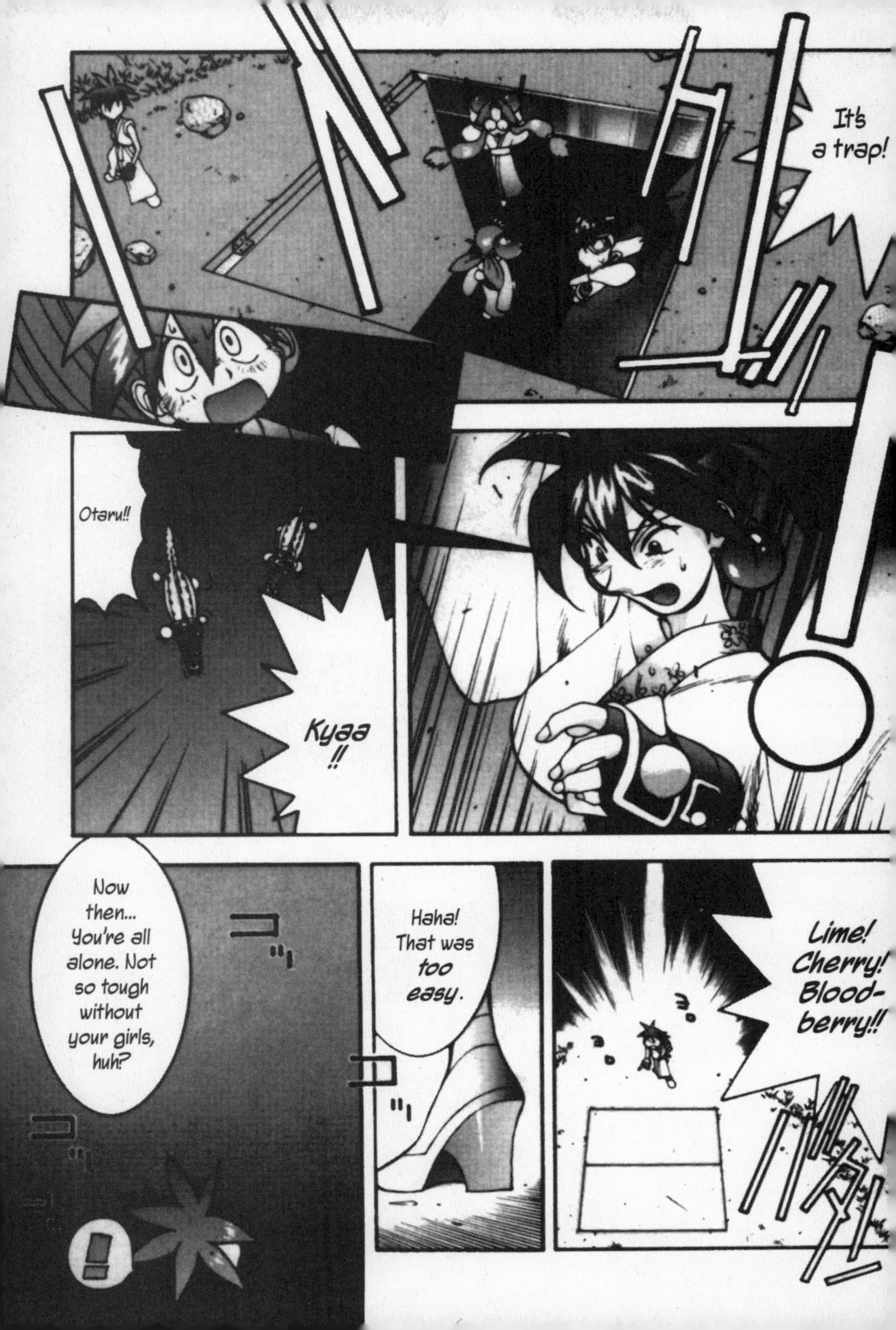
It's a trap!
Otaru!!
Kyaa !!
Lime! Cherry! Blood-berry!!
Haha! That was too easy.
Now then... You're all alone. Not so tough without your girls, huh?

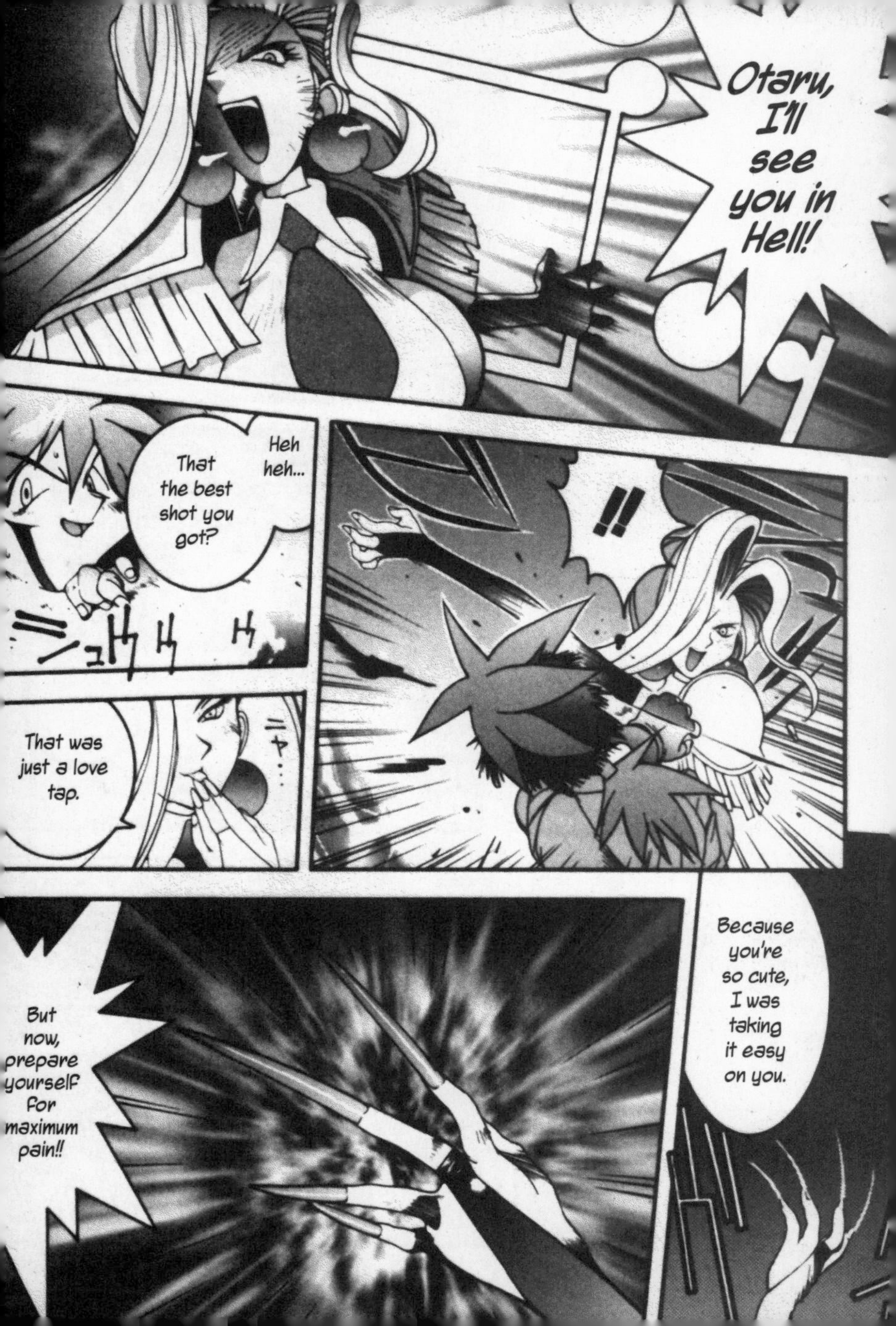
Otaru, I'll see you in Hell!
!!
Heh heh...
That the best shot you got?
That was just a love tap.
Because you're so cute, I was taking it easy on you.
But now, prepare yourself for maximum pain!!

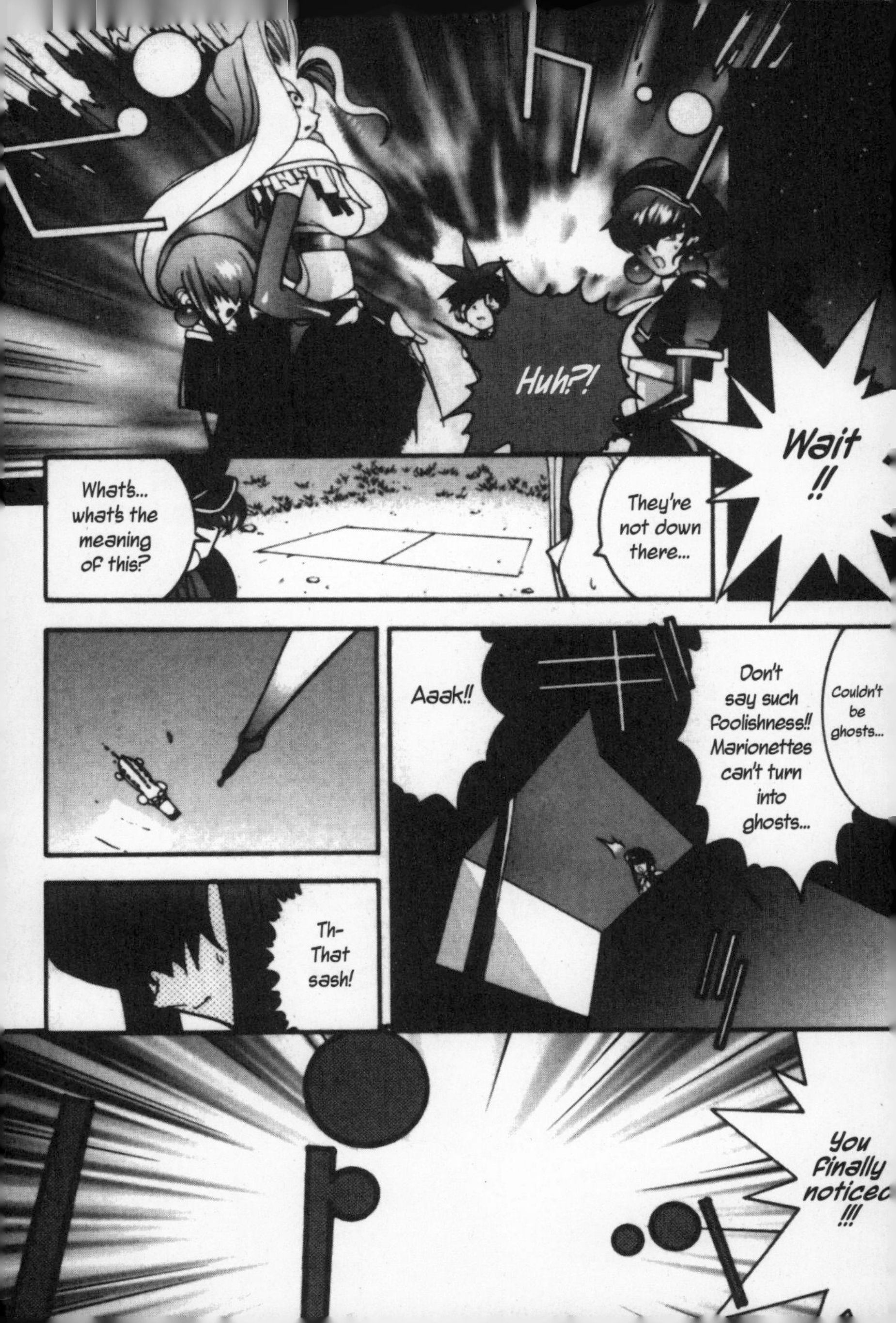
Huh?!
Wait!!
They're not down there...
What's... what's the meaning of this?
Couldn't be ghosts...
Don't say such foolishness!! Marionettes can't turn into ghosts...
Aaak!!
Th- That sash!
You finally noticed!!!

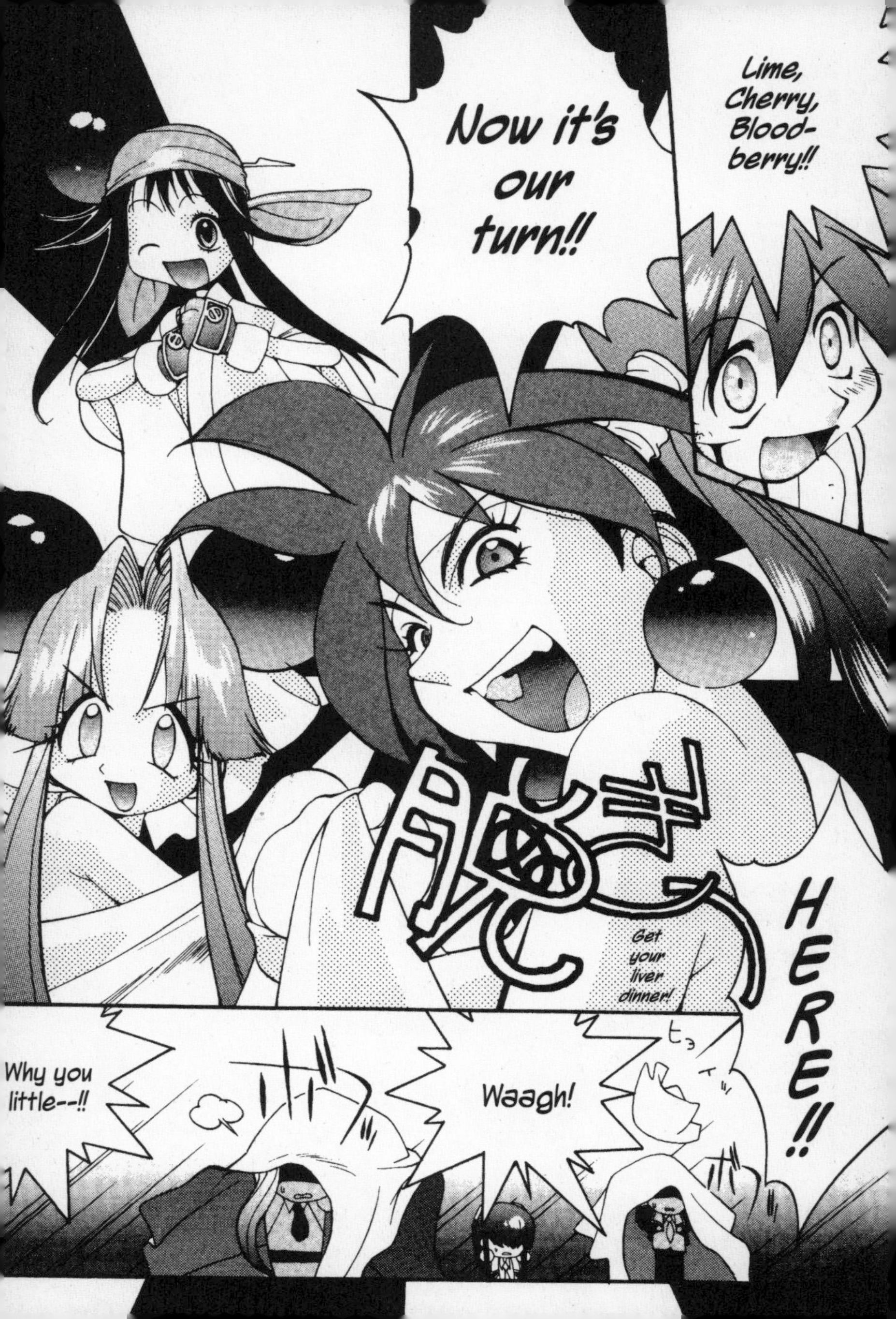
Lime, Cherry, Blood-berry!!
Now it's our turn!!
HERE!!
Get your liver dinner!
Waagh!
Why you little--!!

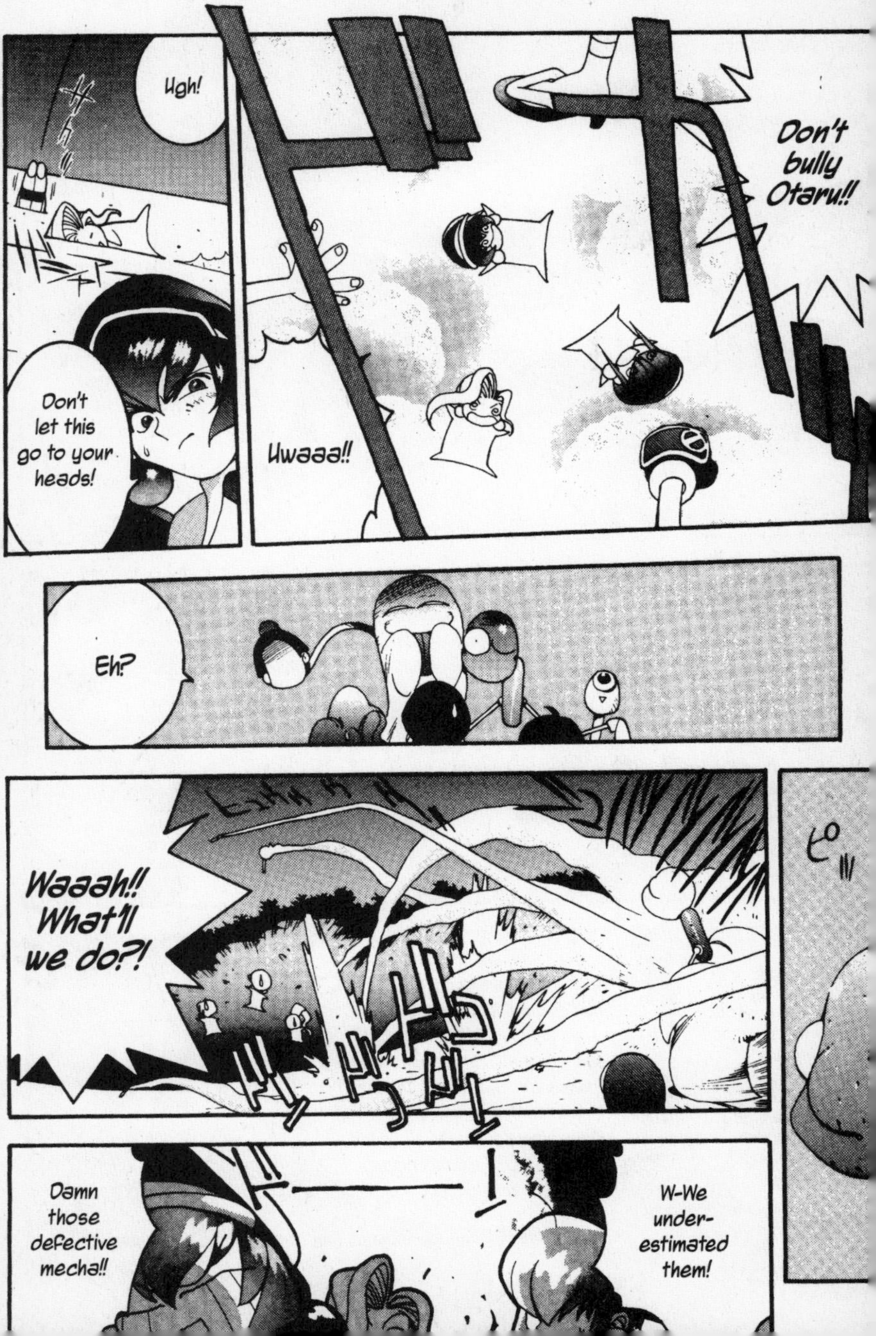
Don't bully Otaru!!
Uwaaa!!
Ugh!
Don't let this go to your heads!
Eh?
Waaah!! What'll we do?!
W-We under-estimated them!
Damn those defective mecha!!

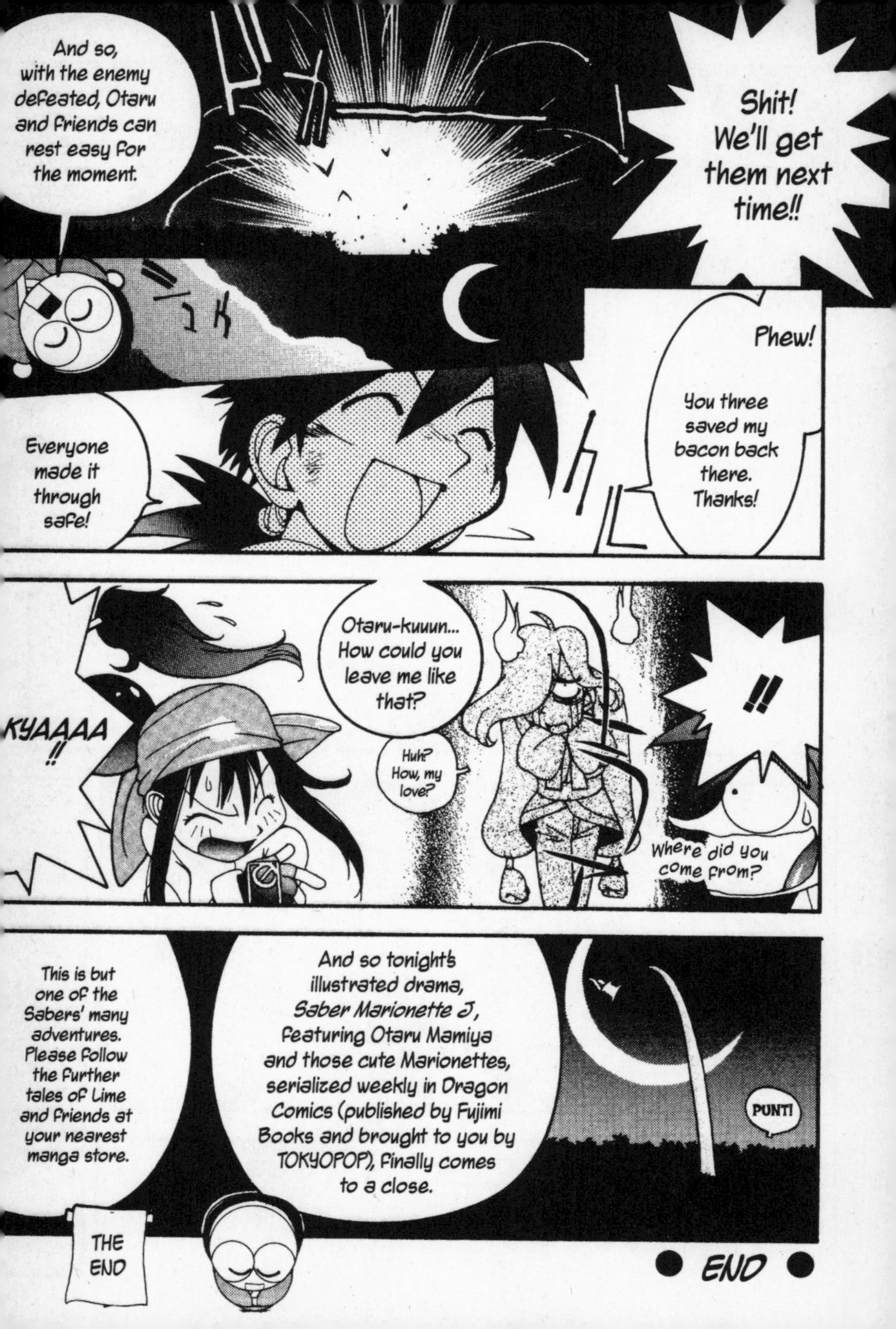
Shit! We'll get them next time!!
And so, with the enemy defeated, Otaru and friends can rest easy for the moment.
Phew!
You three saved my bacon back there. Thanks!
Everyone made it through safe!
!!
Where did you come from?
Otaru-kuuun... How could you leave me like that?
Huh? How, my love?
KYAAAA !!
PUNT!
And so tonight's illustrated drama, *Saber Marionette J*, featuring Otaru Mamiya and those cute Marionettes, serialized weekly in Dragon Comics (published by Fujimi Books and brought to you by TOKYOPOP), finally comes to a close.
This is but one of the Sabers' many adventures. Please follow the further tales of Lime and friends at your nearest manga store.
THE END
• END •

Saber Marionette J

Otaru and Saber Marionettes Lime, Cherry and Bloodberry go on a dire mission to destroy the main computer of Gartland! Along the way, they are ambushed and viciously attacked by the Saber Dolls, whose loyalties still lie with the villainous Faust. Can Otaru stop his arousal-induced nosebleeds long enough to save his homeworld?

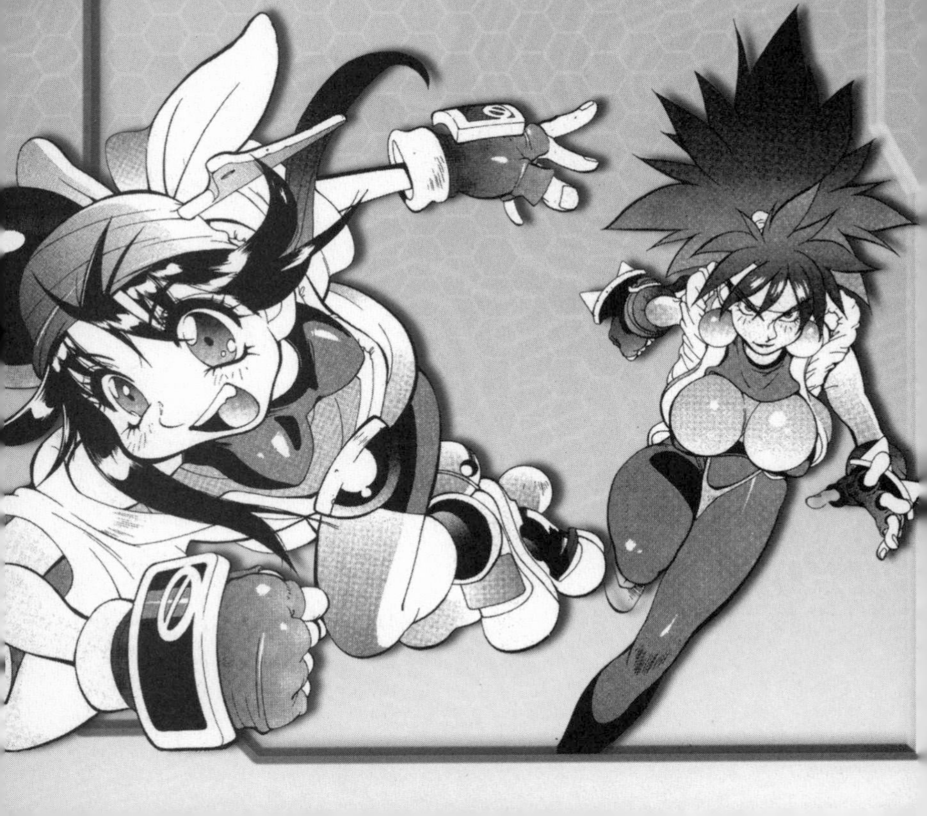

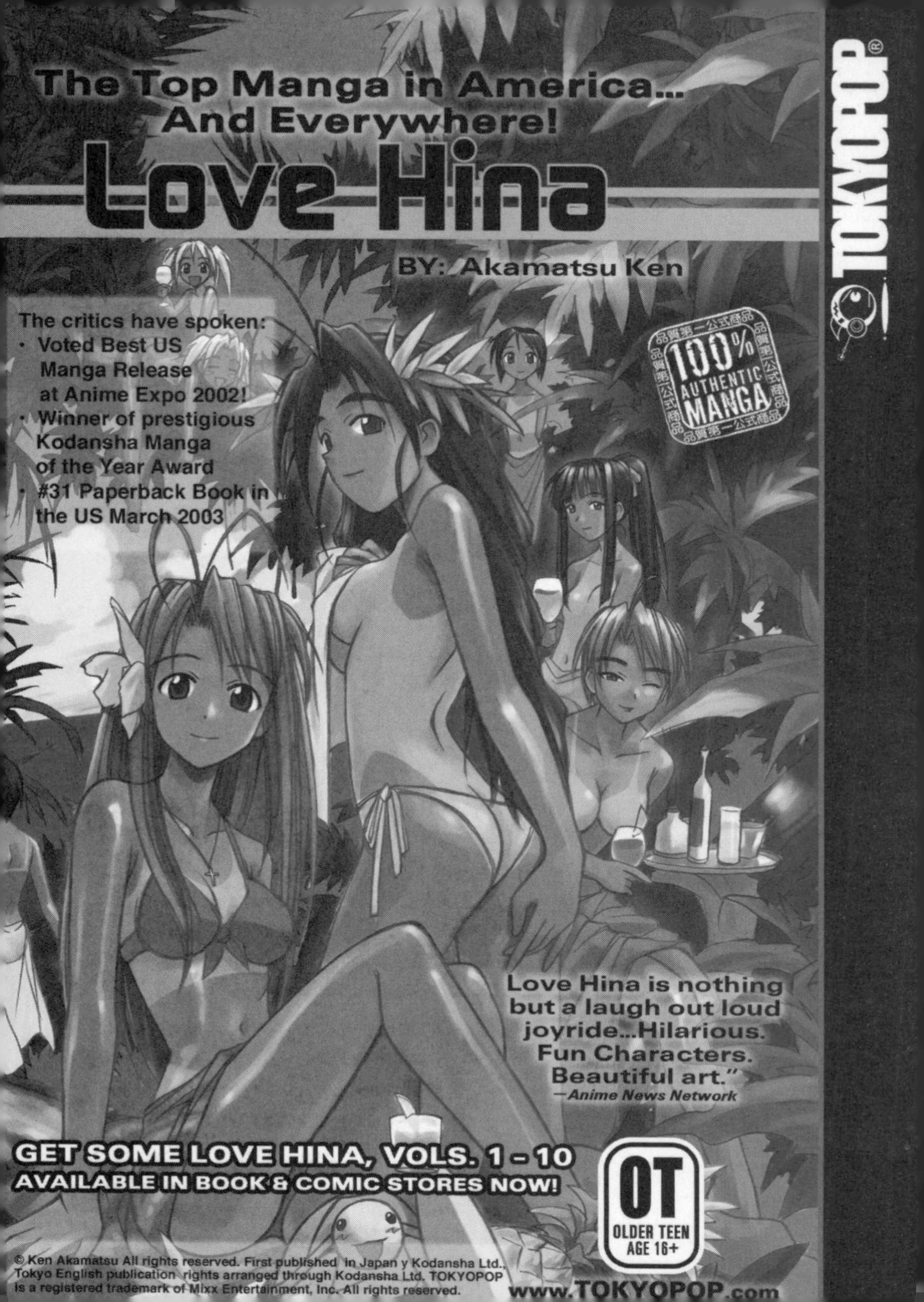
The Top Manga in America...
And Everywhere!
Love Hina
BY: Akamatsu Ken
The critics have spoken:
• Voted Best US Manga Release at Anime Expo 2002!
• Winner of prestigious Kodansha Manga of the Year Award
• #31 Paperback Book in the US March 2003
100% AUTHENTIC MANGA
TOKYOPOP®
"Love Hina is nothing but a laugh out loud joyride...Hilarious. Fun Characters. Beautiful art."
—Anime News Network
GET SOME LOVE HINA, VOLS. 1 - 10
AVAILABLE IN BOOK & COMIC STORES NOW!
OT
OLDER TEEN AGE 16+
© Ken Akamatsu All rights reserved. First published in Japan y Kodansha Ltd., Tokyo English publication rights arranged through Kodansha Ltd. TOKYOPOP is a registered trademark of Mixx Entertainment, Inc. All rights reserved.
www.TOKYOPOP.com

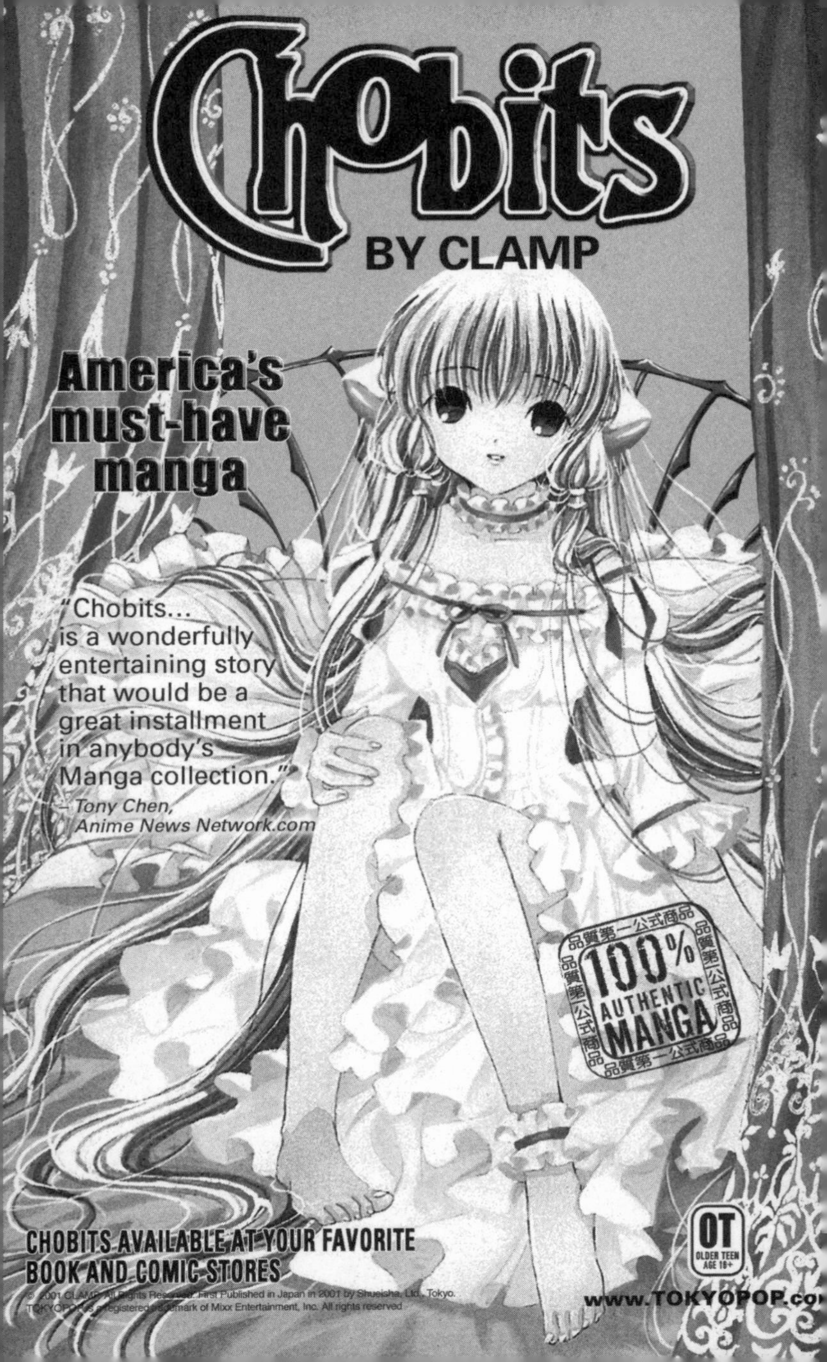

Chobits
BY CLAMP
America's must-have manga
"Chobits... is a wonderfully entertaining story that would be a great installment in anybody's Manga collection."
– Tony Chen, Anime News Network.com
品質第一公式商品
100% AUTHENTIC MANGA
CHOBITS AVAILABLE AT YOUR FAVORITE BOOK AND COMIC STORES
© 2001 CLAMP. All Rights Reserved. First Published in Japan in 2001 by Shueisha, Ltd., Tokyo.
TOKYOPOP is a registered trademark of Mixx Entertainment, Inc. All rights reserved
OT
OLDER TEEN AGE 16+
www.TOKYOPOP.co

SAMURAI DEEPER キョ

BY: AKIMINE KAMIJYO

100% AUTHENTIC MANGA

The Action-Packed Samurai Drama that Spawned the Hit Anime!

Slice the surface
to find the assassin within...

SAMURAI DEEPER KYO AVAILABLE AT YOUR FAVORITE BOOK & COMIC STORES NOW!

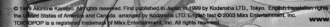

STOP!

This is the back of the book.
You wouldn't want to spoil a great ending!

This book is printed "manga-style," in the authentic Japanese right-to-left format. Since none of the artwork has been flipped or altered, readers get to experience the story just as the creator intended. You've been asking for it, so TOKYOPOP® delivered: authentic, hot-off-the-press, and far more fun!

DIRECTIONS

If this is your first time reading manga-style, here's a quick guide to help you understand how it works.

It's easy... just start in the top right panel and follow the numbers. Have fun, and look for more 100% authentic manga from TOKYOPOP®!

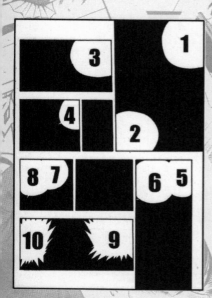